EVALUATION
METHODOLOGY
—— BASICS ——

To my husband, Susumu, and to
our long-awaited little girl, due in July 2004

EVALUATION METHODOLOGY BASICS

THE NUTS
AND BOLTS
OF SOUND
EVALUATION

E. JANE DAVIDSON

SAGE Publications
Thousand Oaks ▪ London ▪ New Delhi

For information:

Sage Publications, Inc.
2455 Teller Road
Thousand Oaks, California 91320
E-mail: order@sagepub.com

Sage Publications Ltd.
1 Oliver's Yard
55 City Road
London EC1Y 1SP
United Kingdom

Sage Publications India Pvt. Ltd.
B-42, Panchsheel Enclave
Post Box 4109
New Delhi 110 017 India

Printed in the United States of America

Library of Congress Cataloging-in-Publication Data

Davidson, E. Jane.
Evaluation methodology basics: The nuts and bolts of sound evaluation /
E. Jane Davidson.
    p. cm.
Includes bibliographical references and index.
ISBN 0-7619-2929-0 (cloth) — ISBN 0-7619-2930-4 (pbk.)
    1. Evaluation research (Social action programs) 2. Evaluation—Methodology.
I. Title.
H62.D254 2005
001.4—dc22   2004008544

This book is printed on acid-free paper.

04   05   06   07   08   10   9   8   7   6   5   4   3   2   1

Acquisitions Editor:	Lisa Cuevas Shaw
Editorial Assistant:	Margo Crouppen
Production Editor:	Diane S. Foster
Copy Editor:	D. J. Peck
Typesetter:	C&M Digitals (P) Ltd.
Proofreader:	Cheryl Rivard
Indexer:	Teri Greenberg
Cover Designer:	Janet Foulger

CONTENTS

———•◦•———

PREFACE

There are several evaluation books that present a survey of the various evaluation approaches, models, and theories; provide guidance for facilitating or managing the evaluation process; and/or explore some of the important theoretical, ethical, practical, and political issues in evaluation. These are an excellent source for giving the relative newcomer a sense of the diverse approaches and ideas within the evaluation community.

There are also numerous texts that guide readers through the process of using social science research methods to answer evaluation questions. The steps involved (with some variations) are typically clarifying evaluation questions, developing an appropriate research resign, identifying or developing measures, collecting data, and presenting findings.

Evaluation, however, is much more than "applied social science research." E-*valu*-ation, as the term implies, involves not only collecting descriptive information about a program, product, or other entity but also using something called "values" to (a) determine what information should be collected and (b) draw explicitly evaluative inferences from the data, that is, inferences that say something about the quality, value, or importance of something. Put another way, research can tell us "what's so," but only evaluation can tell us "so what."

Evaluation theorists for years have advised us to "take into account" all relevant values and to use them in the interpretation of data collected as part of an evaluation (House & Howe, 1999). But especially for the relatively new evaluator (even one who is knowledgeable and experienced in research methodology), there is not a lot of guidance about how this is done.

Scriven has made by far the greatest contributions to the development of a unique logic and methodology that is truly evaluation specific. He addresses head-on the issue of which values should be considered relevant in an evaluation and where they should be applied (e.g., Scriven, 1991).

What is "evaluation-specific logic and methodology"? It is a set of principles (logic) and procedures (methodology) that guides the evaluation team in the task of blending descriptive data with relevant values to draw explicitly evaluative conclusions. An explicitly evaluative conclusion is one that says how good, valuable, or important something is rather than just describing what it is like or what happened as a result of its implementation.

Evaluation-specific methodology is absolutely essential for answering truly evaluative questions such as whether a certain program, policy, or product is (a) just good enough to buy, fund, or support; (b) significantly better than that; (c) clearly better than the other two options we are considering (or might have considered); and/or (d) an excellent example of "best practice." In contrast, evaluation-specific methodology is *not* necessary for answering nonevaluative research questions, that is, those that are not directly concerned with quality, value, or importance.

WHO AND WHAT THIS BOOK IS FOR

This book is designed primarily for the many practitioners who find themselves thrown into evaluation roles without the benefit of formal evaluation training. Even those with a good grounding in applied research methods find that there is a whole lot more to putting together a good evaluation than meets the eye. For these people, and for students of evaluation (who struggle with many of the same issues and often plan to be practitioners as well), this is the straight-talking evaluation methodology book you have been dying to add to your bookshelf.

The purpose of this book is to provide a "nuts-and-bolts" guide that covers some of the practical and methodological basics of doing an evaluation. It is designed to lead the evaluation team (which may include people internal to the organization, external contractors, and/or other key stakeholders) through the steps involved in doing a good evaluation.

The focus is on evaluation-specific logic and methodology (which address the issues described previously) rather than on what is already covered well in social science research texts (e.g., the development of measures and instruments for collecting data). From "Where do I start?" to "How do I pull all of this information together into a report for my client?" this book provides a step-by-step guide, including checklists, rubrics, and rules of thumb for doing a real evaluation.

Topics covered in this book include the following:

- How to identify the right criteria for your evaluation (using needs assessment and other strategies)
- How to figure out which criteria are more important than others
- How to blend a mix of qualitative and quantitative data with relevant standards and values to draw explicitly evaluative conclusions (i.e., say something specific about quality or value)
- How to pull together information about all of the strengths and weaknesses to answer the fundamental evaluation questions for the client
- How to evaluate an evaluation

WHAT IS NEW OR FRESH ABOUT THIS APPROACH?

Although the work presented in this book does seek to bring some fresh insights and ideas, it stands on the shoulders of some veritable giants in the field to whom I owe a debt of gratitude. In particular, the pioneering work of Scriven on the conceptualization of evaluation's unique logic and methodology has provided a solid theoretical foundation for what I have attempted here. No one has thought more deeply or critically about what evaluation really is, how it is different from other undertakings, and what very specific procedures are required to answer truly evaluative questions than has Scriven.

The work of both Carol Weiss and Michael Quinn Patton on the utilization of evaluation have also been highly influential in the development of the ideas in this book. The same is true of the contributions from the various authors and practitioners who use program theory in evaluation (particularly the innovative work of those who have critiqued and improved on theory-based evaluation, such as Patricia Rogers and Carol Weiss). I have also drawn quite heavily on my knowledge of personnel evaluation and other developments from industrial and organizational psychology, organization development, and organizational learning. Finally, the practical know-how gleaned from working on real-world projects alongside colleagues at The Evaluation Center (especially Daniel Stufflebeam, James Sanders, and Gary Miron) has been invaluable for the development of new ideas, as has the experience of grappling with applied evaluation problems myself.

What I have attempted here is to combine a number of ideas from these supposedly diametrically opposed theoretical "camps" in the evaluation field and to augment them with some of the tools, techniques, and ideas I have developed myself and with colleagues. My goal was to spell out a coherent approach that draws on the best of the best, adds its own twists to fill the gaps, and includes practical nuts-and-bolts guidelines and tools that could be applied in a real-world setting.

Although Scriven's work is widely respected in the field and many of the concepts he has introduced are in common use (e.g., formative evaluation, summative evaluation, goal-free evaluation, meta-evaluation), it has always puzzled me that far fewer people seem to apply evaluation-specific logic and methodology in practice. One possible explanation is that the depth and sophistication of Scriven's writing in this area make it a challenging read for the relative newcomer—although an incredibly valuable one for those who make the effort. But even for those who do, many people still find it hard to *visualize* what evaluation logic and methodology would really "look like" in practice. One of my goals in this book is to help fill this gap, albeit with my own interpretations of how best to apply the concepts.

A second major barrier to getting evaluation logic and methodology more widely integrated into evaluation practice, in my view, has been the lack of per- ceived linkages to the various other evaluation approaches that have contributed so much to the field. For example, there has been a persistent misconception that these fundamental principles and procedures apply only to independent evalua- tions (i.e., evaluations that do not include organizational members on the evalu- ation team). The methodologies explained in this book are designed to be just as useful as a guide for a facilitated participatory or collaborative evaluation as for a fully external noninteractive evaluation (i.e., one that does not include stake- holders on the evaluation team). Although many writers tend to promote the use of one approach or the other, I take the view that both approaches are valuable, depending on what primary need the evaluation is addressing (e.g., building organizational learning capacity, meeting accountability requirements) and on the time and resources available to get the evaluation done.

Another common (and completely incorrect) view is that the use of evaluation logic and methodology is somehow the antithesis of **theory-based evaluation** (i.e., evaluation that uses as its guiding framework the mechanism by which the program is expected to achieve its effects). In fact, this is one of the more powerful blends possible and is one of the key avenues I have pursued in an effort to develop some of the new evaluation methodologies that are presented in this book.

THE SIMPLICITY–COMPLEXITY TRADE-OFF

The intended approach of this book is to present the methodology that is specific to evaluation in as simple and straightforward a way as possible so that readers can see clearly how it works. There are, of course, many circumstances in which the evaluation waters are a lot muddier than might appear to be implied in much of this book. In particular, the higher up into the policymaking stratosphere we go (especially with public policy), the more we are dealing with difficult trade-offs among conflicting stakeholder values that cannot easily be resolved with, say, a high-quality needs assessment. Rather than confuse the newcomer with the nested cans of worms one might pry open here, I have (for the most part) deliberately chosen to set these issues aside while we first get on with the important task of understanding the basics of evaluation methodology.

This book is not intended to be a replacement for the more in-depth theoretical contributions already made by Scriven, Weiss, Patton, Rogers, Stufflebeam, or any of the others whose work I have drawn on. At the end of each chapter, a set of additional readings is listed for readers who wish to delve deeper into the concepts presented.

WHAT IS "THE TRUTH" IN EVALUATION?

One of the major points of departure among evaluators as they approach their work is grounded in how they view the notion of "truth" in evaluation. I take a fairly practical position on this that goes roughly as follows. Evaluation findings are "demonstrably true" when a solid mix of evidence supports a conclusion at or above the level of certainty required in that decision-making context. Does that mean that I think something has been "proven" to a 100% level of certainty so that it can be called an absolute truth in the strictest sense of the word? Certainly not. Every decision-making context has somewhat different requirements for the level of certainty needed for evaluation findings (similar to the standards of proof used to determine criminal responsibility vs. civil responsibility). In some cases, the stakes are very high and we need to be very sure indeed about our findings, at least "beyond reasonable doubt." In other cases, such a high level of certainty is not required and a "balance of evidence" standard of proof would be more appropriate. Most of my evaluation work to date has required levels of certainty somewhere between those two levels.

Those readers who have had a smattering or more of philosophy will recognize this as a *postpositive perspective*. In this book, quality or value is treated as a real (i.e., factual) attribute of things within a certain context, but one that is often hard to pin down. Getting "certain enough" answers to evaluation questions involves some serious detective work, including using multiple methods to unearth and synthesize the multiple perspectives that together can get us a close enough approximation to the truth.

The principle of obtaining multiple perspectives to get close enough to the truth applies not just to data collection but also to the all-important "values" side of evaluation. This issue is discussed in some detail in Chapter 6. Although some people might advocate addressing the values question in an opening chapter, based on my experience in teaching evaluation to relative newcomers to the profession, I am assuming that most people will want to get into the nuts and bolts before they tackle any tricky philosophical issues. However, those who find themselves distracted by this burning unanswered question should skip ahead to Chapter 6 early on and then come back to the nuts and bolts.

A MULTIDISCIPLINARY APPROACH

The purpose of this book is to contribute to the development of the "core" of evaluation—that which makes evaluation unique and that applies across multiple contexts, fields, and types of evaluands. To maximize relevance for a variety of applications, I have included diverse examples from program, policy, and project evaluation; personnel selection; performance appraisal; and product and service evaluation. This is not to say that each of these receives equal treatment in the book; the examples are much more skewed toward the evaluation of programs to reflect the interests of the largest audience.

ACKNOWLEDGMENTS

I thank the many reviewers who provided useful critiques on earlier drafts of all or part of this book, including Lori Wingate, Justin Menkes, Christopher Nelson, Daniel Stufflebeam, James Sanders, Paul Clements, Thomaz Chianca, Thomas Cook, Michael Quinn Patton, Lois-Ellen Datta, Doug Leigh, and Greg Roberts.

ONE

WHAT IS EVALUATION?

———•◦•———

Aspromised in the preface, this book's approach is to give you a "bare-bones," nuts-and-bolts guide about how to do an **evaluation.**[1] Although we will not be spending a huge amount of time on evaluation theory, it is certainly a good idea to start with a clear notion of what it is we are getting ourselves into.

BASIC DEFINITIONS

In terms of the evolution of the human race, evaluation is possibly the most important activity that has allowed us to evolve, develop, improve things, and survive in an ever-changing environment. Every time we try something new—a farming method, a manufacturing **process,** a medical treatment, a social change **program,** a new management team, a **policy** or **strategy,** or a new information **system**—it is important to consider its value. Is it better than what we had before? Is it better than the other options we might have chosen? How else might it be improved to push it to the next level? What did we learn from trying it out?

> Professional evaluation is defined as the **systematic** determination of the **quality** or **value** of something (Scriven, 1991).

Things that we might (and should) evaluate systematically include the following[2]:

- **Projects,** programs, or organizations
- Personnel or performance

1

- Policies or strategies
- Products or services
- Processes or systems
- Proposals, contract bids, or job applications

There is a fundamental logic and methodology that ties together the evaluation of these different kinds of evaluands. For example, some of the key learnings from the evaluation of **products** and personnel often apply to the evaluation of programs and policies and vice versa. This *transdisciplinary* way of thinking about evaluation provides a constant source of innovative ideas for improving how we evaluate. For this reason, this book contains illustrative examples drawn from a variety of settings and evaluation tasks.

Evaluations are generally conducted for one or two main reasons: to find areas for improvement and/or to generate an **assessment** of *overall* quality or value (usually for reporting or decision-making purposes). Defining the nature of the evaluation question is key to choosing the right methodology.

Some other terms that appear regularly in this book are merit, worth, quality, and value. Scriven (1991) defines these as follows:

Merit is the "intrinsic" value of something; the term is used inter-changeably with *quality.*

Worth is the value of something to an individual, an organization, an institution, or a collective; the term is used interchangeably with *value.*

This distinction might seem to be a fine one, but it can come in handy. For example, in the evaluation of products, **services,** and programs, it is important to critically consider the extent to which improvements in *quality* (e.g., adding more "bells and whistles") would actually provide enough incremental *value* for the individuals and/or organization concerned to justify their cost.

More often than not in evaluation, we are looking at whether something is "worth" buying, continuing to fund, enrolling in, or implementing on a broader scale. Accordingly, most "big picture" evaluation questions are questions of value (to **recipients**/users, funders/taxpayers, and other relevant parties) rather than of pure merit. There are exceptions, however, and that is why I have kept both considerations in play.

FITTING EVALUATION APPROACH TO PURPOSE

For any given evaluation, a range of possible approaches is available to the practitioner and the **client**. The option that is most often discussed in evaluation circles pertains to whether an evaluation should be conducted independently (i.e., by one or more outside contractors) or whether the program or product designers or staff should be heavily involved in the evaluation process.

If the primary purpose of the evaluation is for *accountability,* it is often important to have an **independent evaluation** conducted (i.e., nobody on the evaluation team should have a significant vested interest in whether the results are good or bad). This is not always a requirement (e.g., managers in all kinds of organizations frequently report on the performance of their own units, products, and/or people), but this credibility or independence issue is definitely one to consider when choosing how to handle an accountability-focused evaluation.

There are many cases where independence is not essential, but building **organizational learning capacity** is key; that is, a primary goal is to improve **organizational learning** (i.e., the organization's ability to learn from its successes and failures). In such cases, an evaluation can (and should) be conducted with a degree of **stakeholder** participation. Many high-quality professional evaluations are conducted collaboratively with organizational staff, internal human resources consultants, managers, **customers** or recipients, or a combination of these groups.

A **learning organization** is one that acquires, creates, evaluates, and disseminates knowledge—and uses that knowledge to improve itself—more effectively than do most organizations. The best learning organizations tend to use both independent and **participatory evaluations** to build learning capacity, gather multiple perspectives on how they are doing, and keep themselves honest (Davidson, 2003).

THE STEPS INVOLVED

Whether the evaluation is conducted independently or in a participatory mode, it is important to begin with a clear understanding of what evaluation is and what kinds of evaluation questions need to be answered in a particular case. Next, one needs to identify relevant "values," collect appropriate data, and systematically combine the values with the descriptive data to convey, in a useful and concise way, defensible answers to the key evaluation questions (see Exhibit 1.1).

Exhibit 1.1   Overview of the Book's Step-by-Step Approach to Evaluation

CHAPTER 1	Understanding the basics about evaluation

↓

CHAPTER 2	Defining the main purposes of the evaluation and the "big picture" questions that need answers

↓

CHAPTER 3	Identifying the evaluative **criteria** (using needs assessment and other techniques)

↓

CHAPTER 4	Organizing the list of criteria and choosing sources of evidence (mixed method data)

↓

CHAPTER 5	Dealing with the causation issue: how to tell the difference between **outcomes** or **effects** and coincidental changes not caused by the evaluand

↓

CHAPTER 6	Values in evaluation: understanding which values should legitimately be applied in an evaluation and how to navigate the different kinds of "subjectivity"

↓

CHAPTER 7	Importance weighting: figuring out which criteria are the most important

↓

CHAPTER 8	Merit determination: figuring out how well your evaluand has done on the criteria (excellent? good? satisfactory? mediocre? unacceptable?)

↓

CHAPTER 9	Synthesis methodology: systematic methods for condensing evaluative findings

↓

CHAPTER 10	Putting it all together: fitting the pieces into the Key Evaluation Checklist framework

↓

CHAPTER 11	Meta-evaluation: how to figure out whether your (or someone else's) evaluation is any good

THE INGREDIENTS OF A GOOD EVALUATION

The overarching framework used for planning and conducting an evaluation and presenting its results is Scriven's (2003) Key Evaluation Checklist (KEC) with a few modifications and simplifications. This is a guiding framework for the evaluation team members (be they organizational members, **external evaluators,** or a mix) to make sure that all important ingredients that will allow valid **evaluative conclusions** to be drawn are included.

The KEC should be thought of both as a checklist of necessary ingredients to include in a solid evaluation and as a framework to help guide evaluation planning and reporting. Because the KEC was designed primarily for application to program evaluation, some of the points might need reframing when the KEC is used for other **evaluands** or **evaluees** (the term used in personnel evaluation). In a posting to a listserv on November 16, 2002, Scriven describes how and why the KEC was developed:

> The Key Evaluation Checklist evolved out of the work of a committee set up by the U.S. Office of Education which was to hand out money to disseminate the best educational products to come out of the chain of Federal Labs and R&D Centers (some of which still exist). The submissions were supposed to have supporting evidence, but these documents struck me as frequently making a few similar mistakes (of omission, mostly). I started making a list of the recurring holes, i.e., the missing elements, and finished up with a list of what was needed in a good proof of merit, a list which we used and improved.

A brief overview of the KEC is shown in Exhibit 1.2. Each line of KEC checkpoints represents another layer in the evaluation. We begin with the Preliminaries (Checkpoints I–III), which give us some basic information about the evaluand and the evaluation. From there, we move to the Foundations (Checkpoints 1–5), which provide the basic ingredients we need, that is, descriptive information about the program, who it serves (or should serve), and the values we will apply to evaluate it. The third level, which Scriven called the Sub-evaluations (Checkpoints 6–10), includes all of the explicitly evaluative elements in an evaluation (i.e., where we apply values to descriptive facts to derive evaluative conclusions at the analytical level). Finally, we reach the Conclusions section (Checkpoints 11–15), which includes overall answers to the evaluation questions plus some follow-up elements.

Exhibit 1.2 The Key Evaluation Checklist (modified from Scriven's 2003 version)

I. Executive Summary One- to two-page overview of the evaluand and findings	**II. Preface** Who asked for this evaluation and why? What are the main evaluation questions? Who are the main audiences?	**III. Methodology** What is the overall design of the evaluation (e.g., quasi-experimental, participatory, goal free) and (briefly) why?
1. Background and Context Why did this program or product come into existence in the first place?	**2. Descriptions and Definitions** Describe the evaluand in enough detail so that virtually anyone can understand what it is and what it does. **3. Consumers** Who are the actual or potential recipients or impactees of the program (e.g., demographics)?	**4. Resources** What resources are (or were) available to create, maintain, and help the program or policy succeed? **5. Values** On what basis will you determine whether the evaluand is of high quality, valuable, and so forth? Where will you get the criteria, and how will you determine "how good is good"?
6. Process Evaluation How good, valuable, or efficient is the evaluand's content (design) and implementation (delivery)?	**7. Outcome Evaluation** How good or valuable are the **impacts** (intended and unintended) on immediate recipients and other impactees? **8 & 9. Comparative Cost-Effectiveness** How costly is this evaluand to consumers, funders, staff, and the like, compared with alternative uses of the available resources that might feasibly have achieved outcomes of similar or greater value? Are the costs excessive, quite high, just acceptable, or very reasonable?	**10. Exportability** What elements of the evaluand (e.g., innovative design or approach) might make it potentially valuable or a significant contribution or advance in another setting?
Preliminaries	**Foundations**	**Sub-Evaluations**

6

11. Overall Significance

Draw on all of the information in Checkpoints 6 through 10 to answer the main evaluation questions (e.g., What are the main areas where the evaluand is doing well, and where is it lacking? Is this the most cost-effective use of the available resources to address the identified needs without excessive adverse impact?).

Conclusions

12. Recommendations and Explanations
[optional]
A more in-depth analysis of why/how things went right/wrong, perhaps including recommendations for improvement

13. Responsibilities
[optional]
A more in-depth analysis of exactly who or what was responsible for good or bad results (Note: This is very tricky and is usually not the kind of territory you want to get into unless you are highly skilled.)

14. Reporting and Follow-up
Who will receive copies of the evaluation report and in what form (e.g., written, oral, detailed versions, executive summary)?

15. Meta-evaluation
A critical assessment of the strengths and weaknesses of the evaluation itself (e.g., How well were all of the Key Evaluation Checklist checkpoints covered?) and conclusions about its overall utility, accuracy or validity, feasibility, and propriety (see the Program Evaluation Standards for details)

SOURCE: Adapted and reprinted by permission by Michael Scriven.

Scriven (1991) asserts that evaluations should generally cover all of these checkpoints (except for Checkpoints 12 and 13, which are optional) to draw valid conclusions. Each point listed in the KEC is backed by a carefully thought-out rationale showing why omission of the particular point is likely to compromise the validity of conclusions. Although this should not be taken to mean that all checkpoints must *always* be included in all evaluations, it does mean that decisions to omit certain elements should be carefully justified. This is particularly important for Checkpoints 5 through 9 and 11, which form the core of the evaluation.

Obviously, there is a lot more to the KEC than one can fit on a one-page summary. Throughout this book, we work through many of the KEC checkpoints, paying particular attention to the truly evaluative ones (from Checkpoint 5 [Values] through Checkpoint 11 [Overall Significance]), which is where **evaluation-specific logic and methodology** come into play. Later, in Chapter 10, we return to the KEC and show how all of the information we have covered fits into the big picture.

It is important to note that the KEC can be applied to a participatory or **collaborative evaluation** just as easily as it fits into the conduct of an independent evaluation being done for accountability. Whether the evaluation is a facilitated collaborative effort or not, the evaluation team members (be they external or **internal evaluators**) still need some guidelines for figuring out what should go into an evaluation to make sure that it provides the most accurate answers to the most important questions.

IDENTIFYING THE EVALUAND, ITS BACKGROUND, AND ITS CONTEXT

Before we plunge into the nuts and bolts of evaluation design, it is a good idea to first clarify what it is you plan to evaluate (i.e., your evaluand). This might seem like an incredibly basic question, but it trips up a lot of people. For your first evaluation, it is important to choose something manageable to which you could reasonably expect to gain access.

A clear and accurate description of your evaluand should appear under Checkpoint 2 (Descriptions and Definitions) of the KEC and should also have a brief mention in your evaluation report's Executive Summary (Checkpoint I). Equally important is to gain a solid understanding of the evaluand's Background and Context (Checkpoint 1). These three checkpoints are the focus of this chapter (Exhibit 1.3).

Exhibit 1.3   The Checkpoints Where the Evaluand, Its Background, and Its Context Are Described

---

I. Executive Summary
One- to two-page overview of the evaluand and findings

1. Background and Context	**2. Descriptions and Definitions**
Why did this program or product come into existence in the first place?	Describe the evaluand in enough detail so that virtually anyone can understand what it is and what it does.

When completing the Descriptions and Definitions checkpoint, the evaluation team should not just use brochures or Web sites to find out what the evaluand is *supposed* to be like; instead, the team should describe it as it *really* is. This usually involves, at a minimum, a firsthand visit and some interviewing of key stakeholders. The information presented under this checkpoint should be purely descriptive in nature; that is, you should not make comments here about the merits of the evaluand or its design.

At the same time, the evaluation team should conduct a preliminary investigation to find out what it was that led to the development of the evaluand in the first place and any underlying rationale for how or why it was intended to address the original need, problem, or issue. This information will go under the Background and Context checkpoint.

ADVICE FOR CHOOSING YOUR FIRST EVALUATION PROJECT

Whether you are attending an evaluation class or just trying to figure out for yourself how to put together an evaluation, a key part of the process will be working through an example of your own as you go through this book. This process can be made easier or harder depending on what you choose as your first project. Here are a few tips for choosing a project that will allow you to get the most out of this book:

1.   Make life easier for yourself by choosing an intervention, program, or the like that is designed to benefit *people* in some way. In this book, we talk a lot about assessing the needs of recipients and impactees, so it helps if these are (a) a clearly defined group and (b) human. Try to avoid abstract evaluands or very complex systems. You can get into these later.

2.   For this exercise, the evaluand should be a "live" program or intervention that is currently in existence and that you can go and see with your own eyes. Inanimate objects, distant programs, things you have only seen on the Internet, and things that no longer exist are not good ideas for first projects because they make it harder to get access to "the clients" (an important part of getting a feel for evaluation).

3.   Do not tackle something that could have political ramifications for you (or for your instructor if you are a student). Examples might include your boss's pet project, another professor's class, and university administrative systems (these are too complex anyway).

4.   It is better if you can choose something of which you are *not* a current, recent, or future recipient or consumer (e.g., a graduate program in which you studied, a workshop you attended). Although the "inside perspective" might seem to be advantageous at first, people tend to get way too distracted with their own personal perspectives or agendas and end up missing a lot of important issues and not doing so well on their evaluation projects.

If you are already working in evaluation, you no doubt have plenty of evaluands from which to choose. For students who need to track down an evaluand, the following are some ideas for evaluands to consider as first-time evaluation projects:

- A community health program
- A workplace wellness initiative
- A school counseling service
- An internship program
- An AIDS prevention program
- A jail diversion program for first-time offenders

- A training program or workshop
- A summer camp
- A performance management and reward system
- A mentoring program
- A distance learning course
- A fast-track program for high-potential employees or students
- An organizational change intervention
- A distribution system for a particular product
- An executive recruitment service

After you have identified an appropriate evaluand, work through the exercises at the end of this chapter. These will yield a draft of Checkpoints 1 and 2 of the KEC.

NOTES

1. Definitions of the key terms used in this book may also be found in the Glossary.

2. This list is an elaboration of Scriven's (1991) list of the Big Six categories of evaluand, expanded here to be more inclusive of the various terminology used across different fields.

ADDITIONAL READINGS

Entries in Scriven's (1991) *Evaluation Thesaurus:*
- Consultant
- Contextually evaluative
- Cost-free evaluation
- Criterion
- Descriptive
- Evaluand
- Evaluate/Evaluation
- Introduction: The nature of evaluation

Davidson, E. J. (2002). The discipline of evaluation: A helicopter tour for I/O psychologists. *The Industrial–Organizational Psychologist, 40*(2), 31–35. Available online: http://siop.org/tip/tip.html

Fetterman, D. M. (2000). *Foundations of empowerment evaluation.* Thousand Oaks, CA: Sage.

Patton, M. Q. (1997). *Utilization-focused evaluation* (3rd ed.). Thousand Oaks, CA: Sage.
Rose, D. S., & Davidson, E. J. (2003). Overview of program evaluation. In J. E. Edwards, J. C. Scott, & N. S. Raju (Eds.), *The human resources program evaluation handbook* (pp. 3–26). Thousand Oaks, CA: Sage.
Scriven, M. (1993). *Hard-won lessons in program evaluation* (New Directions for Program Evaluation, No. 58). San Francisco, CA: Jossey-Bass.

EXERCISES

1. Clearly identify your evaluand, that is, what you plan to evaluate (or to just write an evaluation plan for). Explain, on half a page or less, what it is (be sure to include the points that follow).
   a. Is it a program, policy, product, service, system, or something else?
   b. Who exactly does it (or should it) serve (e.g., customers, **consumers,** recipients, people in need, **target market**)?
   c. Who is in charge of it?

2. Try explaining what you have written to a colleague to make sure that it makes sense. (Common mistakes here include prematurely specifying what criteria you plan to use [e.g., saying that you are going to evaluate something "in terms of X"], choosing something far too complex for your first evaluation [e.g., having two or more nested evaluands such as a project within a program within a system], and commenting on the merits of the evaluand [at this stage you should be purely descriptive].)

3. Interview key stakeholders to gain an understanding of your evaluand's background and context.
   a. Find out why your evaluand came into existence in the first place—to address what need or problem?
   b. What rationale can you find (from documentation, interviews, or other methods) that reveals how or why your evaluand was supposed to meet this need or address this problem?
   c. What other events were happening at the time (e.g., political environment, legislation, technological developments, cultural issues), and how did they lead to the development of your evaluand at that time?

TWO

DEFINING THE PURPOSE
OF THE EVALUATION

————•◦•————

Having identified and described the evaluand, the first task in designing an evaluation is to determine its main purpose and the "big picture" questions that need to be answered. This feeds directly into Checkpoint II of the Key Evaluation Checklist (KEC), the Preface (Exhibit 2.1).

Exhibit 2.1   The Preface Checkpoint of the KEC

> **II. Preface**
> Who asked for this evaluation and why? What are the main evaluation questions? Who are the main audiences?

In the initial contact with the client, you will need to document who asked for this evaluation and why. As you scope the project, you should also be looking to clearly define the evaluation's purpose, its main audiences, and the big picture questions that need to be answered:

A. What is (are) the main purpose(s) of the evaluation?
    i.   To determine the *overall* quality or value of something
    ii. To find areas for improvement
    iii. Both of the above

B. What is (are) the big picture question(s) for which we need answers?

    i. Absolute merit or worth (e.g., How effective/valuable/ meritorious is/was this? Is/Was it worth the resources [e.g., time, money] put into it?)

    ii. Relative merit or worth (e.g., How does it compare with the other options or candidates?)

Having a good understanding of both the broad purpose ("A" in the preceding outline) and the big picture questions that you need to answer ("B" in the outline) is a crucial first step before jumping into any kind of design. The evaluation methods you will use all hinge on getting this right. In the next few sections, we run through a few examples of when each purpose and type of question might fit the situation to help you get a good feel for this.

At the end of this chapter, you will identify the big picture questions that you need to answer about the evaluand and the primary audience for the answers. Note that the primary audience usually consists of more people than the person who initially asked for the evaluation. The various stakeholders you talk to may have some specific questions for you to answer, but they might not always be clear about which options under A and B in the outline apply. Your job as evaluator is to probe what it is that the organization really needs to know and to communicate this in a way that makes sense to your audience. (This usually means not using jargon such as *absolute* and *relative merit*.)

EVALUATIONS FOR DETERMINING OVERALL QUALITY OR VALUE

There are many reasons why it may be important to determine the *overall* quality or value of a program, policy, project, organization, product, service, or period of individual, team, or business unit performance. This is sometimes called **summative evaluation** (Scriven, 1981). Broadly speaking, it encompasses evaluations that are done primarily for reporting and decision-making purposes other than improvement of the evaluand itself. Some specific examples of instances where you might need to determine the overall value of something include the following:

- For accountability to funders, managers, or shareholders: what someone has to show for money, resources, or funding allocated (this may include demonstrating **return on investment** [ROI])

- For go/no-go decisions: when deciding whether a particular intervention, product, or service is worth buying, implementing, or continuing to fund
- For making choices among alternatives: when selecting from several options (e.g., interventions you are considering implementing, products you are considering buying, job candidates or consultants you are considering hiring)
- For allocation decisions (e.g., how large a bonus to give each employee in a department; how much funding to allocate to several projects, business units, or grants; how to divide up scholarship money)
- For competitive analysis: benchmarking products, services, or practices against those of **competitors** to see where they stand in the market, where they are superior, and where they fall short
- For use as a marketing tool: documenting the impact of products or services to show prospective clients or customers evidence that a particular product or service is superior to others they are considering

Many of these reasons overlap, and for a particular evaluation it is quite likely that more than one of them applies. Whether you work as an internal evaluator, an evaluation consultant, or a buyer of evaluation services, the main point you should draw from this list is that summative evaluation is not just about accountability reporting. Rather, it is an essential source of useful in-house information for learning about what works, building competitive advantage, and making prudent decisions.

Systematic evaluation of products, services, programs, and other entities has been around for many years, but only in certain sectors. For example, rankings and ratings of cars, electronic products, appliances, airlines, business schools, and universities are readily available (albeit with different levels of quality) for the consumer who wants to make an informed decision. It is gradually becoming easier to obtain information about the effectiveness of medicines and of social, educational, and health programs. But in sharp contrast, there are several areas (e.g., consulting) where evidence about the effectiveness of products, services, programs, and interventions is still strangely absent despite its value for marketing, continuous improvement, and decision-making purposes.

Quick Exercise: What Kinds of Evaluations Are Out There?

1. Take a look at Web sites and brochures for the leading organizations in your field. To what extent do they make mention of the quality or value of what they do (e.g., programs or interventions offered, products or services delivered)?

2. What evidence do these leading organizations offer in favor of their claims? Classify it using the scheme in Table 2.1. How convincing do you think this evidence is? Why?

Table 2.1   How Organizations Promote Their Products, Services, and Programs to Prospective Clients

Level	Strategy	Example
Bare minimum	Product/Service listing	"These are the products/ services we provide"
Standard practice	Brand recognition	"These are the 'big name' organizations we have worked with"
Promising practice	Selective testimonials	"These are testimonials from satisfied clients"
Superior practice	Documentation of actual results	"These are the actual results/ impacts we have documented for our intervention/product"
Exemplary practice	"Bring it on!"	"These are the results/impacts documented by an independent evaluator"

EVALUATIONS FOR FINDING AREAS FOR IMPROVEMENT

Many practitioners will argue that the primary purpose of *all* evaluation should be for the purpose of improvement. As we have seen from the preceding examples, that is definitely not the main point in many cases, although it is certainly important at times.

Evaluation for the purpose of improvement—often called **formative evaluation** (Scriven, 1981)—is useful in two main cases:

- To help a relatively new product, service, or program "find its feet" or to help a relatively new staff member get up to speed
- To explore ways of improving a "mature" product, service, or program

Helping a New Evaluand Find Its Feet

All of us have, at some time or another, started in a new job and experienced the inevitability of needing to spend time making a few mistakes and "learning the ropes" before we get "up to speed." The same is true for a new product, practice, program, or policy. In general, the more innovative and interesting the new initiative, the more glitches that occur early on and the longer it takes to achieve peak performance.

This is an important principle for all programs and organizations: If, over a period of time, you find that you have absolutely no errors or glitches, it is very likely that you are not pushing the innovation envelope far enough.[1] In fact, Jack Welch, the former chief executive officer of General Electric, advocated "fast failure," pointing out that those firms that reach failure before their competitors have the chance to be the first to learn about a new product, market, or technology.

Part of being able to innovate and learn, then, involves (a) having some way of figuring out what works best (i.e., evaluation) and (b) accepting the fact that negative results are valuable because they teach you something. For a true learning organization, the practice of recognition (and the **performance appraisal** system) reflects this reality; that is, innovators and experimenters are not "crucified" for getting negative results.

Improving a Mature Evaluand

Formative evaluations of mature products, services, or programs are also an important undertaking. As we know, the pace of change in the new millennium means that the tried-and-true "best practices" of yesteryear become outdated at an alarming rate. Technological advances are one of the more obvious things that keep us continually on our toes. But shifting demographics and the changing needs and demands of customers, clients, communities, and the workforce also have a dramatic impact on what works as new generations and subcultures emerge and merge in our increasingly diverse and international society.

The organization that fails to recognize the constantly changing environment can very quickly end up like the "boiled frog" that did not realize the water had changed temperature until it was too sluggish to make a jump for safety (Villiers, 1989). One way of staying ahead of the game is to have the organization's evaluative finger firmly on the pulse of customer needs, never assuming that what has worked in the past and is working in the present will automatically work in the future.

Keeping in touch with the community or the market (i.e., the needs of your customers, recipients, or users) also requires a mind-set that values negative results and does not create incentives for people to "bury" the learnings that could be gleaned from them. When you find out that some aspect of your heretofore successful product or program now needs to be changed, you should rejoice. Identifying ways in which to improve something tried-and-true is the key to avoiding stagnation.

Pop Quiz: Do Organizations Need Summative Evaluation?

Respond to the following comment from a manager in an organization you work with (on half a page or less, single-spaced): "All of our evaluations are geared exclusively toward improving our programs, policies, and practices. We have no need for any kind of evaluation that looks at the overall quality or value of something."

QUESTIONS ABOUT ABSOLUTE VERSUS RELATIVE QUALITY OR VALUE

Broadly speaking, there are two types of evaluation questions: those that ask about the quality (i.e., merit) or value (i.e., worth) of something in *absolute* terms and those that ask about the quality or value of something in *relative* terms. Questions about the absolute quality or value of something (sometimes called **grading**[2]) may include the following:

- Is this intervention, product, or individual good enough to implement, buy, or hire (i.e., up to minimum requirements)?
- How should this level of performance be characterized (on a particular **dimension of merit** or overall)? Is it excellent? Good? Satisfactory? Poor? Completely unacceptable?

In contrast, questions about the relative quality or value of something are always asked in comparison with one or more other evaluands (e.g., interventions, products, job candidates). This evaluative activity is sometimes called **ranking,** even though it does not necessarily result in a strict numerical rank for each evaluand. Examples include the following:

- Which of these three pilot interventions is the most cost-effective and should be implemented throughout our organization?
- Who are the top 10% of our employees or students?

Now, how does this absolute–relative distinction link with the two main evaluation purposes (formative and summative) outlined earlier? It is easy to see how the preceding categories fit with summative evaluation. But even when the main purpose of the evaluation is formative, the absolute–relative merit questions will still apply at least to *aspects* of the evaluand (e.g., performance on a specific outcome), if not always to the entire entity itself. Table 2.2 shows example evaluation questions under each category of the resulting 2 × 2 matrix.

Table 2.2   Example Evaluation Questions for Looking at Absolute Versus Relative Merit or Worth for Each Evaluation Purpose

Purpose of Evaluation	*"Grading" Questions*	*"Ranking" Questions*
Demonstrating or assessing overall quality or value (summative)	Is this national health intervention worth what it costs (in terms of time, money, and other resources)?	Which of these three executive development interventions we tried was the most cost-effective?
Finding areas for improving an existing evaluand (formative)	How well does the content of this training program (coverage, breadth, and depth) match the real needs of our minority trainees?	How do the initial improvements in manufacturing efficiency compare with those achieved elsewhere in the industry?

Pop Quiz: True or False?

Respond to the following comment from a colleague (on half a page or less): "Sometimes evaluation has nothing to do with determining the quality or value of something. Sometimes it is done to find areas for improvement. That means your original definition of evaluation is completely wrong."

SUMMARY AND FINAL COMMENTS

The very first step when designing an evaluation is to identify your purpose. Do you need to demonstrate to someone (perhaps yourself) the overall quality or value of something? Do you need to find areas for improvement? Or, do you need to do both (if so, which purpose is primary)?

Second, you need to figure out whether your primary evaluation questions relate to (a) the absolute merit or worth of your evaluand or aspects of it (e.g., Is it worth implementing nationwide? How should we rate this aspect of it?) or (b) the relative merit or worth of your evaluand (e.g., How does it compare with the other options? Which of these is the best?).

Evaluation is something that prudent individuals, groups, organizations, and countries make a point of doing as part of good quality management. It is the only way in which to accomplish the following:

- Find out whether the resources we pour into something (including our own blood, sweat, and tears) are really yielding the greatest possible benefit
- Help a new product, program, or intervention to find its feet or help a new employee to get up to speed as quickly as possible
- Know for sure how good products and services are relative to their competitors (regardless of whether we are the maker of those products, the buyers of those products, or a "consumer watchdog")
- Avoid becoming the boiled frog whose earlier success bred fatal complacency
- Avoid reinventing the wheel (perhaps even a wonky one) because we did not bother to learn from our own (and others') successes and failures

Now that we have figured out why we are here and what (in big picture terms) our client needs to know, it is time to try putting that into practice. In the next chapter, we start plunging into the nuts and bolts of how we are going to do this evaluation.

NOTES

1. Of course, there are limits to how far it is prudent to push the envelope in some industries (e.g., in nuclear power plants where safety is paramount). In such cases, the innovation and experimentation part of organizational learning might need to be taken offline until the new method or product is perfected.

2. Credit is due to Scriven (1991) for the distinction between grading and ranking tasks in evaluation. He also includes "scoring" and "apportioning" as two other evaluative tasks. I have left those out at this stage to help keep things simple.

ADDITIONAL READINGS

Entries in Scriven's (1991) *Evaluation Thesaurus:*
- Formative
- Grading
- Interocular significance
- Merit
- Ranking/Rank ordering
- Reasons for evaluation
- Significance
- Statistical significance
- Summative
- Worth

Davidson, E. J., Howe, M., & Scriven, M. (in press). Evaluative thinking for grantees. In M. Braverman, N. Constantine, & J. K. Slater (Eds.), *Foundations and evaluation: Contexts and practices for effective philanthropy.* San Francisco: Jossey-Bass.

Denton, J. (1998). *Organisational learning and effectiveness.* London: Routledge.

DiBella, A. J., & Nevis, E. C. (1998). *How organizations learn.* San Francisco: Jossey-Bass.

Dodgson, M. (1993). Organizational learning: A review of some literatures. *Organizational Studies, 14,* 375–394.

Preskill, H., & Torres, R. T. (1999). *Evaluative inquiry for learning in organizations.* Thousand Oaks, CA: Sage.

Senge, P. M. (1990). *The fifth discipline: The art and practice of the learning organization.* New York: Currency Doubleday.

EXERCISES

1. Comment on the following statement: "Formative evaluation (i.e., evaluation designed to inform decisions about *improving* a program or another evaluand) looks at design and implementation issues rather than at outcomes. Summative evaluation is when you look at outcomes." Is this (a) always true, (b) sometimes true (if so, when?), or (c) never true? Explain. (A suggested answer to this question is provided in the "Answers to Selected Exercises" section.)

2. Identify *two or three key evaluation questions* for your evaluand. For each one, provide brief answers for each of the following (on half a page or less for all of them combined):
   a. In answering this question, do you need to assess overall value or find areas for improvement? (If both apply, prioritize [i.e., rank] the purposes.)
   b. Is the evaluation question you have identified primarily one about *absolute* or *relative* merit or worth? If relative merit or worth, relative to what?
   c. Who wants to know the answer to this question and why? (If there is more than one answer, choose the top two or three audiences and prioritize who you will target.)
   d. Refer back to the KEC. For which checkpoint have you just written a draft?

◄ THREE ►

IDENTIFYING
EVALUATIVE CRITERIA

———•◆•———

In the first two chapters, we identified our evaluand, what "big picture" questions need to be answered about it, and who needs to know. Now it is time to roll up our sleeves and get into some of the nuts and bolts. One of the most important activities in putting together a solid evaluation is identifying the evaluative criteria or **dimensions of merit.** These are the attributes (e.g., features, impacts) of the evaluand that we will look at to see how good (or how valuable, how effective, etc.) it is.

The evaluative criteria are most relevant in five of the Key Evaluation Checklist (KEC) checkpoints: Consumers, where we identify who might be affected by the evaluand; Values, where we explain broadly how we define what is "good" (or what is "valuable"); Process Evaluation, where we evaluate the content and implementation of an evaluand; **Outcome Evaluation;** and Comparative Cost-Effectiveness. These checkpoints are reproduced in Exhibit 3.1.

Before we start exploring the strategies available for identifying evaluative criteria, it is worth spending a few minutes on the following question: Why not just use goals? After all, this is one of the most common strategies used by both managers and evaluators, that is, seeing whether the evaluand did what it was supposed to do.

23

Exhibit 3.1   The KEC Checkpoints That Are Most Relevant to the
                    Identification of Evaluative Criteria

Foundations	**3. Consumers** Who are the actual or potential recipients or impactees of the program (e.g., demographics)?	**5. Values** On what basis will you determine whether the evaluand is of high quality, is valuable, and so forth? Where will you get the criteria, and how will you determine "how good is good"?

Sub-Evaluations	**6. Process Evaluation** How good, valuable, or efficient is the evaluand's content (design) and implementation (delivery)?	**7. Outcome Evaluation** How good or valuable are the impacts (intended and unintended) on immediate recipients and other impactees?	**8 & 9. Comparative Cost-Effectiveness** How costly is this evaluand to consumers, funders, staff, and so forth, compared with alternative uses of the available resources that might feasibly have achieved outcomes of similar or greater value? Are the costs excessive, quite high, just acceptable, or very reasonable?

WHY NOT JUST USE GOALS?

One of the first places many people start when they are asked to evaluate something is to find out what it was supposed to do and then check to see whether it did that. It is quite legitimate for management to want some information about performance relative to preset targets, and an evaluator is certainly the kind of person who has the expertise to collect such information. But as evaluators, we also must consider whether this information alone will allow us to draw valid conclusions about how well the product, project, or program is doing.

Before we get into a discussion of this, a quick point of clarification is in order. Most evaluands have some overarching purpose that we might refer to as a "goal." But that is not the kind of goal we discuss in this section. Rather, the term is used here to refer to the *specific objectives* that many evaluands have in place, complete with *preset targets* that might or might not be achieved.

Well-thought-out goals (in the sense of specific measurable targets to be achieved) can often take us part of the way toward working out how good (or how valuable, how effective, etc.) an evaluand is. Unfortunately, even the best ones have the potential to fall short in several important respects. Let's use an example to see why. Suppose that we had a hypothetical evaluand (called Program X) with three specific measurable goals. Suppose that Program X achieves one goal exactly, makes a near miss on another, but far exceeds target performance on its third goal (Exhibit 3.2).

Exhibit 3.2   Performance of Program X Against Its Three
                          Specific Goals

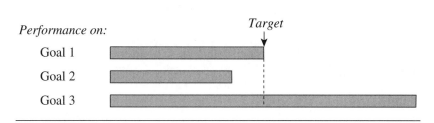

Table 3.1 lists some of the challenges encountered if one takes a strictly goal achievement-oriented approach to evaluating Program X.

The long and the short of it is that goals with specific targets can be handy guides when they exist but that even the best ones still need to be tweaked and/or supplemented with other criteria if they are to be used in an evaluation. What we really need is something more bulletproof that will allow us to take into account all of the issues listed previously and will even deal with the situation when there are no preset goals or targets or when we decide to do the evaluation in *goal-free* mode.

Table 3.1   Problems With Using Preset Targets or Goals as the Only
                  Criteria

Problem	*Example*
Overruns and shortfalls	Should we (a) call Program X a "failure" because it missed one of its targets, (b) say that it did very well because it exceeded one of its targets by much more than it missed on another, or (c) something in between?
Goal difficulty	What if the goal that Program X barely missed (Goal 2) was a particularly challenging one, whereas the goal it far exceeded (Goal 3) was easy?
Goal importance	What if the easy target was actually the more important one (i.e., it was more valuable to meet that goal than to meet the other one)? (How would we find out independently whether it was or was not? More on that in Chapter 7.)
Side effects	What if Program X also had an excellent side effect that was not included in the list of goals? Should we disregard that? If not, how would we know whether it compensated for the target it missed?
Synthesizing mixed results	What if we need to rank (or choose between) two programs, one of which is Program X and the other of which exactly met each of the three targets without exceeding any? On what basis could we say that one is better than the other?
Reasonableness of target levels	Suppose you find out that Program X came in "on budget" (i.e., met its cost goal), but then you find out that it cost five times as much as any comparable project that achieved roughly the same thing. (A similar problem occurs if Program X goes just over a very lean budget.)
Ignoring process: Do the ends justify the means?	What if Program X came in on budget by forcing the project staff to work overtime every weekend for 3 months so that in the end the top three team members quit their jobs and went to work for a competitor?

Problem	Example
Whose/Which goals to use?	Suppose different people (program designers, management, and the staff who implemented the program) have very different versions of what the goals really are (i.e., what they are *really* trying to achieve). Whose/which goals should you evaluate against? *Related issues:* How will you handle the politics of choosing one set of goals over another? What will you do if you chew through your entire evaluation budget just finding out what the goals are?

NOTE: These points draw on Scriven's (1991) list of problems with goal achievement evaluation, with some adaptations and further explanations.

In **goal-free evaluation** (GFE), the evaluation team deliberately avoids learning what the goals are (or were) so as to avoid being overly focused on intended outcomes. The rationale behind this approach is that both intended and unintended effects are important to include in an evaluation. Therefore, it is important to find all effects, and it is of little consequence whether any identified effects happened to be intended or unintended.

Because the human mind inevitably pays more attention to what it knows it is looking for, concentrating on intended effects can lead the evaluation team to miss seeing some of the unintended effects. By leaving the search for effects (i.e., outcomes) open-ended and not focused primarily on goals (i.e., intended effects), GFE often picks up more side effects than does goal-based evaluation (GBE).

GFE is sometimes called **needs-based evaluation** because a **needs assessment** is one of the primary tools used to identify what effects (both positive and negative) should be investigated.

IDENTIFYING CRITERIA: BASIC CONCEPTS AND TOOLS

Identifying the right criteria for an evaluation is similar to deciding what symptoms to look at when determining what (if anything) is wrong with a patient and how serious it is:

- We have a relatively limited time frame in which to make the diagnosis.
- If we miss something, we could easily make the wrong diagnosis.
- If we place importance on things that are not relevant to overall health, we could make an inaccurate diagnosis.
- Some *types* of symptoms represent more serious problems than do others.
- The *severity* of symptoms is important. Slight deviations from healthy levels are not as serious as those that are way off the mark.
- Sometimes it is *combinations* of symptoms that indicate a far more (or less) serious condition than each individual symptom would suggest.
- Sick patients are sometimes in denial about their symptoms or simply do not notice them, so there is a need to verify what they tell us (when possible) and to look for what they do not tell us.
- There could be several things wrong with the patient.
- In the end, we must put a lot of complex information together and come up with a final diagnosis (so that we know whether to admit the person to a hospital immediately or to send him or her home with some medication).

Unlike medicine, evaluation is not a discipline that has been developed by practicing professionals over thousands of years, so we are not yet at the stage where we have huge encyclopedias that will walk us through any evaluation step-by-step. Even if we did, such "book knowledge" would not be enough. Like medicine, evaluation is an art and a craft as well as a science. Becoming a good evaluator involves developing the pattern-spotting skills of a methodical and insightful detective, the critical thinking instincts of a top-notch political reporter, and the bedside manner and holistic perspective of an excellent doctor, among many other skills.

For the beginner, this lack of structured guidance can be a real headache. Although doing evaluation in the real world involves many complexities, there are (thankfully) a number of fairly straightforward nuts-and-bolts tools that evaluators can use to get started.

When it comes to building a criterion list, there are a few tools and procedures that are either essential or very useful:

- A needs assessment
- A simple **logic model** that links the evaluand to the **needs**

- An assessment of other relevant values
- Checklists for thinking of other relevant criteria under the headings of Process, Outcomes, and Cost
- A strategy for organizing your criterion checklist

In the rest of this chapter, we run through what these tools and procedures are and how to use them. By the end, you should be able to draw up a good initial criterion list for whatever it is you plan to evaluate. Of course, you will often find that you need to tweak the list once you get into the evaluation proper because, for example, there may be some effects or issues that you did not anticipate. But the main thing is to go into the evaluation with a well-thought-out plan so that you know what you need to know, where to get that information, and how you are going to put it together when you write up (or present) your report.

For those readers with a particular interest in **policy evaluation,** the identification of criteria follows many of the fundamental principles described here but can be more complex in several ways. For example, one often must weigh very difficult conflicting values such as whether being able to freely choose a school for one's child is intrinsically valuable even if that choice leads to poorer educational outcomes for the child (Miron & Nelson, 1992). Colleagues who work in the areas spanning evaluation and public policy have recommended two books that complement the methods described here and help to span the gap between traditional **policy analysis** and evaluation. These are listed as Additional Readings at the end of this chapter.

NEEDS ASSESSMENT FUNDAMENTALS

The very basic idea behind needs assessment is as follows. Having a positive impact on end users (also referred to as **consumers** or **impactees**) is (or should be) the fundamental purpose that justifies the creation or existence of all products, services, programs, and policies in the first place. The primary *consumer* is the person or entity who buys or uses a product or service, enrolls in or is the recipient of a program, is directly affected by a government policy, and so forth. (There may also be some others affected indirectly or unintentionally, hence the use of the more inclusive term *impactees.*)

If we can understand what the true needs of consumers or impactees are, this gives us a solid basis for finding out how well a program is doing by seeing how well it is helping to meet those needs. In other words, needs that we identify become the outcome criteria we use for the evaluation. Furthermore, the data collected during the needs assessment phase can often double as **baseline data** if we wish to track change in certain outcome variables.

Before launching into a needs assessment, then, a useful first step is to figure out who our consumers or impactees are. We had a shot at this in the exercise at the end of Chapter 1, but let's clarify a few key points and double-check to make sure that we have this right.

IDENTIFYING CONSUMERS OR IMPACTEES

In general, consumers (or impactees) are those people for whom something changes (or should or might change) as a result of a particular product, service, program, or policy.

Occasionally, products, services, programs, or policies are designed to prevent change rather than to effect change (e.g., cosmetics that slow or prevent the signs of aging). In such cases, the impacts, effects, or outcomes are the lack of change that otherwise would have occurred and the impactees are the users or receivers of the products, services, or programs.

Recall the KEC, where Checkpoint 3 states that an important part of evaluation is to correctly identify the consumers. When we talk about consumers or impactees, we are referring to those people for whom something changes (or should or might change), or for whom something is prevented from changing, as a result of our product, program, or policy. At this point, we do not include the **upstream stakeholders** (i.e., the people who worked on the design, implementation, and/or management) under the heading of consumers or impactees; rather, we include just the people "downstream," that is, **downstream consumers** (Exhibit 3.3).

Consumers can be divided into two groups: (a) immediate users or recipients and (b) other downstream impactees (Exhibit 3.3). **Immediate recipients** are the people who actually bought a product, signed up for a program, or received services directly from the evaluand, whereas downstream impactees are those who were not **direct recipients** but who were affected nevertheless. Downstream

Exhibit 3.3   Upstream Stakeholders Versus Downstream Consumers

Upstream Stakeholders   *Downstream Consumers*

Designers   EVALUAND   Immediate   Other downstream
                                       recipients   impactees

        Manufacturers   Salespeople
        Implementers   Customer service

impactees need not be individuals; instead, they could be the unit or organization where direct recipients work, the local community, or society in general.

Table 3.2 gives some examples of the different types of consumers for programs, policies, and products. When listing consumers, you should always include not only those who actually received the product, service, or program but also those who potentially could have or should have done so. This is because the extent to which a program or service actually reached those who most needed it is part of what makes a good program or service. If we consider just the impact on those who happened to be reached, we might be missing a big chunk of the story. In product evaluation terms, it may be helpful to think of the categories of immediate consumers as the "potential target markets."

Quick Exercise: Identifying Consumers

1. At the top of a new page, write a one-sentence description of your evaluand (you can draw this from the exercise at the end of Chapter 1, tweaking as necessary in light of what you have learned since).

2. Create a table like Table 3.2 (except that you will only need one row), and identify the actual and potential immediate recipients or users of your chosen evaluand. Next, list the potential downstream impactees. (Do this on half a page or less, single-spaced.)

3. Discuss what you have written with a colleague, and critique each other's work. (Common mistakes include mentioning upstream stakeholders such as program staff and salespeople [we will consider them elsewhere] and "throwing in the kitchen sink" [limit your list to two or three main groups in each category unless there are really compelling reasons to include more].)

Table 3.2   Examples of Consumers Identified for Different Evaluands

Evaluand	Immediate Recipients (actual or potential)	Downstream Impactees (actual or potential)
After-school chess program	Children who attended the program; other children in the area who do not currently attend other after-school activities	Siblings and families of children who attended the program; the local community
Executive coaching intervention	Executives who received coaching; other executives or managers within the company who did not receive coaching	Executives' direct reports; the senior management team; the chief executive officer; shareholders; the organization as a whole
Policy to decrease legal drinking age from 21 to 18 years	People 18 to 20 years of age	Parents and siblings of 18- to 20-year-olds; the police; bar and restaurant managers; the general public (especially those who patronize bars)
New 1-kg (2-pound) lightweight portable printer	Professionals and academicians who are frequent travelers or who have a "just-in-time" approach to doing presentations; people in small apartments or dormitories	Colleagues; clients; the organizations where primary consumers (immediate recipients) work
Farm irrigation project	Farmers who received irrigation; farm workers; farmers and other landowners in the area who did not receive irrigation	Adjacent landowners; produce vendors; the surrounding community (e.g., people who consume farm produce, local businesses)

Pop Quiz: Timing of the Needs Assessment

> It is likely that you will run into a few people who will tell you that the only time a needs assessment is appropriate is at the design stage of the program, project, product, or policy. Once the evaluand has been launched, it is way too late for a needs assessment. You need to have a good answer for this one. What should it be? (Jot it down on half a page or less.)

Needs Versus Wants

There are two critically important things you must know to design a good needs assessment. One is the fundamental difference between **wants** and needs. The other is what the distinctions are among the different kinds of needs, not all of which we are concerned with in a needs assessment.

Importantly, a true need might *not* be something that someone desires or is conscious of needing. It might even be something that is definitely not wanted. A seriously dehydrated person wandering in the desert might strongly desire a beer on arrival at an oasis, but what he or she really needs is water.

A *need* is something without which unsatisfactory functioning occurs.[1]

In contrast, a *want* is a conscious desire without which dissatisfaction (but not necessarily unsatisfactory functioning) occurs.

Let's try a more complex example to demonstrate the distinction between wants and needs. If you ask 14-year-olds whether they really need to know how to do algebra, they might tell you that it is one of life's cruelest inventions and a completely unnecessary one at that. What they are expressing in this case are wants and not needs. It is a fact that, in virtually all societies around the world, some understanding of algebra (and mental arithmetic) is essential to make sure that one does not get "ripped off" when buying timber for building a house or when buying food for one's family. Getting ripped off is clearly unsatisfactory functioning, so a certain level of knowledge in algebra and arithmetic is a need.

The Context Dependence of Needs

Another important point here is that needs are highly context dependent, with context having many dimensions such as geographical, cultural, and historical. A century ago, we did not need to be able to get from one side of the Pacific Ocean to the other in less than a day, but in today's business environment, that is expected. A firm doing business overseas would fall way behind its competitors (a clear example of unsatisfactory functioning) if representatives traveled only by sea and took weeks to get to their overseas customers. The context has changed, and the need has changed with it. As another example, basic living condition needs are defined differently in different countries because "satisfactory functioning" is defined differently.

If needs are context dependent, does that mean that they all are arbitrary? Not at all. Common sense and good evaluation practice dictate that we need to clearly define the context and justify why we classify certain things as needs. If there is disagreement on this, so much the better. It can help to spark an important dialogue about how "need" should be defined in a particular context, and this is an extremely important conversation to have.

This is not meant to imply that you, as an evaluator, are somehow infallible. Evaluation is a tough job that is difficult to get right, and you should *always* be open to the possibility that you have missed something, incorrectly assumed something, included something irrelevant, or made some other blunder. What we try to do throughout this book is make the evaluation's methods and findings as **systematic** (step-by-step and thorough), **objective** (free from unacceptable bias), and **transparent** (easy to follow) as possible. This makes it easier for you and others to pinpoint exactly where you might have gone wrong as you drew your evaluative conclusions.

> ## The Evaluative Attitude:
> ## An Important Attribute for an Evaluator
>
> Remember that if your critic is right, change what you have written or said. If your critic is wrong, see whether you can find a way to explain what you have written or said better so that others do not jump to the wrong conclusion as well.
>
> All serious criticism is valuable because it allows you to correct and/or clarify. Knowing this, and actively seeking out such criticism, is central to being a good evaluator. After all, useful criticism is what we sell, so seeking it out ourselves is "walking the talk."

Different Kinds of Needs

We have distinguished needs from wants. Now we need to make sure that we understand the different kinds of needs. Basically, there are three dimensions on which we can distinguish needs.

> The main dimensions that distinguish the different kinds of needs are as follows:
>
> 1. Conscious needs versus unconscious needs
>
> 2. Met needs versus unmet needs
>
> 3. Performance needs versus instrumental needs[2]

The distinction between *conscious needs* and *unconscious needs* is a fairly straightforward one—the things we know we need versus the things we do not know we need. And, as pointed out earlier, there are things that we *think* we do not need but that we actually do need. The term *unconscious* is not meant to imply that these needs are not known to anyone; rather, it just implies that the needs are not known to the person who has the needs.

A trickier distinction is that between *met needs* and *unmet needs.* The idea here is that just because someone already has something does not mean that he or she does not need it. Suppose that a group of rural farmers has good irrigation to their crops. Does this mean that irrigation is not needed? It is true that irrigation is not an unmet need in this case, but it is certainly something that, if taken away, would probably cause seriously unsatisfactory functioning, including possible crop loss.

Why bother with looking at needs that are already met? Whatever we are evaluating is designed to address unmet needs, right? Yes, but do not forget unintended consequences. A good evaluand is something that not only adds good things (e.g., services, products, opportunities) but also does not take away something important in the process. For example, building a new factory in an economically depressed town may provide employment for local people, thereby addressing an unmet need. But what if it also drains most of the town's water supply and/or seriously pollutes the air, thereby taking away the previously met needs of clean air and water? Evaluation involves not only looking at how well problems (unmet needs) were addressed but also looking at whether any new problems or benefits were caused.

The third (and most difficult) distinction is that between ***performance needs*** and ***instrumental needs.*** A performance need is a state of existence or level of performance that is required for satisfactory functioning. Roughly, it is a "need to do" something, a "need to be" something, or a "need to be able to do" something. In contrast, an instrumental need is the product, tool, or intervention that is required to address the performance need.

If we say that traveling executives need lightweight laptop computers, that is an example of an instrumental need. If we say that these executives need to be able to access e-mail and files while on the road, that is the performance need. The important thing to notice here is that the performance need is a lot easier to argue as a defensible fact than is the instrumental need. After all, one could also access e-mail and files through a handheld computer or personal digital assistant (PDA) or by using business centers or Internet cafés. If an executive has possession of or access to one of these, he or she might not need a laptop at all.

In short, the performance need is the *actual or potential problem,* whereas the instrumental need is the *proposed solution.* In needs assessment, we are concerned with the performance needs and not the instrumental needs. As we will see, this has major implications for needs assessment methods.

NEEDS ASSESSMENT METHODS: A TWO-PHASE APPROACH

Needs assessment, as conceptualized here, consists of two phases:

1. Identifying and documenting performance needs (severity documentation phase)
2. Investigating the underlying causes of performance needs (diagnostic phase)

Identifying and Documenting Performance Needs

The first phase of the needs assessment is the most intuitive one for most people. Typically, it involves starting with the "presenting needs," that is, the unmet performance needs that have caught the attention of stakeholders. For example, perhaps a community has noticed an increase in drug abuse by teenagers or a school is concerned about a high dropout rate among its students.

The first step is to document the extent of this presenting need by gathering some hard evidence (usually quantitative data) about the magnitude of the problem. This might involve asking police for records of teen drug arrests or examining school records to find out how high the dropout rate is. In many cases, it is helpful to locate some comparative information (e.g., similar statistics from earlier years, data from similar communities in the city or state) to gain a comparative sense of the severity of the problem.

The second step is to flesh out this information by finding out more about the individuals in need. Is the drug use (or the tendency to drop out of school) more prevalent among boys or girls or within a particular demographic group (e.g., age, ethnicity, socioeconomic status)?

The third step is to look for other types of performance needs apart from the one or two that were originally noticed. Have there also been problems with truancy, violence, bullying, or other crimes? This step often involves a combination of open-ended inquiry, such as asking parents, teachers, police, and community members, and collection of hard data (statistics) as corroborating evidence.

Not all evaluations require such extensive documentation of the nature and extent of the needs within a particular population. But at the very least, the evaluation team should make some effort to lay out the evidence of the need that led to the development of the evaluand in the first place.

By the end of this first phase, the evaluation team should have a clear picture of the nature and extent of the needs within the target community. The next phase involves delving deeper to understand the underlying causes of those needs.

Investigating the Underlying Causes of Performance Needs

One big problem that is frequently encountered in organizations is a premature jump to instrumental needs. For example, suppose that there is a problem with poor employee performance. Very often, people jump straight to the conclusion that a training program is needed to address the performance problem, go ahead and implement it, and then wonder why it does not work.

One method that may be useful for helping people to understand the nature of this problem is to use a logic model to illustrate (and then discuss) the assumption being made.

A **logic model** is a diagram that illustrates the cause-and-effect mechanism(s) by which an evaluand meets (or is supposed to meet) certain needs or achieves (or is supposed to achieve) certain effects.

Program theory is a description of the mechanism by which the program is expected to achieve its effects. A program theory can be expressed in a narrative or picture, or it can be depicted in a simple logic model.

The term **program logic** is often used in cases where the program theory is very simple or straightforward.

Let's use an example to illustrate. Suppose that you have been asked to evaluate a training program that had been put in place by a manager or human resources person to address a performance problem among a certain group of employees. What is the assumed underlying need? Why is a training program thought to be the correct solution? Let's map it out using a logic model (Exhibit 3.4).

Exhibit 3.4   Identifying the Underlying Assumption Linking Treatment to Performance Needs

If we implement this		*We will address this underlying need*		*Which should solve our performance problem*
Training program	→	?	→	Improved performance

What is assumed to be the underlying cause of the performance problem whenever training is proposed as the solution? That would be a skill deficit (Exhibit 3.5).

Exhibit 3.5   Underlying Assumption Linking Treatment to Performance Needs

Part of conducting a good needs assessment is the task of checking any assumptions such as this to find out whether or not they are the true cause of a performance need. Sometimes the cause is quite different from what was assumed (in which case the wrong intervention was implemented), and sometimes there is more than one cause of the performance need (in which case it is likely that only a partial solution was implemented).

When checking assumptions regarding needs, it is a good idea to use a logic model to map out each of the possible underlying needs (or causes of the performance need) so that they can be systematically checked and confirmed or ruled out. In the case of an employee performance problem, a list of possible causes (or underlying needs) would include the following:

- Skill deficit
- Lack of knowledge or understanding
- Lack of extrinsic motivation (incentives)
- Lack of intrinsic motivation (interest)
- Lack of resources
- Work–family conflict
- A negative psychosocial work environment

Each of these underlying problems would need to be addressed by a somewhat different intervention. Exhibit 3.6 shows the intervention that might be implemented in response to each of the above underlying needs. For example, if a major cause of the performance problem were a lack of intrinsic motivation (or interest in the work), one possible intervention would be something called job enrichment—removing some of the job's structure/control, increasing accountability, adding more challenging assignments, and finding other ways to make the work more meaningful and interesting.

Exhibit 3.6   Interventions Needed to Address the Various Possible Underlying Needs (causes of poor performance)

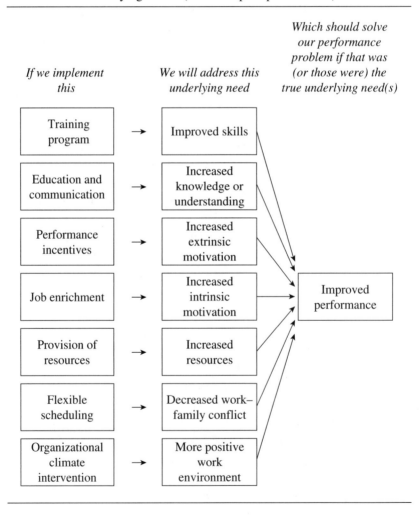

Clearly, it is preferable to look into the underlying causes of identified performance needs at the program design stage. However, if this has not been done, the evaluator will need to check whether all important underlying needs were met, regardless of whether they were identified originally. In many cases, there is more than one cause of a performance need (or the causes are different for different people), and a multifaceted solution (or different solutions for different people) is required.

The use of a logic model in this way also has benefits further down the line. It helps to identify not only the *final outcomes* that are needed (e.g., improved performance) but also the *intermediate outcomes* that should be checked on to see whether whatever was causing the performance need has been addressed. We explore the use of logic models more in Chapter 5 when we learn how to deal with the causation issue.

Pop Quiz: Different Kinds of Needs

Suppose that you are asked to do a needs assessment for either an after-school program for urban youth or a PDA for high school students.

If you asked potential participants or users, "What do you need?" What kinds of needs would you most likely be tapping into? (circle one type of need on each line)

- Conscious needs or unconscious needs?
- Met needs or unmet needs?
- Performance needs or instrumental needs?

On a separate piece of paper, list the types of needs that you would still be missing after asking that question.

The key point of the preceding pop quiz is to realize that the information you can get from asking potential participants about their needs is just the tip of the iceberg. Much of the most important information must be gathered in some other way. In the next section, we look at some of the strategies available for drilling into the iceberg.

NEEDS ASSESSMENT DESIGN, STRATEGIES,
AND METHODS: A SIMPLE EXAMPLE

As we saw in the previous sections, a good needs assessment must be concerned with performance needs—conscious and unconscious, met and unmet.
Let's illustrate how to do this with an example from a program with which the
author has worked. A community organization runs a grantsmanship workshop
to help members of local community organizations and schools learn how to
write grants and obtain funding for programs and activities that benefit the
community. Participants are also offered follow-up technical assistance after
the workshop as they develop and submit their proposals for funding.

To figure out what outcomes to look at, we first need to identify our
consumers[3]:

• *Actual or potential program recipients.* These include (a) people who
have participated (or are participating) in the grantsmanship workshop and
(b) other community organization or school members who would potentially
benefit from participating in the workshop.

• *Downstream impactees.* Most important, these include the organizations where the participants work and the communities they serve. In the case
of schools, this means the students, their families, and the wider community.
In the case of community organizations, this means the communities that are
served by those organizations.

For this particular evaluation, the documentation of the extent of the needs
was relatively minimal. The reason for the development of the program in the
first place was to find ways in which to help strengthen the local community.
In particular, local knowledge revealed that several local community organizations and schools had ideas and energy to contribute to the community but
lacked the funding to be able to do so. Based on this information, it was determined that there was at least enough need to justify offering a grantsmanship
workshop.

The more important part of the needs assessment for this program was the
diagnostic phase. Here, we took the primary purpose of the program and drew
a simple logic model that showed the mechanisms by which the program
should fulfill its purpose. This particular model (Exhibit 3.7) is a simplified
version of the original that was constructed by the program director (who had

extensive expertise in grant writing and firsthand knowledge of the participants' needs) in collaboration with the author. Thus, the logic model represents the director's view of how the program should work, but with some input from an evaluator.

Exhibit 3.7   Simple Logic Model for the Grantsmanship Workshop

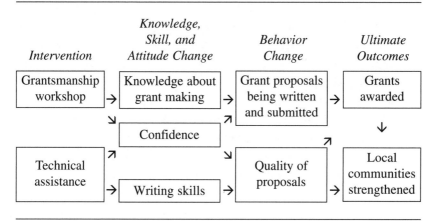

Starting with the program's purpose (the ultimate outcomes identified on the right-hand side of the model), the director was able to use her knowledge of grant writing and of the local community to work backward through the model to identify the underlying needs. To be awarded grants, the participants needed to write and submit high-quality grant proposals. To write and submit high-quality grant proposals, people needed certain knowledge about grant making, confidence that they could put together proposals, and writing skills.

The logic model identifies several different kinds of needs, ranging from knowledge, skills, and attitudes needed to create and submit high-quality grant proposals with a good chance of being funded to the ultimate long-term need (stronger communities). The logic model also helps the evaluation team to identify which outcomes we can reasonably expect to see improvements in early on (e.g., increased knowledge, better skills, improved attitudes) and which outcomes would be futile to assess too early (e.g., grants awarded, strengthened communities).

To identify the specific knowledge that participants needed about grant making, the director compiled an initial list, based on the steps to putting together a good proposal, when she designed the workshop. After running the workshop, she identified one or two other areas of required knowledge, and these elements were added to the list. The final list of required knowledge was as follows:

- Knowing what kinds of things can and cannot get funded by grants
- Knowing where to find grants
- Knowing about other funding opportunities and sources apart from grants
- Knowing that behind every charity or foundation, there were people wanting to make the world a better place; that is, understanding the perspectives or missions of foundations and of people reviewing proposals
- Knowing the elements that go into grant proposals
- Knowing how to write grant proposals (e.g., structure, steps involved)
- Knowing how to design a grants pursuit plan and schedule
- Knowing whether a person's community organization or school was ready to pursue grants and other funding opportunities

In addition to this knowledge, the director noted after running the first workshop that confidence was a major barrier to people getting started on developing proposals. Finally, it made sense to us that some basic level of writing skills was required to be able to develop good proposals. These skills might be developed somewhat as part of the workshop and follow-up, but participants were also encouraged to draw on help when they needed it.

I have deliberately chosen a simple example here to show clearly how the pieces fit together. In this case, having access to a specific individual with good content knowledge and some basic evaluation training (a 3-day workshop) made the development of a logic model and the identification of needs relatively straightforward. The evaluator's role in this case was to draw out this information, help hone the thinking, and package it in a way that could be applied immediately to an evaluation.

To connect this to the early theory of needs assessment, remember that we needed to cover both met needs and unmet needs, that is, the needs that may already be met in some people but unmet in others and that need to be addressed for the workshop to achieve its purpose. In this case, the met needs are the knowledge, skills, and attitudes that give rise to "satisfactory functioning or better"—the characteristics of those who are writing successful grants already. The unmet needs correspond to any current lack of knowledge, skills, or attitudes that gives rise to unsatisfactory functioning—the barriers to writing successful grants.

NEEDS ASSESSMENT DESIGN, STRATEGIES, AND METHODS: OPTIONS FOR MORE COMPLEX CASES

For a much larger budget program, the first phase of the needs assessment (documenting the magnitude of the need) often must be significantly more detailed than that just described. The key for this example would be an investigation of (a) untapped potential to deliver programs to the community and (b) evidence that the community needs the programs that could be offered.

The diagnostic phase of a more detailed needs assessment would seek to identify the reasons for the untapped potential in the community organizations. In the grantsmanship workshop example, knowledge of the underlying needs was already at the director's fingertips. But in another situation, the evaluation team might need to do some detective work to identify what distinguishes people in the community who are already pulling in good grants from those who are not yet able to succeed at that level.

Recall that in a needs assessment, it is important to look at both conscious and unconscious needs. *Conscious needs* are those that the actual or potential workshop participants themselves are aware of, whereas *unconscious needs* are those that we need to track down by other means (e.g., by asking experts in grant making or reviewers of proposals). This is why a needs assessment should never consist of only a survey of potential workshop participants asking what they think they need. According to the director of this particular program, many participants vastly underestimated what they needed to know to write grants and have them funded.

Critical Point: Working With Stakeholder Input

Whenever you are working to gather input from stakeholders (as with this needs assessment task), bear in mind that your job is not just to collect their opinions and report those as the needs. Some of the things that people tell you will not be legitimate needs (e.g., things that will advance them in their careers or get them some political mileage, "hobby horses" that are not grounded in any valid link to needs, things that they are simply not knowledgeable about). There is no need to figure all of this out while you are gathering the information, but be sure to increase your awareness of such things and make a brief note of anything that strikes you as needing further thought later.

As a guide for designing needs assessments, Table 3.3 lists some strategies we can use to identify each of these different kinds of needs (met, unmet, conscious, and unconscious), as applied to the grantsmanship workshop example. Some of these are repeated from the earlier discussion and are presented here for easier reference. As mentioned previously, the information unearthed by a needs assessment identifies the outcomes we should look at when evaluating the program.

Table 3.3   Strategies for Identifying Different Kinds of Performance
Needs for Participants in a Grantsmanship Workshop

	Conscious Needs	*Unconscious Needs*
Met Needs	Ask graduates of the workshop and other grant writers (especially those who hailed from similar community settings) what skills, knowledge, and experience gained in grantsmanship training have been most useful in helping them to succeed in getting funding.	Ask experts and proposal reviewers about the skills, knowledge, and other characteristics of the best grant writers with whom they have ever worked. Identify the community organizations that are most successful at maintaining and growing their funding streams. Ask what knowledge, skills, and other capabilities have made them successful and what they seek out when hiring grant writers.
Unmet Needs	Ask grant writers what skills, knowledge, and experience they really needed when they first started trying to write grants but had not learned in any formal training they received. Ask grant writers about instances when they have seen other relatively new grant writers do poorly. What skills and/or knowledge were they missing that were most problematic?	Ask people who employ grant writers for examples of people they have hired who turned out to be incapable of doing the job they were hired to do. What was missing from these individuals' repertoires? Ask employers and clients what knowledge, skills, and abilities are hardest to find when they are looking for good grant writers.

	Talk to highly experienced and top-performing grant reviewers, identify the elements of a high-quality proposal, and map out the knowledge and skills required to complete each element.
General Sources (all four types)	Do some "job shadowing"; that is, observe grant writers with different skill levels in action while they are in the process of identifying sources of funding, writing, and submitting proposals. Note areas of excellence and of problematic performance.
	Look at examples of proposals produced by grant writers. What were their strengths? Where were they lacking?

Note that the diagnostic phase of the needs assessment is an inherently open-ended inquiry. That is why qualitative methods are most prevalent here. In contrast, the earlier documentation of performance needs in the community usually focuses on the magnitude of needs that are thought to exist. That is why the methods used for the first phase of the needs assessment are typically more quantitative.

IDENTIFYING OTHER RELEVANT CRITERIA

Once you have identified the main needs for the program, your next step is to think through what other considerations might be relevant to this evaluation. Table 3.4 lists the main possibilities that should be considered in addition to needs (Scriven, 2003) and shows how they would be applied to a grantsmanship workshop with follow-up technical assistance.

The list of criteria in Table 3.4 should be kept alongside the list we generated from the earlier logic model-based needs assessment. You may have noticed some overlap between the two. That is not a problem. Together, the two lists will form the main ingredients for generating a complete list of criteria under the headings of Process Evaluation, Outcome Evaluation, Comparative Cost-Effectiveness, and Exportability (KEC Checkpoints 6–10). We address this in the next chapter.

Table 3.4   Other Relevant Considerations for Identifying Relevant
                 Criteria (from the Key Evaluation Checklist) Applied to the
                 Evaluation of a Grantsmanship Workshop

Consideration	Relevant Aspects for Case Example
Criteria of merit from the definitions and standard use	[At the basic level, what does it mean to have completed a workshop on grantsmanship? What should it consist of or include at a minimum? What outcomes should be assessed?] ❑ Content/Design: Inclusion of all major steps required to identify and obtain funding ❑ Outcomes: Grants written, submitted, and funded
Legal requirements	❑ Implementation: Selection of people into the workshop is in compliance with the law ❑ Implementation: Participant and staff legal rights are protected (e.g., zero incidence of sexual and other forms of harassment) ❑ Implementation: Financial and other accountability
Ethical requirements	❑ Implementation: Fairness or equity with which workshop participant and staff needs and concerns are handled
Fidelity to alleged specifications ("authenticity," might need an "index of implementation")	❑ Content/Design: Extent to which actual program reflects what is advertised to participants and the grant-writing profession as a whole (and, presumably, what was specified in the original design, although one should not penalize a program for improving on the original design)
Personal and organizational goals, if not goal free; alignment with organizational strategy	❑ Content/Design: Fit with or contribution to the organization's strategic goals ❑ Content/Design: Fit with or contribution to the goals of the participants and their community organizations
Professional standards	❑ Content/Design: Meets any relevant content guidelines (e.g., professional association guidelines)

Consideration	*Relevant Aspects for Case Example*
Logical (e.g., consistency)	❑ Content/Design: Workshop makes sense "as a package" (i.e., not disjointed or inconsistent)
Legislative	❑ [This one might not apply in this case but is worth checking if the program is in compliance with relevant legislation.]
Scientific/ Technical	❑ Content/Design: Content of workshop corresponds to current knowledge in grant writing; no flawed, incorrect, or badly outdated content ❑ Outcomes: Proposals produced by participants are highly rated by experts and proposal reviewers
Market	❑ Content/Design: Attractive to prospective participants (i.e., generates sufficient enrollment)
Expert judgment	❑ [For those aspects of program quality that are not able to be assessed in other ways,] the extent to which recognized grant-writing experts consider this to be a good workshop
Historical/ Traditional/ Cultural standards	❑ Content/Design and implementation: Relevance to participants' communities ❑ Implementation: Respect for diverse cultures and viewpoints as well as understanding of the key issues in the contexts where they [plan to] work ❑ Implementation: Teaching approach fits reasonably well with local norms and culture-linked learning styles (although one should not penalize a program for having learning experiences that bring in a perspective from outside the culture)

NOTES

1. This is an adaptation of Scriven's (1991) definition of a need as "anything essential for a satisfactory mode of existence or level of performance" (p. 242).

2. This is from Scriven (1991), except that Scriven uses a medical metaphor, referring to the latter as "treatment needs" (p. 242).

3. There might be more needs to consider than those of the groups listed here (e.g., needs of other staff within the participant organizations, employers within the community), but let's keep things simple by focusing on the needs of the program recipients and downstream impactees.

ADDITIONAL READINGS

Entries in Scriven's (1991) *Evaluation Thesaurus:*
- Consumer
- Consumer-based evaluation
- Critical competitors
- Goal achievement evaluation
- Goal-based evaluation
- Goal-free evaluation
- Monitoring
- Needs assessment
- Objectives
- Terror

Altschuld, J. W., & Witkin, B. R. (2000). *From needs assessment to action: Transforming needs into solution strategies.* Thousand Oaks, CA: Sage.
Bickman, L. (1987). The functions of program theory. In L. Bickman (Ed.), *New directions for program evaluation* (No. 33, pp. 5–18). San Francisco: Jossey-Bass.
McCrae, D., & Whittington, D. (1997). *Expert advice for policy choice.* Washington, DC: Georgetown University Press.
Munger, M. C. (2000). *Analyzing policy: Choices, conflicts, and practice.* New York: Norton.
Rogers, P. J., Hacsi, T. A., Petrosino, A., & Huebner, T. A. (Eds.). (2000). Program theory in evaluation: Challenges and opportunities [special issue]. *New Directions for Evaluation, 87.*
Scriven, M. (1974). Prose and cons about goal-free evaluation. In W. J. Popham (Ed.), *Evaluation in education: Current applications* (pp. 34–42). Berkeley, CA: McCutchan.
Weiss, C. H. (1997, Winter). Theory-based evaluation: Past, present, and future. *New Directions for Evaluation, 76,* 41–56.
Witkin, B. R., & Altschuld, J. W. (1995). *Planning and conducting needs assessments.* Thousand Oaks, CA: Sage.

EXERCISES

1. (a) What is the purpose of doing a needs assessment as part of an evaluation of a mature program? What is it for? How does it fit into the

evaluation? (b) Are there any evaluations for which a needs assessment might not be necessary? If so, describe them. If not, why not? (A suggested answer to this question is provided in the "Answers to Selected Exercises" section.)

2. On two pages or less, outline how you would go about conducting a needs assessment for your chosen evaluand. Identify your primary consumers and downstream impactees, and indicate how you would identify met and unmet needs as well as conscious and unconscious needs.

3. Draw up a table like Table 3.4. Keep the left-hand column the same, but in the right-hand column, outline how each of the considerations listed applies to the evaluand that you identified at the end of Chapter 1.

FOUR

ORGANIZING THE CRITERIA AND IDENTIFYING POTENTIAL SOURCES OF EVIDENCE

———————

In the previous chapter, we worked through the main sources for identifying the evaluative criteria, that is, those aspects or attributes that distinguish a good or valuable evaluand from a poor or not so valuable one. In this chapter, we bring them together and organize them so that we can see where they will fit into a final report. We also identify sources of evidence we can use to assess the evaluand on each criterion.

The criteria (or dimensions of merit) used to determine the quality or value of the evaluand fall under the Sub-evaluation checkpoints (Checkpoints 6–10) of the Key Evaluation Checklist (KEC): Process, Outcomes, **Comparative Cost-Effectiveness,** and Exportability. These are reproduced in Exhibit 4.1.

For each of Checkpoints 6 to 9, the evaluation team members need to generate an initial list of criteria they will use to evaluate process, outcomes, and comparative cost-effectiveness. Next, there may be a need to trim the list if the evaluation budget and timeline will not support such a detailed evaluation. Finally, during the course of the evaluation (and as part of the **rolling design**), unanticipated criteria may be added to the list and existing criteria may be modified. The evaluation needs to maintain this open-ended aspect to ensure that all important elements are captured and that any changing or unanticipated circumstances are responded to appropriately. Checkpoint 10 (Exportability) is

Exhibit 4.1   The Sub-evaluation Checkpoints of the Modified KEC

6. Process Evaluation	7. Outcome Evaluation	8 & 9. Comparative Cost-Effectiveness	10. Exportability
How good, valuable, or efficient are the evaluand's content (design) and implementation (delivery)?	How good or valuable are the impacts (both intended and unintended) on immediate recipients and other impactees?	How costly is the evaluand to consumers, funders, staff, and so forth, compared with alternative uses of the available resources that might feasibly have achieved outcomes of similar or greater value? Are the costs excessive, quite high, just acceptable, or very reasonable?	What elements of the evaluand (e.g., innovative approach or design) might make it potentially valuable or a significant contribution or advance in another setting?

often a purely open-ended question that is best asked by thoughtful reflection and expert input once the findings start to emerge from the other checkpoints.

The next few sections are intended to guide the evaluation team through the construction of criterion lists for the evaluation of process, outcomes, and cost, drawing on the groundwork we did in the previous chapter. Also included are some ideas for what to list as useful comparisons (to address the issue of comparative cost-effectiveness) and as possibilities for exportability.

THE IMPORTANCE OF CHOOSING
MULTIPLE SOURCES OF EVIDENCE

Evaluation is an intensely political undertaking that can spark some rather extreme psychological and emotional reactions. These reactions are at their peak when feedback is less positive than expected. Even a conclusion such as the following can give rise to an amazing deluge of personal attacks that are quite disproportionate to the nature of the feedback: "Basically, this is a very solid policy/program/project. But there are just a few areas where improvement is needed."

Why are the politics and psychology of evaluation important here? It reminds us of—and keeps us motivated about—the fact that whatever conclusions we draw (especially if they are negative in any way) must be backed up by solid irrefutable evidence. This gives rise to one of the most important rules in evaluation:

Never draw a conclusion based on a single piece of evidence.

This point cannot be emphasized enough. Sometimes you will need at least three or four independent angles on the same issue to make absolutely sure that you have a clear picture of what is happening. Where do you get these independent angles? From both of the following:

- Different types of data (both qualitative and quantitative)
- Multiple sources of information (e.g., existing documentation, observations, input from more than one group of stakeholders)

This basic principle is also called **triangulation.** When applying it in evaluation, it is important not only to collect data using different methods and sources but also to use those data together to draw conclusions about how well the evaluand is doing. This means going way beyond simply analyzing the data separately and presenting them as they are. If there are areas of divergence between what is found from one method, source, or perspective and another, this needs to be explored and explained. You might need to collect more data, and that is where the rolling design comes in handy.

A rolling design is basically an open-ended continuous improvement approach to doing evaluation. Instead of rolling out a major evaluation data collection effort all at once, we do so in phases. Starting with something roughly equivalent to a pilot (i.e., a small-scale initial data collection effort) and then expanding the scope each time, we evaluate the findings as we progress through each stage and take opportunities between phases to continuously improve the data collection instruments and methods so as to make sure that they capture any important information that arises along the way.

THE PROCESS EVALUATION CHECKPOINT

When we evaluate the "process" of a program or policy, we are talking about taking a critical look at the quality or value of everything about the program (what it is and does) *except* outcomes and costs. The elements of process that need to be evaluated fall into the following three categories:

- Content (what the evaluand consists of, i.e., its basic components or design)
- Implementation (how well or efficiently the evaluand was implemented or delivered to the consumers who needed it)
- Other features (any other elements or features that make the program good or bad but that are not covered in the first two points and are not outcomes or cost-related criteria)

Our task now is to take these three categories and feed into them all of the process-relevant ingredients we generated from the needs assessment and the list of other relevant sources of value, adding any extra considerations as necessary. If the list of criteria is quite large, it will be important to cluster the criteria into subcategories so that the list is organized and easier to understand. This may best be done by sticking pieces of paper with the criteria written on them to a board or wall where they can be moved around and organized.

Table 4.1 shows a sample list of **process evaluation** criteria for the grantsmanship workshop used as an example in the previous chapter. Each of the items in the middle column is drawn directly from Chapter 3, where we used relevant values and standards to generate a list of criteria. An extra column has been added to indicate some possible sources of evidence regarding program performance on those criteria.

As mentioned earlier, there is often a need to pare down the initial criterion list to make sure that the evaluation task can be completed within the allowed time frame and budget. Many of the items in Table 4.1 are overlapping or could be summarized more briefly, and some of the items are likely to fall outside the scope of a small-scale evaluation (e.g., financial and other accountability, fit with the organization's strategic goals, attractiveness to prospective participants). Through some judicious pruning and blending, the evaluation team should be able to come up with a shorter list of criteria that captures all of the important elements of Table 4.1 but is much more manageable (Table 4.2).

Table 4.1 Criterion List for Process Evaluation of a Grantsmanship Workshop

Category	Subcategories and Criteria	Sources of Evidence
Content evaluation	❑ Inclusion of all major steps required to identify and obtain funding ❑ Extent to which actual program reflects what was advertised to participants ❑ Fit with or contribution to the organization's strategic goals ❑ Fit with or contribution to the goals of the participants and their community organizations ❑ Meets any relevant content guidelines (e.g., professional association guidelines) ❑ Workshop makes sense "as a package" (i.e., not disjointed or inconsistent) ❑ Content of workshop corresponds to current knowledge in grant writing; no flawed, incorrect, or badly outdated content ❑ Attractiveness to prospective participants (i.e., generates sufficient enrollment) ❑ Relevance to participants' communities ❑ Compliance with professional standards	❑ Expert review ❑ Participant feedback ❑ Comparison relative to any standards
Implementation evaluation	❑ Selection of people into the workshop is in compliance with the law ❑ Financial and other accountability ❑ Basic legal and ethical considerations (e.g., participant and staff legal rights are protected, fairness/equity) ❑ Respect for diverse cultures and viewpoints and understanding of the key issues in the contexts where they work (or plan to work) ❑ Teaching approach fits reasonably well with local norms and culture-linked learning styles and was engaging/interesting for participants	❑ Review by the organization's lawyer or legal department ❑ Expert review ❑ Participant feedback ❑ Comparison with relevant standards

Table 4.2   Condensed Version of Criterion List for Process Evaluation of
                  a Grantsmanship Workshop

Category	Subcategories and Criteria	Sources of Evidence
Content evaluation	❑ Accurately covers all major steps required to identify and obtain funding; consistent with grant-writing "best practice" ❑ Fit with the needs or goals of the participants and their community organizations	❑ Expert review (e.g., check against any relevant content guidelines issued by professional associations) ❑ Participant feedback on fit with needs and adequacy of coverage
Implementation evaluation	❑ Basic legal and ethical considerations (e.g., fairness/equity to participants) ❑ Respect for—and a teaching approach that fits—the represented cultures and viewpoints and the contexts where they work (or plan to work)	❑ Participant feedback ❑ Review by an expert in culture-linked learning styles

The shorter list of process evaluation criteria is clearly more feasible for the small program described here. However, it is always a good idea to keep the longer list on hand in case the evaluation team encounters some important aspect of process that is not covered in the reduced list. In addition, the evaluation report should state briefly how the scope of the process evaluation was reduced and the rationale behind the inclusion or exclusion of criteria, that is, why certain elements were considered to be inside or outside the bounds of the evaluation.

THE OUTCOME EVALUATION CHECKPOINT

Outcomes or impacts (this book uses these terms interchangeably, but see the Glossary for further explanation) are things that happen—or are prevented from happening—as a result of the program. Outcomes can affect anyone listed (or who should have been listed) under the Consumers checkpoint. That means all intended and unintended recipients, users, or impactees such as workshop participants, those who dropped out, those who completed the workshop successfully, their employers and colleagues, and their siblings and other family members.

As we noted under process evaluation, most evaluations will not have the time or budget available to investigate in-depth impacts on all **potential impactees;** however, one should definitely include current and past participants and, in the grantsmanship workshop example, their employers (or the community organization with which they work). If anything substantial turns up, the evaluation team can investigate it further. If not, at least the possibility was investigated.

The procedure for generating a criterion checklist for outcomes is very similar to that for process evaluation. First, create a broad-brush list that incorporates the outcome variables from the logic model you have drawn (for the grantsmanship workshop example, see Chapter 3). Use these as your main criteria. Add any **subcriteria** you may have identified (e.g., the list of knowledge about grant making that we generated after creating the logic model). Finally, add any other variables drawn from the needs assessment (i.e., your investigation of met, unmet, conscious, and unconscious performance needs). The list generated by the evaluation team might resemble that in Table 4.3.

Note that the categories in Table 4.3 are drawn directly from the outcome columns in the logic model (Chapter 3), omitting the right-hand column because these outcomes are too far downstream to realistically include in an early evaluation. The criteria in Table 4.3 are the boxes in the logic model, whereas the subcriteria under Knowledge about grant making are included in the list that was generated after developing the logic model based on stakeholder input. In this case, the resulting table is not too cumbersome and does not need to be condensed.

Table 4.3 Criterion List for Outcome Evaluation of a Grantsmanship Workshop

Category	Criteria and Subcriteria	Sources of Evidence

Knowledge, skill, and attitude gain	❑ Knowledge about grant making:
	   ✓ Knowing what kinds of things can and cannot get funded by grants
	   ✓ Knowing where to find grants
	   ✓ Knowing about other funding opportunities and sources apart from grants
	   ✓ Knowing that behind every charity or foundation were people wanting to make the world a better place (i.e., understanding the perspectives or missions of foundations and of people reviewing proposals)
	   ✓ Knowing the elements that go into a grant proposal
	   ✓ Knowing how to write a grant proposal (i.e., structure and steps involved)
	   ✓ Knowing how to design a grants pursuit plan and schedule
	   ✓ Understanding whether the person's community organization or school was ready to pursue grants and other funding opportunities
		❑ Participant self-assessment of knowledge, confidence about writing a proposal, and writing skills before and after the workshop
		
		 ❑ Instructor assessment of knowledge gain in participants

	❑ Confidence	
	❑ Writing skills	
Application of knowledge, skill, and attitudes	❑ Grant proposals being written and submitted	❑ Self-reports from participants about proposals in progress or submitted ❑ Assessments by workshop facilitator (based on contact with participants)
	❑ Quality of proposals	❑ Assessments by grants expert

THE COMPARATIVE COST-EFFECTIVENESS CHECKPOINT

Any program, no matter how it is funded, needs to have cost included in its evaluation. Even if it generates extremely valuable outcomes, these must always be considered in terms of what it cost to obtain them. Cost includes not only monetary costs but also time, effort, space, and **opportunity costs** (i.e., the activities that might have taken place if these resources had not been devoted to the program).

To help make the consideration of cost a bit more systematic, a useful tool to use is Scriven's (1991) "cost cube." The cost cube considers three dimensions of cost: types of costs, costs to whom, and costs when (Exhibit 4.2).

Exhibit 4.2 Cost Cube for the Grantsmanship Workshop

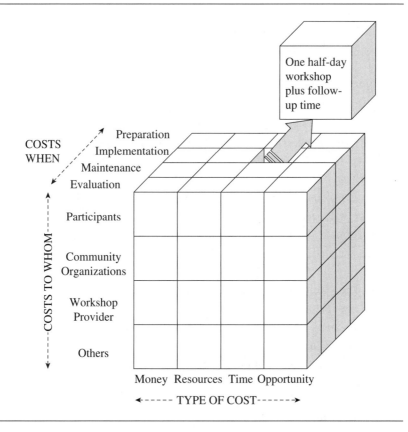

Not all of the "to whom" parties listed will have elements in each of the cubes shown (e.g., workshop participants will not incur money costs for evaluating the program). Nevertheless, the cost cube can be a very useful tool for making sure that all important costs are considered. In some evaluations, one particular slice of the cube will be much more important than the rest of the cube.

What do we do with all of these costs once we have listed them? Recall that all of the Subevaluation checkpoints (6–10) in the Key Evaluation Checklist (KEC), including cost, need to be addressed in an explicitly evaluative way. This means that we are seeking to answer cost evaluation questions such as the following:

- Are/Were the costs really excessive, quite high, acceptable/reasonable, or extremely cheap?
- How costly is/was this evaluand to consumers, funders, staff, and so forth, compared with alternative uses of the available resources that might feasibly have achieved outcomes of similar or greater value?

Note that these questions go right to the heart of the "good value" or "poor value" issue and do not just stop at the surface with the questions, "Did the evaluand stay within budget?" or "What were the costs?" A thorough treatment of cost evaluation will question whether the budget itself was excessively high or low and whether there were more cost-effective alternatives that should have been considered.

To determine how the cost of the evaluand stacks up relative to alternatives, we will need a list of comparisons (or "critical competitors") and some information about their relative costs. Scriven (1991) suggests thinking through the alternatives under four broad categories:

- The "Rolls Royce" (an exemplary intervention or evaluand and an example of what is widely regarded as "best practice" or state-of-the-art)
- The "Shoestring" (a creative low-budget option)
- "A Little More" (an option that has slightly more resources allocated to it)
- "A Little Less" (a slightly more streamlined or economical version of the evaluand)

With this list added to the mix, we now have the main ingredients needed to complete the Comparative Cost-Effectiveness checkpoint. The cost cube provides us with a three-dimensional tool for identifying the important descriptive data, whereas the list of comparisons will allow us to place these costs in the context of what else was available. Later, we will need to combine both of these pieces of information with a set of relevant values or standards to find the answers to the explicitly evaluative cost evaluation questions discussed previously. This part of the evaluation is called the merit determination step and is covered in Chapter 8.

THE EXPORTABILITY CHECKPOINT

When considering the Exportability checkpoint, the evaluation team needs to consider what elements of the evaluand (e.g., innovative design or approach) might make it potentially valuable or a significant contribution or advance in another setting. For example, suppose that the evaluand is a manufacturing process using a highly innovative technology that dramatically reduces quality problems relative to any other process tried previously. Not only does the process have value for the company using it, but the idea could potentially be applied in other contexts, perhaps completely revolutionizing manufacturing processes around the world. From a commercial perspective, the company might consider setting up a consulting unit that assists other companies in upgrading their manufacturing operations.

In many ways, the Exportability checkpoint evaluates the significance of the evaluand as an advancement in the field. A good example of this, also from the manufacturing sector, is Six Sigma methodology. This approach to quality management was originally developed by General Electric, Motorola, and a few other companies. Now many of these companies sell training and certification in Six Sigma methodology, allowing trainees to qualify at different levels of expertise such as "green belts" and "black belts."

Note that it is not always the case that the evaluand has significant value outside its current context. However, it is always worth considering the possibility under this checkpoint and then skipping it in the final report if there is nothing worth noting.

ADDITIONAL READINGS

Entries in Scriven's (1991) *Evaluation Thesaurus:*
- Cost analysis
- Fallacy of irrelevant expertise
- Multiplism
- Opportunity cost
- Outcome evaluation
- Proactive evaluation
- Process evaluation
- Technicism

Levin, H. M., & McEwan, P. J. (2001). Introduction to cost analysis. In H. M. Levin & P. J. McEwan (Eds.), *Cost-effectiveness analysis: Methods and applications* (2nd ed., pp. 1–30). Thousand Oaks, CA: Sage.

Patton, M. Q. (2002). *Qualitative research and evaluation methods* (3rd ed.). Thousand Oaks, CA: Sage.

Patton, M. Q. (2003). *Qualitative Evaluation Checklist.* Available online: http://evaluation.wmich.edu/checklists/

Pyzdek, T. (2003). *The Six Sigma handbook: A complete guide for greenbelts, black-belts, and managers at all levels* (2nd ed.). New York: McGraw-Hill.

Stake, R. (1995). *The art of case study research.* Thousand Oaks, CA: Sage.

EXERCISES

1. Create a criterion list for the Process Evaluation checkpoint of your evaluation plan. Be sure to follow the process used in this chapter, step-by-step, to make sure that you have not missed anything important. (Hint: A common mistake here is to describe the process by which you plan to conduct the evaluation. That is not what you are being asked to do. Rather, you are being asked for the criteria you would use to figure out whether the content and implementation of your evaluand are any good or not.)

2. Suppose that you have been asked to evaluate a training program designed to help young unemployed people seek and obtain work effectively. Although the "proof of the pudding" is in whether the participants actually find jobs, one other important outcome (a bit further upstream) is the quality of the résumés they produce while they are in the program.

    a. How would you go about defining what makes a "good" résumé (based on the sources we covered in Chapter 3)? (Note that for this exercise, you will be unable to define this in terms of outcomes, e.g., "A good résumé is one that gets the person a job." Rather, you need to create guidelines for evaluating the actual piece of paper before you know whether the person has a job or not.)

    b. List at least three types of evidence you would gather from different sources (specify the sources) to evaluate the participants' résumés (on half a page or less).

    c. Suppose that a cost-conscious program manager suggests that you are being wasteful and should use just a single indicator instead. How would you respond (on half a page or less)?

3. Create a criterion list for the Outcome Evaluation checkpoint of your evaluation plan.

4. Use the cost cube to identify the most important costs that should be considered for your evaluand. Identify at least four critical competitors with which you will compare your evaluand to assess comparative cost-effectiveness.

5. Identify some areas of potential exportability for your evaluand.

⊰ FIVE ⊱

DEALING WITH THE
CAUSATION ISSUE

—•◦•—

No discussion of evaluation nuts and bolts is complete without some
mention of the **causation** issue. Although this is a relatively simple
concept to grasp in everyday life, causation is both one of the most difficult
and one of the most important issues in evaluation. Even if we observe changes
that are consistent with the expectations or goals of a program or another
evaluand, we cannot correctly refer to these as "impacts" or "outcomes" unless
we can demonstrate that the evaluand was at least a primary cause of those
changes.

Strategies for inferring causation form a key part of what should be written into the Methodology checkpoint of the Key Evaluation Checklist (KEC)
(Exhibit 5.1). The choice of evaluation design affects the evaluation team's
ability to make causal inferences. Causation is also relevant for the Outcomes
checkpoint because identifying anything as an outcome is saying that it was
caused by the evaluand.

One of the great challenges with causation is that the further down the
causal chain (toward what we might call "ultimate outcomes") one goes, the
more other factors come into play. For example, the career success of a university graduate can be attributed not only to the quality of education he or she
received but also to the quality of mentoring and advancement opportunities
after graduation, support from family, aptitude or intelligence, and many other
factors. The fact that so many variables are in play makes it quite difficult to pin
down whether career success (and other downstream changes) is substantially

Exhibit 5.1   The KEC Checkpoints for Which the Causation Issue Is Most
Relevant

III. Methodology
What is the overall design of the evaluation (e.g., quasi-experimental,
participatory, goal free)? Explain why (briefly).

7. Outcome Evaluation
How good or valuable are the impacts (both intended and unintended) on
immediate recipients and other impactees?

---

due to the evaluand (in this case, the program from which the student graduated) or can be attributed mostly to other factors.

Although the causation issue is incredibly important, demonstrating causal links can seem like an impossible task, especially for evaluators with limited time and resources (most of us likely fall into that category). For this reason, many people abandon the issue altogether, either by tacking on a bunch of disclaimers to their evaluations or by downplaying the importance of causal analysis.

Here is the good news: There is some practical light at the end of the causation tunnel, and the tunnel is not nearly as long and treacherous as legend has it. To deal with the causation issue, we need to answer four important questions in the following order:

- How certain does the client need us to be to say that the evaluand "caused" a certain change?
- What are the basic principles for inferring causation?
- What types of evidence do we have available to help us identify or rule out possible causal links?
- How should we decide what blend of evidence will generate the level of certainty needed most cost-effectively?

CERTAINTY ABOUT CAUSATION

Many readers of this book may have noticed that in the academic literature, research conclusions are often so laced with disclaimers about causation that one wonders whether it is possible to demonstrate causal links at all. Why would an evaluator on a limited budget even bother trying? The trick here is to understand two things. First, there are some major differences between the standards of proof being used by academics and what may be appropriate for us to use. Second, many of the methods used to address causation in the empirical literature are, quite frankly, pretty weak on the causal inference front.

Every profession has its own "dialect," including special terminology and rules regarding how to talk about things. For academics in the hard sciences and at least most of the social sciences, the norms dictate that even if researchers have evidence that makes them 99% sure that something is true, they still cannot say that they "know" or have "proved" it. Instead, the language is always framed in a cautious way, for example, "The evidence appears to suggest . . ." or "We found tentative support for . . ." This is in sharp contrast to the way in which we (and our clients) use terms such as *know* and *certain* in everyday conversation.

Organizational reality in for-profit, not-for-profit, and many government settings is that most decision makers would say that they *knew* something— and were prepared to make decisions on the basis of that knowledge—if they were, say, 70% or 80% certain based on the evidence. Of course, this varies a bit from setting to setting and from decision to decision, but most would agree that this sounds about right.

Our task as evaluators is to provide timely answers about the quality or value of products, programs, policies, and other evaluands, often to help people make decisions. These may be internal decisions about how to improve something or consumer decisions about which product to buy or which school to attend. Because each decision-making context requires a different level of certainty, it is important to be clear up front about the level of certainty required. Then, rather than throwing in the methodological kitchen sink or skipping the causal inference step, we will be in a much better position to strategically put together a blend of methods that will meet that certainty requirement (Davidson, 2003).

Some of the research in the academic literature tends to be somewhat lacking in evidence for making causal inferences. There are two reasons for this. One is that many researchers use wholly quantitative or wholly qualitative methods in their studies. The other reason is that in quantitative studies, researchers often lack the opportunity to use large samples, control groups, and random assignment. In such cases, quantitative methods alone tend to be woefully inadequate for attributing causation, as are many all-qualitative designs. So, those disclaimers about causation that we see in such single-method (i.e., all-quantitative or all-qualitative) research are almost certainly justified. Moreover, they are attributable to shortcomings in the research design itself rather than to the impossibility of solving the problem.

INFERRING CAUSATION: BASIC PRINCIPLES

> What are we trying to do when we infer causation? There are two basic principles here. First, look for evidence for and against the suspected cause (i.e., the evaluand). Second, look for evidence for and against any important alternative causes (i.e., rival explanations).

When considering whether the evaluand caused the observed changes, the evaluation team members need to consider what evidence, if present, would help to convince them that this was the case. Conversely, if such evidence were absent, to what extent would that convince them that the evaluand was probably not the cause?

Equally important in causal analysis is the careful consideration of any and all important rival explanations for the observed changes. But how do we know which rival explanations are most important and how many we need to eliminate? That all depends on what level of certainty you need in your decision-making context. Sometimes you will need to eliminate only the "primary suspects," that is, the most likely alternative explanations. Sometimes you will need to rule out just about anything that anyone can suggest.

Probably the best way in which to approach this task is with a stepwise process. The first step is to put yourself in the shoes of the harshest critics you can imagine and think what objections they might raise to your claim that the evaluand caused a particular effect. Using a mix of strategies from the next section, gather enough evidence to confirm or rule out that rival explanation. Then consider what the next objection is likely to be. Repeat the process until all remaining alternative explanations are unlikely enough that they do not threaten your conclusions given the level of certainty needed to make them.

Usually, the more politically charged or controversial something is, the more likely it is that there will be opponents, many of whom will attack the methodology of the evaluation if they do not like the conclusions. And the harder people attack, the more solid your answers need to be. For this reason, the level of certainty required may change depending on what you uncover in the evaluation.

Even if a fairly high level of certainty is required, the trick is not to focus on a single "Rolls Royce" method for causal inference (e.g., an elaborate experimental design with multiple controls). Rather, you should use a strategic mix of methods that have different strengths and that *together* will give you enough evidence to be certain enough that the link is (or is not) causal. This principle (using methods with different strengths to complement each other) is called *critical multiplism* (Shadish, 1994).

INFERRING CAUSATION: EIGHT STRATEGIES

Some academics, among others, frequently say that the only way in which to infer causation is with the use of randomized **experimental designs.** This is sometimes met with a response from practitioners that such methods are simply not feasible in real-world settings. This is not true.

There is good news on both fronts for evaluators who need to know whether the changes they are seeing really are outcomes (i.e., changes attributable to the evaluand)—and that is all of us. The fact of the matter is that experimental designs (or at least **quasi-experimental designs**) are actually quite viable more often than we might expect. But even when they are not, there are several other practical strategies, some of which make use of some very powerful qualitative methodologies, that can be used to supplement or even replace the use of experimental and quasi-experimental designs.

The following subsections describe a range of methods for inferring causation, from very simple commonsense strategies to some more complex methods. For a small-scale evaluation, even some modest evidence about causation could prove to be sufficient. For more high-stakes evaluations, the evaluation team will need to draw on a range of methods to attain the level of certainty required.

Strategy 1: Ask Observers

Suppose that someone asked you to name the four or five most important factors that led to the development of your current professional skill set. Most of us could easily identify which experiences were the most important and which ones had nearly no effect whatsoever. For the powerful learning experiences we have in our careers, there is no doubt in our minds that the experiences were primary *causes* of the learning. In many cases, we can also identify important contextual factors or we can point to a combination of experiences that culminated in a quantum leap in knowledge. And we can just as easily list a number of courses, books, conferences, and work assignments that added very little (i.e., where there was virtually no causal link).

It is amazing how "arm's length" we are as we look at the impacts of things on people's lives, especially in quantitative research. We gather pre- and posttest measures, and then use regression and other statistical tools to partial out the extraneous effects of this and that, without ever considering that perhaps we should start by just asking the question directly. In qualitative research, such evidence is perhaps more likely to be collected, but it is often not treated as explicit evidence of causation.

The "ask observers" strategy includes two possibilities. The first is to directly ask people who were supposedly affected by the evaluand (i.e., actual or potential impactees). The second possibility is to ask those who were in a position to observe the effects on impactees (e.g., coworkers, parents, teachers, trainers).

There are two ways in which to infer causation by just asking the people who were supposedly affected by the evaluand. One is to first gather some data about changes in outcome variables (e.g., reduced absenteeism, improved performance) and then to identify those people who experienced (a) little change, (b) some change, and (c) substantial change (positive or negative). In a follow-up interview or survey, the evaluation team members could ask, for example, "We noticed that you have had a substantial decrease in the number of times you were absent from or late to work during the past few months. Can you tell us a little about why that is?" The answer would tell you whether the individual believed that the evaluand was the primary cause or not and/or the extent to which other factors (e.g., contextual factors, other events) might also have contributed to the change. Note that the use of an open-ended question here allows respondents to list other causes that the evaluation team might not even have considered.

The other way in which to gather causal information from those directly affected by the evaluand is to actually work causation into the survey or interview questions themselves. So, instead of asking people to rate their level of knowledge before and after completing a training or educational program, you might ask directly, "How much has your knowledge increased *as a result of* participating in this program?" (Include the italics in the survey item to make sure that respondents pay attention to it.) To probe other causes of knowledge gain, you might ask, "Did anything else besides the program increase your knowledge in this area over the same period of time?" To get at side effects, you might ask, "Please describe anything else that has happened to you or someone you know *as a result of* participating in this program." This way, you are not simply asking what has changed since before the program; instead, you are asking directly about the things that people know or believe were caused by the program.

Some researchers may argue that causation-rich questions such as these are leading, that is, that they implicitly direct the respondent to answer in a particular way (usually positive). It is true that we need to be careful about question wording when designing interview instruments or questionnaires, bearing in mind that in most cases, it is quite obvious what the evaluation team is trying to get at. But do not forget that these same questions, if well constructed, can also provide the opportunity for the respondent to say, "My knowledge of X increased during that time, but not because of that program." The arm's-length pre- and postquestionnaire that does not ask about causation eliminates the opportunity for people to even mention this.

A great example that incorporates both of these "just ask people" strategies just described is Brinkerhoff's (2003) Success Case Method. All participants in a particular program are given a 5-minute questionnaire on which they are asked whether or not they have been able to achieve enhanced performance as a result of the program and, if so, to give an example. Claims of dramatic improvement are then cross-checked against hard data to identify the true success cases, and a sample of these individuals are then interviewed in-depth to find out what it was that allowed them to get so much out of the program. In this case, the causation question is not just *whether* the program produced the effect but also *what other factors* enabled or inhibited the effect.

Some might argue that the individual might not be a reliable witness to help answer the causation question. In rare cases, this may be true. However, there are few evaluands that are so subtle in their effects that the recipient does not even notice their influence, so it seems remiss to exclude the views of the very people who likely saw things happen with their own eyes or experienced change directly. Of course, in most cases, other evidence will also be required to make justifiable causal inferences.

The "ask observers" method is not limited to those who were themselves changed. Often it is possible to identify people who observed a cause produce an effect in someone (or something) else. For example, parents of very young children can often directly observe the influence of particular experiences on their children (e.g., whether children mimic violent acts after watching a certain television show). A spouse might be in a good position to observe whether a violent offender's behavior was affected by a counseling session. Or an observer in a mathematics class might be able to see directly whether children learn faster and are more engaged when a new practical exercise is used to illustrate a concept.

Strategy 2: Check Whether the Content
of the Evaluand Matches the Outcome

Here is another super simple commonsense strategy for inferring causation. Suppose that a treatment program for alcoholics taught participants several very specific strategies they could use to avert potential relapses. Also, suppose that participants in this program really did have very few relapses after completing the program. If the program were truly the cause of the lack of relapses, the evaluation team would expect to find that the alcoholics who avoided relapses used the strategies they had been taught in the treatment program rather than other strategies they knew previously or had picked up elsewhere. In other words, the content of the evaluand should quite often be reflected in some of the outcomes themselves if the evaluand did indeed cause the observed change.

When using this method, it is equally important to look for counterexamples. In this case, that means other strategies that were not learned in the program but that were used successfully to avert relapses. Where (or from whom) were these strategies learned? This information may point to one or more additional causes of alcoholics' success that were not attributable to the specific program. The existence of these additional causes does not negate the value of the program. However, if all potential relapses were prevented using strategies other than those taught in the program, and especially if relapses were not prevented in several cases where the taught strategies were used, this would call into question the value of the relapse avoidance strategies (and perhaps of the entire program).

Strategy 3: Look for Other Telltale Patterns
That Suggest One Cause or Another

In addition to looking to see whether early outcomes (e.g., the behavior changes just described) match the content of the evaluand, it is often possible to identify other telltale patterns that suggest a particular cause. These patterns, or "signature traces," are described by Scriven as the key to making causal inferences using the *modus operandi method*. This method uses the detective metaphor to describe the way in which potential causal explanations are identified and tested. Scriven describes how chains of causal events often leave signature traces that the evaluator tracks down by moving both up and down the causal chain. Starting with the observed effects, or "clues," one can move up the causal chain, identifying what might have caused them.

In the opposite direction, one can start with the evaluand itself, or the "suspect," and trace down the causal chain to see what impacts it might have had and through what mechanisms. If evidence is consistent with the expected "trace" left by a particular causal chain, confidence in that chain as the correct causal explanation is increased. Evidence that contradicts the expected trace eliminates that causal chain as a possibility, and missing evidence makes the explanation more doubtful.

The modus operandi method works best for evaluands that have highly distinctive patterns of effects. For example, a faith-based marriage counseling program, if effective, not only would result in partners using strategies taught within the sessions to improve their marriages but also would be likely to yield a telltale pattern of distinctive side effects. We might expect participants to report increased spiritual enlightenment and stronger connections with the relevant faith community. We might also expect to see less tolerance of attitudes and behaviors that are inconsistent with participants' faith. In contrast, improvements in marital relationships that were due not to the faith-based element but rather to the regular counseling would not be expected to yield such a pattern.

In some cases, there is not a great deal known about the patterns we should expect if a certain evaluand is likely to cause a particular effect. In such cases, it can be useful (albeit a weaker option) to draw an analogy with what is known about something similar. So, if the pattern observed closely resembles a known pattern in an analogous case, this can be interpreted as at least partial evidence for a causal link.

Let's use an example to illustrate the use of analogy as partial evidence of causation. Suppose that you had been asked to evaluate a cutting-edge intervention that helped teams of people to critically reflect on their work and generate new ways of doing things. Also, suppose that there was virtually no documentation about what happens when such interventions are successful. As an alternative, the evaluation team might dig for similar interventions that had not been used on teams. Previous research shows that when individuals are taught to critically reflect on their own work (e.g., in executive coaching), they can make transformational improvements in their own performance. The team learning intervention seeks to translate this idea for an interactive team setting. By examining the patterns in executive coaching success cases and seeing whether they are mirrored in the team intervention, it may be possible to use this as indirect evidence for a causal link by drawing an analogy with the individual-level version of the intervention. This evidence alone will not allow the evaluation team to make causal inferences, but it is certainly one additional piece of evidence to add to the pool.

Strategy 4: Check Whether the Timing of Outcomes Makes Sense

In nearly all cases, an outcome should appear only at the same time as or after whatever caused it.[1] With distal outcomes in particular (i.e., those quite far downstream in the causal chain), the evaluation team should expect a considerable delay between the introduction of the evaluand and the appearance of outcomes. In general, the further downstream the outcomes, the longer they should take to appear.

For example, suppose that we were evaluating a community health intervention that focused on improving diet and exercise. We should probably expect to see the following:

- Fairly immediate knowledge and skill gain relating to the subject matter taught as part of the intervention (i.e., we should be able to detect this during and/or immediately after any health education component)
- A short delay (days to weeks) before the knowledge and skills are translated into changed behavior such as improved eating habits and exercise

- A moderate delay (weeks to months) before we could expect to see changes in individual health indicators, such as cholesterol, weight, and blood pressure, as a result of sustained behavior change
- A long delay (probably years) before these changes could be expected to have become widespread enough in the community to affect community-level health statistics such as the incidence of diabetes and heart disease and average life expectancy

Information about expected time frames for outcomes may be found in the relevant literature and from experts in the field. But in many cases, the evaluation team's logic might not be too far off target, so just taking the time to think through the timing issue will probably pay dividends.

There are three ways in which this information can be used to help confirm or disconfirm causal links. First, each identified outcome should be checked to ensure that it did not occur either before the evaluand was introduced or unrealistically quickly afterward. In fact, this is one good reason to check on some of those downstream outcomes at points in time when it should be too early to detect any change.

Second, outcomes should also be checked to see whether the timing of their appearance would be more (or equally) logical relative to other possible causes. For example, suppose that on-the-job performance improved following a well-executed training program that also coincided with the introduction of a performance-linked bonus system. In this case, the evaluation team would look at the timing of the improvements relative to the introduction of the two interventions to try to work out whether one or both of these (and/or something else) were likely to have been a substantial cause of the improvement.

The third strategy for using information about the timing of outcomes is to check whether outcomes further downstream in the logic model did not occur out of sequence, that is, before the outcomes that were expected to lead to them. In the earlier example of a community health program, if participant cholesterol and blood pressure dropped prior to any change in eating or exercising behavior, this makes it unlikely that the observed improvements in health indicators were caused by the program.

For those readers interested in exploring the timing of outcomes in more depth, Lipsey (1989) presents a very useful set of graphs that show different patterns of responses to interventions, including a delayed reaction and an initial response followed by a decay.

Strategy 5: Check Whether the "Dose" Is Related Logically to the "Response"

In the messy real world of evaluation, we are often faced with situations where an evaluand has been implemented inconsistently. For example, the author was once asked to evaluate the effectiveness of a new **management-by-objectives** (MBO) and reward system. A year after the system was rolled out organization-wide, it turned out that approximately a quarter of all staff still had no objectives in place and that the range in the quality of performance objectives was extremely variable across the organization for those who had objectives in place. Although the social scientists in us might throw our hands in the air in frustration in this kind of situation, the shrewd evaluators in us should instantly spot this as an excellent opportunity to check the causal link between the evaluand and its suspected effects.

The dose–response idea (i.e., if more A, then more B) comes from the medical metaphor of drug testing—the higher the dose, the greater the response should be (up to a point). For a performance management system such as the one just described, the more completely and effectively the system had been implemented in a particular work unit, the higher the "dose" (of MBO) for that unit and the greater the expected improvement in performance. If we found that performance had improved more dramatically in units where the system had been poorly implemented (or not implemented at all), this would be evidence that the new performance appraisal system was probably not the cause of the improvement.

When looking at the relationship between the "dose" of the evaluand and the "response" (magnitude of the outcome), it is important to bear in mind that this might not necessarily be a linear relationship. It is very common to have a "ceiling effect" where longer duration or more intensive exposure starts adding little or nothing in incremental value beyond a lower dose. Also, in many cases, there might be an "overdose" where excessive exposure or duration backfires and produces a less than optimal (or a very negative) result. As a simple example, schoolchildren will probably tolerate only so many hours per week of extracurricular reading before they develop a loathing for the activity.

An extension of the dose–response relationship is the situation where multiple doses are given and multiple responses are observed. Evidence for causation is strengthened if the evaluand is implemented in several different contexts and if the effect is observed every time (or nearly every time) the cause is introduced (i.e., when A, always B).

Strategy 6: Make Comparisons
With a "Control" or "Comparison" Group

The dichotomous (on/off) version of the dose–response relationship is the comparison between people who have been recipients of an evaluand and those who have not. This relationship forms the basis for the classic experimental design. In a fully randomized experimental design, participants would be randomly assigned to either a treatment group (receive the evaluand) or a control group (receive nothing or an alternative intervention). Provided that sampling is done carefully and that sample sizes are large enough, randomization helps to make sure that there are no systematic differences between the evaluand recipients and nonrecipients. It is rather like thoroughly shuffling a deck of cards to minimize the chance that one player gets all of the high cards.

In a quasi-experimental design, groups would not be randomly assigned, but the evaluation team would seek out a closely similar comparison group with which to compare results. Careful matching of treatment and comparison groups eliminates or greatly reduces the likelihood that rival explanations exist (e.g., the groups were different from the start). For example, studies of the effectiveness of the death penalty have compared crime rates in adjacent counties across state lines where one state introduces or abolishes the death penalty but the other state does not. Researchers carefully check to ensure that prior crime rates are similar and that the inhabitants of each county are similar demographically, socioeconomically, and in any other important respects to make sure that the comparison is reasonable to make.

Strategy 7: Control Statistically for Extraneous Variables

In the statistical analysis of data from experimental, quasi-experimental, and even single group (dose-response) designs, it is often possible to "control for" certain characteristics of the recipients and/or the contexts that are suspected of being correlated with the outcomes. This is particularly useful in cases where the evaluation team cannot be certain that the control or comparison group (if any) is truly similar in these respects.

For example, suppose that you were evaluating an innovative new method for teaching mathematics in a high school and that you had decided to use a comparison group of classes that were not exposed to the new technique. Even if you were able to randomly assign students to the classes that used and did not use the method, it might still be useful to make sure that prior aptitude in math was not causing the results to look better or worse than they really were. The simple way in which to check this is to compare the treatment and control classes on prior math performance or scores on an aptitude or achievement test to ensure that there was no significant difference. But another more sophisticated strategy is to use a statistical technique called *regression analysis* to "partial out" the effect of prior aptitude in math so that any differences observed were not due to that factor. In this way, the evaluation team can statistically control for characteristics that might cloud the results.

Options and strategies available in the area of experimental, quasi-experimental, and related designs and associated data analysis are very numerous indeed. For some evaluations, these designs are essential. In such cases, if the evaluation team members do not have a specialist to help with the design, they would be well advised to find one. And in the meantime, there are many resources available to give the beginner a simple overview of the principles and enough know-how to design simple experimental studies.

Strategy 8: Identify and Check the Underlying Causal Mechanism(s)

Another commonsense strategy we use a lot in everyday life is to look for an underlying mechanism that will help to make the case for causation more or less convincing. For example, the link between cigarette smoking and lung cancer was for years argued to be purely correlational. However, when research identified several substances known to be carcinogenic in cigarette smoke, it became more difficult to argue that there was not a causal link.

As a second example,[2] suppose that a team of consultants had been brought into an organization to facilitate a team learning intervention. The organization has shown an increase in profitability for the past quarter, and management wants to know whether this was due to the team learning intervention or to something else. How might the evaluation team use causal mechanisms to trace potential causal links?

The logic model in Exhibit 5.2 shows how this hypothetical team learning intervention would probably affect the bottom line. Evidence in favor of a causal link would include (a) an increase in investigation and critical dialogue skills during the intervention and (b) evidence that cost-saving improvements were identified or implemented during the intervention itself. Note that the logic model also includes the important contextual factor of a supportive work environment, which would be required for the success of the intervention.

Exhibit 5.2 Logic Model Connecting a Team Learning Intervention to the Bottom Line

Facilitated team learning intervention	→	Investigation and critical dialogue skills	→	Identification of improvement opportunities	→	Increased productivity and revenue
↘		↓	↗		↗	
Supportive work environment	→	Motivating and meaningful work	→	Commitment and intent to stay with organization	→	Cost savings (efficiency and/ or prevention of turnover)

Evidence against a causal link would include (a) no evidence of improved investigation or critical dialogue skills, (b) no evidence that the intervention had a motivating effect (with most participants complaining that it was boring), and (c) most employees attributing their improved performance to the new incentive system rather than the team learning intervention.

Where would a logic model like this come from, and what would make it more or less useful as a source of evidence for causal inference? An evaluation team with knowledge of team learning interventions (and access to the relevant literature) would be able to create a model that is consistent with cutting-edge knowledge about team learning.

CHOOSING A BLEND OF STRATEGIES TO ADDRESS THE CAUSATION ISSUE

As mentioned earlier, there are times when one must build a virtually bullet-proof case for causation, whereas there are other times when such a high level of certainty is not required. Do you need *all* of the previously discussed evidence in hand to demonstrate causation in a particular case? Usually not. Again, it is prudent to put yourself in the shoes of a tough critic. Identify the most potentially threatening rival explanation and then choose the types of evidence that will most quickly and cost-effectively confirm or dispel that rival explanation. Bear in mind that your analysis could show that something else was in fact a major cause of the observed change(s). Make sure that you hunt specifically for evidence that would *confirm* such a rival explanation; do not just look for evidence that would confirm what you hope to find. This hunt for disconfirming evidence as well as confirming evidence will make your conclusions stronger and more defensible.

The elimination of rival explanations is an iterative process and is one that can be greatly assisted by having a group of "devil's advocates" to help you. Once the first round is complete, identify the next most likely alternative explanation and repeat the process just described. Continue until you have amassed a body of evidence that provides you with enough certainty to draw causal inferences given the political pressure your findings will encounter as well as the decision-making or reporting context you face.

Does the evaluator need to show that there were absolutely no other influences affecting the bottom line at the time? Certainly not; there are always other influences at work in a complex system. The main issue is whether the intervention you are evaluating added a *practically significant impact* above and beyond whatever else was happening at the time that was large enough to justify its cost.

NOTES

1. There are rare exceptions to this, for example, when a premonition is caused by a future event. However, these cases rarely apply in professional evaluations.

2. This example was also used in an earlier article about linking organizational learning to the bottom line (Davidson, 2003).

ADDITIONAL READINGS

Entries in Scriven's (1991) *Evaluation Thesaurus:*
- Causation
- Constructionism
- Etiology
- Evaluability assessment
- Illuminative evaluation
- Naturalistic
- Positivism
- Postpositivism
- Program theory
- Quasi-experimental design

- Relativism
- Theory
- True experiment

Davidson, E. J. (2000). Ascertaining causality in theory-based evaluation. In P. J. Rogers, T. A. Hacsi, A. Petrosino, & T. A. Huebner (Eds.), *Program theory in evaluation: Challenges and opportunities* (New Directions for Evaluation, No. 87, pp. 17–26). San Francisco: Jossey-Bass.

Huberman, A. M., & Miles, M. B. (1998). Data management and analysis methods. In N. K. Denzin & Y. S. Lincoln (Eds.), *Collecting and interpreting qualitative materials* (pp. 179–210). Thousand Oaks, CA: Sage.

Hume, D. (2000). An essay concerning human understanding. In *Essays and treatises on several subjects* (Vol. 2). Leeds, UK: Leeds Electronic Text Centre. (Original work published 1777)

Miles, M. B., & Huberman, A. M. (1994). *Qualitative data analysis: An expanded sourcebook* (2nd ed.). Thousand Oaks, CA: Sage.

Scriven, M. (1974). Maximizing the power of causal investigations: The modus operandi method. In W. J. Popham (Ed.), *Evaluation in education: Current applications* (pp. 68–84). Berkeley, CA: McCutchan.

Shadish, W. R., Cook, T. D., & Campbell, D. T. (2002). *Experimental and quasi-experimental designs for generalized causal inference.* Boston: Houghton Mifflin.

EXERCISES

1. Suppose that you are conducting an evaluation of a training program for long-term unemployed individuals, defined as people who had been out of work for at least 2 years. As part of the same evaluation, you find that 50% of the participants got full-time jobs within 3 months of completing the program. This, of course, is good news. But then a cynical friend of yours points out that the local unemployment rate dropped over the same period of time, so that a general improvement in the job market could just as easily be the reason why these people found jobs.

    a. Which two complementary sources of evidence pertaining to causation would together provide the most powerful counterargument to your friend's claim at the lowest cost? Justify your choices (on three quarters of a page or less).

    b. For each source of evidence, describe what you would expect to find if the program was the primary cause of the participants' finding jobs. What evidence would you expect to see if the general change in economic conditions was the primary cause?

2. For your own evaluand, list the top three rival explanations that might be suggested if you find evidence that needs were met. Lay out which causal inference strategies you will include in your evaluation design to make sure that you can check and rule out (or confirm) these rival explanations. (This information should be incorporated into your Methodology checkpoint.)

SIX

"VALUES" IN EVALUATION

———•◦•———

R ight at the beginning of this book, it was noted that the special thing about evaluation—the part that makes it different from (and harder than) descriptive research—is that it involves more than simply collecting data and presenting results in "value-neutral" (i.e., purely descriptive) terms. E-*valu*-ation involves applying **values** to descriptive data so as to say something explicit about the quality or value of the evaluand in a particular context. Our goal is to do this with a level of certainty that is appropriate for those who might potentially make decisions on the basis of our findings.

The content of this chapter is relevant not only to the Values checkpoint but also to all of the Sub-evaluation checkpoints (6–10) and to the Overall Significance checkpoint of the Key Evaluation Checklist (KEC) (Exhibit 6.1).[1] Under the Values checkpoint, the evaluation team needs to identify broadly the sources of value that were used to determine what should be considered "good," "valuable," or "worthwhile" for this particular evaluand. Then those values are applied to the descriptive data collected about process, outcomes, costs, comparisons, and exportability to draw explicitly evaluative conclusions within each of those checkpoints. Finally, the Overall Significance checkpoint is where the evaluation team needs to weigh all of the strengths and weaknesses and to draw overall conclusions about the evaluand—another task that requires the application of values.

To arrive at explicitly evaluative conclusions, at least three important methodological tasks are required that are not found in purely descriptive scientific research: (a) importance weighting, (b) merit determination, and (c) synthesis. These are the methodology topics we cover in the next few chapters.

Exhibit 6.1   The KEC Checkpoints Where Values Are Most Relevant

---

5. Values
On what basis will you determine whether the evaluand is of high quality or value? Where will you get the criteria, and how will you determine "how good is good"?

---

6. Process Evaluation	7. Outcome Evaluation	8 & 9. Comparative Cost-Effectiveness	10. Exportability
How good, valuable, or efficient is the evaluand's content (design) and implementation (delivery)?	How good or valuable are the impacts (both intended and unintended) on immediate recipients and other impactees?	How costly is this evaluand to consumers, funders, staff, and so forth, compared with alternative uses of the available resources that might feasibly have achieved outcomes of similar or greater value? Are the costs excessive, quite high, just acceptable, or very reasonable?	What elements of the evaluand (e.g., innovative design or approach) might make it potentially valuable or a significant contribution or advance in another setting?

---

11. Overall Significance
Draw on all of the information in Checkpoints 6 through 10 to answer the main evaluation questions, including the following. What are the main areas where the evaluand is doing well, and where is it lacking? Is this the most cost-effective use of the available resources to address the identified needs without excessive adverse impact?

But before moving further into the nuts and bolts of evaluation-specific methodology, it is important to get a solid understanding of the following:

- The nature of the controversy surrounding this part of evaluation that centers on the question, "Aren't values all just subjective?"
- An important source of the disagreement on this issue, that is, the failure to clearly distinguish among three distinct kinds of subjectivity

- The tensions between taking a hard subjectivist line on this issue and the common sense of people (clients) trying to make informed choices and decisions in the real world
- Where the "values" in a solid evaluation really come from

At the end of this chapter, a pragmatic stance on this controversial issue is presented. The main purpose here is to find a way for most of us to wade out of the "values quagmire" and get on with the evaluative tasks outlined in the subsequent chapters.

THE CONTROVERSY

This is the part of the book where we really start getting into controversial territory. There are both professional evaluators and others who strongly believe that the steps from descriptive data to explicitly evaluative conclusions should not be tackled at all by the evaluator. For example, here is a fairly typical line of argument from some prominent applied researchers who subscribe to what Guba and Lincoln (1989) call the "scientific paradigm":

> This book [*Assessing Organizational Change*] is largely silent on the issue of combining outcomes from different domains in order to reach an overall conclusion about the effectiveness of a change effort. This is by design. The decision was made early on to simply report how the organization had changed on a wide array of outcome measures. No common metric was developed, nor was a weighting system developed that argued that gains in some measures are more important than gains in others. The rationale for not doing this is simple and to us persuasive. It is that different constituents value outcomes differently, and thus it is best to let interested parties reach their own overall conclusions. There are also practical problems in trying to translate diverse outcomes to a common metric. (Lawler, Seashore, & Mirvis, 1983, p. 542)

As we can see, Lawler and colleagues (1983) believe that evaluators should steer clear of assigning value or importance to various findings and instead should let stakeholders make their own determinations. In addition, they appear to be asserting that there is simply *no available methodology* that will yield valid and defensible findings, as evidenced by their closing sentence: "There are also practical problems in trying to translate diverse outcomes to a common metric."

Evaluators who subscribe to the **constructivist/interpretivist paradigm** (roughly the opposite of the scientific paradigm) take a somewhat different position. Although they agree with Lawler and colleagues (1983) that evaluative conclusions can never amount to anything more than the application of personal values in the interpretation of data, they tend to embrace this idea and build it into the design rather than leaving the findings in value-neutral terms (Guba & Lincoln, 1989). This view of evaluation sees the drawing of evaluative conclusions as a sensemaking process in which multiple stakeholders participate.

Despite their very different worldviews, evaluators who subscribe to the constructivist/interpretivist and scientific paradigms seem to share two underlying assumptions:

- All evaluative claims (about the value of certain outcomes or attributes, their relative importance, and what mixed results indicate about overall value) are arrived at "subjectively"; more specifically, the values that are applied to descriptive facts (data) to arrive at evaluative conclusions are *personal values.*
- Allowing stakeholders to make up their own minds, either individually or collectively, is the only valid way in which evaluative conclusions can be drawn at all.

In the remainder of this chapter, we critically examine these assumptions and consider some alternative lines of thought. The first task is to clarify a very common source of confusion about the different meanings of the term *subjective.*

THE THREE TYPES OF SUBJECTIVITY

Evaluation is an intensely political activity that is viewed by many as a threat. As a result, evaluators very often run into situations where people are challenging or attacking their work. One of the most common attacks goes directly to the heart of the subjectivity issue and includes statements such as the following:

- "Well, that's just *your* opinion about the program."
- "Yes, but *who defines* 'acceptable performance'?"

- "Who are you to impose *your values* on our program?"
- "Evaluation is just so subjective!"

One important factor here is being clear about the different types of subjectivity that may exist in an evaluation and being sure not to confuse them. Scriven (1991) makes a very useful distinction among three different kinds of subjectivity, two of which might legitimately appear in an evaluation and one of which should not:

- *Subjective 1:* Arbitrary, idiosyncratic, unreliable, and/or highly personal (i.e., based purely on personal preferences or inappropriate cultural biases); the kind of subjectivity that has no place in serious evaluation
- *Subjective 2:* Assessment or interpretation by a person, rather than by a machine or measurement device, of something external to the person (e.g., expert judgment of a trainee's skills in the effective facilitation of discussions)
- *Subjective 3:* About a person's inner life or experiences (e.g., headaches, fears, beliefs, emotions, stress levels, aspirations), all absolutely real but not usually independently verifiable

Subjective 1: Inappropriate Application
of Personal or Cultural Preferences/Biases

When people complain about an evaluation being "so subjective," the insinuation is usually that the conclusions were of the Subjective 1 type, that is, arbitrary or idiosyncratic. And sometimes that is true. Some of the most important examples of the inappropriate application of personal values have appeared in cross-cultural and gender-related evaluation where those doing the evaluations used preconceived frameworks or biases that failed to capture what was really important and/or seriously disadvantaged certain individuals or groups. Some examples include the following:

- Women managers generally are evaluated more negatively when they use an autocratic management style (which is generally viewed as more "masculine") than are male counterparts who exhibit the same behavior.

• Medical researchers evaluating a traditional treatment being used by witch doctors in Africa concluded, based on their observations of patient outcomes, that the treatment was indeed effective. They dutifully recorded the ingredients in the supplied medicine, which they brought back for use in the West. Unfortunately, the exact same concoction was found to be ineffective when given to Western patients. In this case, the researchers' cultural lens had led them to incorrectly identify the evaluand as being only the medication. What they had failed to understand was that the entire treatment also involved elaborate rituals performed by the witch doctors and required belief in both the rituals and the medication on the part of the patients.

In evaluation in particular, there is a grave danger that the application of inappropriate personal or cultural preferences or biases may lead to faulty conclusions and, therefore, misguided decisions. As evaluators, we need to be open to this possibility. If inappropriate values have crept in, we need to track them down and weed them out. Conversely, if important and relevant values (e.g., those that are relevant to the cultural context) have been excluded, we need to identify them and bring them to bear in the evaluation. If we are unfamiliar with the context to the extent that it would limit our ability to clearly identify or understand those values, it is our responsibility to bring onto the evaluation team people who can help us with that. With careful attention to these issues, the result should be an **objective** evaluation, that is, one that is free of inappropriate personal or cultural biases.

Subjective 2: Informed Judgment

In contrast to the first example, evaluations are often accused of being subjective (again, with the insinuation being Subjective 1, i.e., arbitrary or idiosyncratic) simply because there has been some use of human judgment, assessment, or interpretation (i.e., Subjective 2). For example, informed or expert judgment is used when an experienced facilitator rates the performance of trainees learning the art of facilitation on videotaped role-plays.

The key response in this case is to clarify the distinction between the valid use of expert judgment (Subjective 2) and the inappropriate use of personal preferences and biases in an evaluation (Subjective 1). Again, it is possible for expert judgment to be sloppy, and the evaluator should be extremely vigilant about this possibility.

In addition, even well-founded expert judgments need triangulation (i.e., verification of the findings from another source of data and/or from another informant) to ensure that they are **robust.** If the judgments are supported with solid explanations, if other evidence also points independently to the same conclusion, and if the details of any accusations regarding the inappropriate intrusion of personal preferences are thoroughly investigated and found to be baseless, the accusation of subjectivity (in the Subjective 1 sense) can be refuted.

Subjective 3: "About My Life"

There is a third sense in which the term *subjective* is used, and that is in reference to people's inner lives or experiences (e.g., headaches, fears, beliefs, emotions, stress levels, aspirations). These are the kinds of things that are usually not independently verifiable. Nevertheless, one seldom hears accusations that reports of headaches are "just subjective."

This type of subjective data quite often has a legitimate place in evaluation. The most common case is where the outcomes themselves are internal states such as confidence, stress, anxiety, and sense of cultural identity. Thus, subjective measures are essential for the evaluation of any program that produces outcomes such as these.

An extension of Scriven's (1991) third category of subjectivity is the intersubjective experience of a community or group (e.g., culture, sensemaking). These are aspects of group, community, or organizational life that cannot exist independently of people's shared perceptions and intersubjective sensemaking.

The Red Herring: Subjective Measures Versus Objective Measures

An additional source of confusion with the term *subjective* arises when an evaluation is accused of having too many "soft" or subjective measures and not enough "hard" data. Many of the social sciences use the term *objective measures* to refer to quantitative data relating to independently verifiable phenomena, whereas the term *subjective measures* refers to quantitative data relating to Subjective 2 judgments, Subjective 3 experiences, or qualitative data about anything.

This terminology is unfortunate because it leads people to believe that only quantitative measures of independently verifiable phenomena are really rigorous enough to use in an evaluation. However, it is usually essential to incorporate a far wider range of data into good evaluations, including expert judgment, perceptions, subjective experiences, and any number of aspects of the evaluand that are best assessed using qualitative methods. The terms *subjective* and *objective* are not used in the hard/soft data sense in this book.

THE TENSIONS BETWEEN
SUBJECTIVISM AND COMMON SENSE

Accusations about the subjectivity of evaluation assert that all evaluative claims are based on personal values and preferences. These accusations are reflective of a philosophical doctrine called *subjectivism.* According to this doctrine, all evaluative statements (e.g., saying that something is excellent, a waste of money, or better than the alternative) can be neither true nor false; rather, they are simply statements about the feelings of the people making the statements.[2]

For example, subjectivists believe that the statement "This is an excellent school" is not—and can never be—a statement of fact about the school, no matter what evidence is brought forward to support that claim. It can only be a statement of opinion. It is equivalent to the evaluator saying "I like this school" or reporting that lots of people say that they like it.

Although subjectivism is fashionable in academic circles with both quantitative and qualitative researchers right across the social sciences, it has never really caught on in the real world. People moving into new towns frequently ask around about good schools, honest mechanics, competent doctors, and so forth. These questions are not simply about which schools, mechanics, and doctors their new friends, colleagues, and neighbors happen to like personally; they are about which ones really are known to be the best in terms of their performance. In real life, people know for a fact that there is such a thing as good or poor quality or value, and they often seek out this information to help them make good decisions.

As evaluators working in the real world, we have clients and other "right-to-know" audiences who need good answers to their legitimate questions about quality. A community activist working on a shoestring will need to know whether there is any better way in which to channel limited resources to achieve a more powerful and positive impact in the community. A manager might need to know whether the new performance bonus system is worth the money being spent on it.

When people ask for—and pay for—answers to these questions, they typically are not interested in hearing about how subjective evaluation is. Nor are they interested in being told that they will need to wade through statistics and/or narratives, or will need to personally participate in a lengthy evaluation process, to find their own answers. Clients often expect, quite reasonably, that the evaluation team (which may or may not include organizational members) not only should present them with descriptive data but also should finish the job by providing some defensible conclusions about the quality or value of the evaluand (or areas of strength and weakness).[3]

This is not to say that all evaluation tasks are straightforward enough to produce single defensible conclusions. In some cases, it is quite debatable whether and how certain values should be applied. For example, is it more valuable to successfully place into employment 10% of a group of long-term unemployed individuals with poor educational qualifications or to success-fully place 50% of a similar-sized group whose members were better quali-fied and only briefly out of work? To answer such a question requires considerable thought and additional analysis (e.g., long-term impact on recip-ients, their families, and society; the crime rate). In the end, it might not be possible to find a clear answer based on an analysis of potential downstream impacts. Part of the answer might well rest on what the particular community or society values personally or as a collective. Or the evaluation team might need to report on the issue by raising it as a point for discussion rather than making a call on it. In such cases, it is quite legitimate to leave some shades of gray for the readers to sort out by themselves. But that option should not be abused to the point where the evaluator no longer does the groundwork on relevant values.

It is important to stress that there are many cases where we *can* draw well-supported, defensible conclusions about the quality or value of evaluands to a level of certainty that is appropriate for the particular decision-making context. The most important path to being able to achieve this is the very careful iden-tification and application of relevant values. In particular, we need to make sure that this part of the evaluation goes a long way beyond collecting other people's opinions or asking people what their values are.

WHERE DO THE "VALUES"
IN AN EVALUATION COME FROM?

When most people hear the word *values,* they think of the *personal* values that each of us holds individually. But as we have seen in earlier chapters, there are several other sources of values that are not based simply on personal prefer-ences but that help us to figure out the extent to which a certain set of attributes or outcomes is *valuable* in this particular context.

Let's recap from earlier chapters what outcomes and attributes make an evaluand meritorious or valuable:

- The most important recipient, consumer, or user needs have been better met by the evaluand.
- There has been a noticeable positive impact by the evaluand on siblings, families, the community, the organization, and so forth.
- The content or design of the evaluand was scientifically sound and matched to consumer needs.
- The implementation or delivery of the evaluand was in compliance with all legal, ethical, and professional standards.
- There was a minimum of wastage or inefficiency in the time, money, and other resources spent on the evaluand.
- The evaluand was substantially more cost-effective than anything else that could feasibly have been produced or delivered with the available resources.
- The evaluand had other features or attributes that enhanced the experi-ence of the consumers and others.

Now recall the subjectivist assumptions listed earlier in this chapter:

- All evaluative claims are arrived at subjectively; that is, the values that are applied to descriptive facts (data) to arrive at evaluative conclusions are personal values.
- Evaluative conclusions can be drawn only by allowing stakeholders to make up their own minds, either individually or collectively.

It is certainly true that some assessment or interpretation by a human(s) is likely to form part of the evaluation. However, in a good evaluation, this is limited to judgment by well-qualified experts.

The main accusation of subjectivity came from the second part of the first point, which implies that all evaluative conclusions are based on personal values. In fact, none of the sources of value listed previously represents arbitrary or idiosyncratic personal preferences, especially not on the part of the evaluation team. All of the sources of value came from valid sources—actual needs, ethics, professional standards, and so forth.

For those readers who still see themselves as dyed-in-the-wool value relativists, one could also say that the values on which a solid evaluation is based are defensible insofar as there is sufficiently widespread agreement within the relevant context about those values that they can reasonably be treated as givens. But what such a line implies, for example, is that if we were evaluating an orphanage, whether or not children are fed nutritious food, kept warm, treated for illness, and not sexually abused are only defined as "good" things because *enough people agree* that these qualities are good, not because they actually *are* good. However, common sense tells us unequivocally that these are demonstrably part of what it means to be a good orphanage.

Once we realize that a very substantial proportion of the sources of value come from demonstrably defensible sources, we can move away from the notion that ascribing value must inevitably be a job exclusively for stakeholders. Stakeholder input will certainly be useful in the interpretation of certain findings, particularly because some people are in an excellent position to inform the evaluation team about the issues at hand. But now that it is clear that the sources of value are not just personal, we no longer need to view their application as an act of personal judgment.

To be sure, the evaluation team is made up of people, and people are fallible. Again, we must remember three things. First, we are not usually (if ever) looking for 100% certainty in our conclusions; rather, we are seeking just enough to meet the requirements for certainty in the relevant decision-making context. Second, the more the evaluation team keeps this part of the process carefully documented and justified, the less likely its members are to slip carelessly into sloppy evaluation. Third, all evaluations, especially high-stakes ones, should be meta-evaluated (i.e., the evaluations themselves should be evaluated), preferably by independent evaluation experts. The more transparent the application of values, the easier it will be for a meta-evaluator to see any areas of slippage such as false assumptions. That is our goal as we move into the next few chapters on evaluation-specific methodology.

NOTES

1. Note that the Methodology checkpoint has not been included in Exhibit 6.1. People often argue that methodological choices are very "value laden" and that values or preferences used to choose these should be made explicit. This is very good advice. However, this discussion really falls within the realm of *intradisciplinary* evaluation (Scriven, 1991) in that it pertains to what makes the evaluation design and methods good or bad rather than what makes the evaluand good or bad. This chapter focuses on the latter, whereas the former is addressed throughout the book as we evaluate the merits of different evaluation design issues and strategies and how to match them to the information needs of stakeholders.

2. The more extreme forms of subjectivism, which hold that there is no such thing as *any* kind of objective fact (whether descriptive or evaluative), are being excluded here. Although that is arguably included by purists in the thinking of this doctrine, the more frequent—and important—point of contention in evaluation is about the subjectivity of the values part.

3. Some clients specifically ask that evaluation teams *not* draw explicitly evaluative conclusions because the clients prefer to make up their own minds about the findings and (if necessary) to argue for those interpretations within their organizations. That may be a reasonable request in some cases, but it is often true that a particular stakeholder has insufficient time or expertise to wade through all of the relevant findings and often has a vested interest in a particular interpretation. Therefore, the evaluation team needs to carefully consider the likelihood of evaluation misuse when making a decision not to provide explicitly evaluative conclusions.

ADDITIONAL READINGS

Entries in Scriven's (1991) *Evaluation Thesaurus:*
- Bias
- Illicit values
- Neutral
- Objective
- Social science approach
- Subjectivity
- Value-free doctrine
- Value judgment
- Valuephobia

Eagly, A., Makhijani, M., & Klonsky, B. (1992). Gender and the evaluation of leaders: A meta-analysis. *Psychological Bulletin, 111*, 3–22.

Guba, E. G. (Ed.). (1990). *The paradigm dialog.* Newbury Park, CA: Sage.

Guba, E. G., & Lincoln, Y. S. (2001). *Guidelines and checklist for constructivist (a.k.a. fourth generation) evaluation.* Available online: http://evaluation.wmich.edu/checklists/

House, E. R., & Howe, K. R. (1999). *Values in evaluation and social research.* Thousand Oaks, CA: Sage.

Scriven, M. (1975). *Evaluation bias and its control.* Occasional paper series #4, The Evaluation Center, Western Michigan University. Available online: http://www.wmich.edu/evalctr/pubs/ops/ops04.html

Scriven, M. (1993). *Hard-won lessons in program evaluation.* (New Directions for Program Evaluation, No. 58). San Francisco, CA: Jossey-Bass.

Stufflebeam, D. L. (2001). *Evaluation Values and Criteria Checklist.* Available online: http://evaluation.wmich.edu/checklists/

EXERCISES

1. Suppose that a client does not like the findings of your evaluation and says, "Well, that's just *your* opinion about the program. Evaluations are always just so subjective." How would you respond? (A suggested answer to this question is provided in the "Answers to Selected Exercises" section.)

2. Suppose that you have been asked to evaluate a counseling program that is designed to help people overcome phobias. To really understand the participants' experiences, you make extensive use of in-depth interviewing techniques as part of your work. Shortly after you publish the study, an experienced researcher who specializes in (mostly quantitative) applied psychology criticizes it due to its weak measurement, which she claims is "too subjective." The journal editor has given you 150 words of space in which to respond to this accusation. What would you write? (Be diplomatic.)

3. Imagine that you are an internal evaluation specialist who has been asked to devise a performance appraisal system. In your initial meetings with the union and various staff members, there are strong objections to the idea. "After all," says one person, "whose values will you use to decide what counts as good performance?" How would you respond (on half a page or less)?

SEVEN

DETERMINING IMPORTANCE

———•◦•———

A frequent argument from those who *oppose* the notion that part of the evaluation team's job is to be explicit about quality, value, or importance is that no valid methodologies exist for doing so (Lawler, Seashore, & Mirvis, 1983). It is true that the average research methods text leaves the reader pretty well in the dark on this topic. But it is equally true that there has been significant headway made on the evaluation-specific methodologies available for the tasks of importance weighting, merit determination, and synthesis.[1] That is where we are headed in this chapter as well as the next few chapters.

> **Importance determination** is defined here as the process of assigning labels to dimensions or components to indicate their importance.

When referring to importance determination, the term **importance weighting** is sometimes used. Conceptually, this is reasonably accurate. However, it does tend to make people think immediately of numerical weighting systems, which comprise only a small slice of the possibilities here. Whether one uses numbers, words, or symbols to signify importance matters little until we get to the synthesis step.

Importance determination is most relevant to the Sub-evaluation checkpoints and to the Overall Significance checkpoint of the Key Evaluation Checklist (KEC) (Exhibit 7.1). Under the Sub-evaluation checkpoints, the evaluation team needs to determine the relative importance of the various aspects of the evaluand investigated in addition to determining the merit of performance on each of those aspects (this is covered later, in Chapter 8). Under the Overall Significance

Exhibit 7.1   The KEC Checkpoints Where Importance Determination Is
Used

6. Process Evaluation How good, valuable, or efficient is the evaluand's content (design) and imple-mentation (delivery)?	7. Outcome Evaluation How good or valuable are the impacts (both intended and unintended) on immediate recipients and other impactees?	8 & 9. Comparative Cost-Effectiveness How costly is this evaluand to consumers, funders, staff, and so forth, compared with alternative uses of the available resources that might feasibly have achieved outcomes of similar or greater value? Are the costs excessive, quite high, just acceptable, or very reasonable?	10. Exportability What elements of the evaluand (e.g., innovative design, approach) might make it potentially valuable or a significant contribution or advance in another setting?

11. Overall Significance
Draw on all of the information in Checkpoints 6 through 10 to answer the main evaluation questions, including the following. What are the main areas where the evaluand is doing well, and where is it lacking? Is this the most cost-effective use of the available resources to address the identified needs without excessive adverse impact?

checkpoint, all of these strengths and weaknesses are combined together based on their relative importance to draw overall conclusions. Methods for combining these are covered in Chapter 9.

DETERMINING IMPORTANCE: WHAT AND WHY

As we look down any list of evaluative criteria, it is intuitively obvious that not all of the criteria are equally important. The same is true when looking at the performance of an evaluand across various components. Knowing which criteria and/or components are more important is essential for being able to (a) prioritize improvements, (b) identify whether identified strengths or weaknesses are serious or minor, and/or (c) work out whether an evaluand with mixed results is doing fairly well, quite poorly, or somewhere in between. In this section, we examine the distinction between **dimensional evaluation** and **component evaluation** as well as how it affects the importance determination task.

Determining the Importance of Dimensions or Criteria of Merit

Information about the importance of criteria can be used when profiling the performance of an evaluand on several different dimensions or criteria, as shown in Exhibit 7.2. Weak performance on a minor criterion (e.g., Dimension 4) may be no big deal, but weak performance on something really important (e.g., Dimension 1) would be very bad news indeed. Without this information about importance, one might think that Dimension 4 represented the most pressing area for improvement or the evaluand's most serious weakness, when in reality, Dimension 1 should probably be the primary cause for concern.

Exhibit 7.2   Hypothetical Dimensional Profile With Dimension Importance Indicated

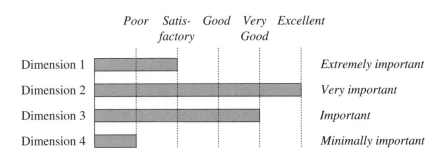

Determining the Importance of Evaluand Components

The same logic applies to component evaluation, where the evaluand is first broken down into components (or pieces), which are considered separately before looking at the overall picture. Both component evaluation and dimensional evaluation are analytical approaches and are distinguished from **holistic evaluation** (which involves considering the evaluand as a whole rather than breaking it down for analysis).

Quick Explanation: Dimensional, Component, and Holistic Evaluation

Dimensional evaluation: A form of **analytical evaluation** in which the quality or value of the evaluand is determined by looking at its performance on multiple dimensions of merit (also called criteria of merit) that pertain to the evaluand as a whole rather than separately to its parts

Component evaluation: A form of analytical evaluation in which the quality or value of the evaluand is determined by evaluating each of the evaluand's components (or parts) separately and then (usually) synthesizing these findings to draw conclusions about the evaluand as a whole. (Each component is usually evaluated on several dimensions of merit that pertain specifically to that component rather than to the evaluand as a whole.)

Holistic evaluation: An approach to evaluation that is either not analytical or not explicitly so and where the quality or value of the evaluand is determined at the whole evaluand level, without explicit analytical consideration of separate evaluand components or dimensions of merit

SOURCE: These terms were coined by Scriven (1991).

Component evaluation is common in the evaluation of policies, programs, or interventions that have several quite distinct parts. For example, suppose that a government policy is introduced with the aim of reducing juvenile delinquency. To achieve this goal, the government might implement several **policy instruments** (components or interventions) such as after-school programs for high-risk youth, more frequent police patrols in areas where juvenile delinquency is rife, counseling and guidance for first-time offenders, and tougher sentences for juvenile recidivists. When evaluating a multifaceted policy or program such as this, it makes sense to make the task more manageable by first breaking the evaluand out into components and considering each one separately before looking at the interactive effects and overall merit of the entire set of policy instruments.

Information about importance may be used when profiling the performance of the evaluand on each of its components (as shown in Exhibit 7.3) and/or when synthesizing the performances on multiple components to draw an overall conclusion about evaluand effectiveness (i.e., figuring out what all of the strengths and weaknesses add up to). Again, the information about importance allows us to (a) identify the components in most urgent need of improvement (if the evaluation is formative) and (b) have some basis for determining the overall merit of a package of interventions, some of which are working better than others (for drawing overall conclusions in a formative or summative evaluation).

Exhibit 7.3   Hypothetical Component Profile With Component Importance Indicated

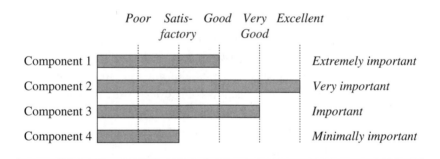

Determining When to Use Dimensional Versus Component Versus Holistic Evaluation

Component evaluation is more appropriate when evaluating policies, programs, or interventions that have several quite distinct parts that are experienced separately by consumers. Some typical examples might include a large-scale international development program consisting of projects implemented in different locations, a government policy that includes multiple policy instruments, and an organizational transformation effort that includes several distinct interventions.

Dimensional evaluation should usually be used when evaluating entities whose quality or value is experienced by consumers on multiple dimensions that pertain to the evaluand as a whole. This approach is typical for single-component programs or interventions and those whose components are experienced by recipients as a package rather than separately. Products also are almost always evaluated dimensionally rather than by their components. For example, cars are usually evaluated with respect to several overall dimensions experienced by the driver (e.g., safety, handling, reliability, fuel economy) rather than by looking separately at the quality of their various components (e.g., engine, braking system, suspension). Of course, evaluative information about product components may be useful, but this information by itself is usually inadequate as a good product evaluation due to the excessive emphasis on technical specifications with little real link to users' needs (see also Scriven's [1991] entry on "technicism").

Holistic evaluation is unusual in the evaluation of programs, policies, and other large complex evaluands. One exception is seen in **connoisseurial evaluation** (also called expertise-oriented evaluation), where an expert provides an overall assessment of the evaluand without explicitly breaking it out analytically. Although we call this form of evaluation *holistic,* it is likely that something implicitly analytical is going on in the mind of the person judging the quality or value of the evaluand. In other words, the individual may be consciously or subconsciously considering the evaluand's merit on several dimensions (or by components) before drawing an overall conclusion. However, in holistic evaluation, merit is being determined in a way that goes beyond subconscious analytical evaluation. A simple example is judging the overall quality of a sample of writing. Although the person making the judgment may consider various aspects of the writing quality (e.g., interesting content, a clear thesis statement, logic arguments, correct grammar and spelling), the overall judgment is inherently holistic and does not consist of merely summing the merit on several dimensions to come to an overall conclusion. In many cases (e.g., grading essays), holistic evaluation actually yields more reliable and valid evaluations than does an analytical approach.

Holistic evaluation is more common in personnel, product, and service evaluation. It is most appropriate when the quality or value of the evaluand is experienced as an entire package, where it is either not possible or not economical to identify dimensions or components that will give a complete picture, and where reasonable (or better) reliability and accuracy can best be obtained by using judgments. Examples include the evaluation of student essays, customer service, classroom teaching, leadership potential, athletic performance, and cosmetics.

DETERMINING IMPORTANCE: SIX STRATEGIES

There are basically six strategies available for determining the importance of evaluative criteria or components:

1. Having stakeholders or consumers "vote" on importance

2. Drawing on the knowledge of selected stakeholders

3. Using evidence from the literature

4. Using specialist judgment

5. Using evidence from the needs and values assessments

6. Using program theory and evidence of causal linkages

Each of these strategies has advantages and disadvantages that make it a better choice in certain situations than in others. In this section, we look at how each one works and when to use it.

Strategy 1: Having Stakeholders or Consumers "Vote" on Importance

Many evaluators tackle the importance issue by gathering **stakeholder** input and using a kind of voting system to decide what is important. This may be a single-step, "cast your vote" approach (e.g., asking people in a survey or an interview to rate the importance of certain evaluand aspects or components), or it may be a consensus-seeking approach (e.g., an initial vote followed by a facilitated discussion among key stakeholders until agreement is reached).

Who gets to vote? Inclusion of a full range of stakeholder opinions is typical in evaluations with a strong democratic and inclusive focus and is also more likely in evaluations employing data collection methods that allow broad coverage (e.g., surveys). A small-group participatory evaluation that is more limited in scope might involve only a selected subgroup of staff within a particular unit or program. In product and service evaluation, it is more common for input to be gathered exclusively from consumers, using more of a "market research" approach. For example, one might ask people with disabilities what service attributes they consider most important in the delivery of community-based health care.

The "stakeholder vote" approach is probably the most commonly used one in both participatory and **nonparticipatory evaluations** that tackle the importance weighting issue. However, it is by no means the only option, whether the evaluation is being conducted in participatory mode or not. Before deciding whether the stakeholder vote approach is appropriate, it is important to consider the following *assumptions* that one makes when opting for it:

- Each person asked is sufficiently well informed and interested in the issues to make an assessment of importance (perhaps after some discussion if a deliberative method is used).
- The most important aspects of the evaluand are whatever aspects the participating stakeholders *believe* are important. There is no more valid way in which to determine importance in this case.
- Of those individuals whose input is sought, no particular stakeholder's or stakeholder group's assessment of importance is more credible or well informed than that of another.

It is important for the evaluation team to consider the circumstances under which these assumptions would and would not be valid. In some evaluations, certain stakeholders might not be sufficiently well informed or deeply interested to work out what *should* be considered important (e.g., due to lack of technical or content knowledge and/or time to devote to deliberation). For example, not all stakeholders would have an opinion as to the relative importance of criteria in the evaluation of a technology-based knowledge management system; instead, some (or most) might provide some initial input about the information they need from such a system and then leave the details to those with some technical expertise.

In other situations, stakeholder beliefs about what is important might be at odds with the facts. Suppose that you asked students who have just entered a doctoral program in evaluation to rate the relative importance of the knowledge and skills they will learn in the program. Although students with significant work experience in evaluation might be able to give well-based opinions on the matter, many will be not at all attuned to the kinds of knowledge and skills they will need to practice effectively in the profession. In cases like this, what certain stakeholders believe to be true may quite simply be misguided or based on insufficient knowledge.

Similarly, there are occasions where a certain group of stakeholders' views should be given greater consideration than a "one person, one vote" strategy would allow. For example, the viewpoints of elders in an indigenous community might provide a deeper understanding of the local issues and priorities than would the viewpoints of younger people in the same community or of a government worker designing programs for that community. In situations where certain stakeholders are better informed than others, it may be advisable to weight input differentially or to filter out input that is less reliable. But more often than not, it is best to consider some alternative methods of weighting performance such as the remaining five strategies detailed in this section.

Strategy 2: Drawing on the Knowledge of Selected Stakeholders

An alternative to the stakeholder vote method of importance determination is the strategy of using selected stakeholder input to *guide* the assignment of importance weightings by the evaluation team. In the stakeholder vote method, we assumed that "importance" was roughly equivalent to "whatever most people think is important." But here we are seeking to go beyond that. We are not simply collecting opinions and reporting the "average" opinion; instead, we are selectively collecting input from various well-informed sources and combining that information in an attempt to determine what *really is* important, taking all of the relevant perspectives and considerations into account.

The methodology for doing this can range from fairly simple to quite complex, depending on the need for precision in the particular decision-making context. At the simplest level, one might identify the one or two best-informed stakeholders and conduct a brief interview that probes their relevant knowledge. For example, when determining the relative importance of the main skill sets needed by doctoral students, the evaluation team might identify certain stakeholders who are in a position to be particularly well informed (e.g., employers of graduates; university, community college, and polytechnic professors or lecturers), gather their input, and then take it into consideration when importance weights (either numerical or nonnumerical) are assigned.

When using this method for determining importance, it is necessary to consider, from an evaluation perspective, what it is that makes a particular aspect of an evaluand "important." Figuring out what importance should mean in a particular evaluation is not a trivial exercise. However, one relatively simple and usually valid option is to conceptualize importance in terms of potential impact. For example, the evaluator might ask stakeholders the following two questions: "How beneficial would it be overall if the evaluand did very well on this dimension or component?" and "How detrimental would it be overall if the evaluand did very poorly on this dimension or component?" The idea here is that the most important dimensions or components are the ones that can make or break the evaluand, whereas the less important ones are just pluses and minuses, that is, nice if you have them but no big deal if you do not.

When determining the importance of a particular criterion, an additional consideration is identifying whether or not there is any level of performance that would be unacceptably low, regardless of how well the evaluand did on other criteria. The minimum acceptable level of performance on a particular criterion is called the **bar** (Scriven, 1991). For example, most programs, products, policies, and job vacancies have a bar on cost. Even if quality is extremely high on all other dimensions, there are limits to what can be spent (in terms of time, money, and other resources).

It is possible to set up a matrix to help with importance determination and identification of bars (or minima). A sample that could be adapted for use in various evaluations is shown in Table 7.1.

Table 7.1   A Simple Matrix for Determining the Relative Importance of Components or Criteria Based on Stakeholder Knowledge

		How detrimental would it be overall if the evaluand did *very poorly* on this dimension or component?		
		Not Noticeably Detrimental	*Noticeably Detrimental*	*Unacceptably Detrimental*
How beneficial would it be overall if the evaluand did *very well* on this dimension or component?	*Somewhat Beneficial*	Somewhat important	Important	Important (and set a bar)
	Very Beneficial	Important	Very important	Very important (and set a bar)
	Extremely Beneficial	Very important	Extremely important	Extremely important (and set a bar)

NOTE: A *bar* is a defined minimum level of criterion performance below which the evaluand is considered completely unacceptable, regardless of performance on other criteria.

When deciding whether to use stakeholder knowledge *alone* to guide importance determination, it is important to consider the assumptions that one must make (or the conditions that must be met) to use this methodology:

- The particular stakeholders who provide input regarding the probable impact of various evaluand attributes or outcomes must be sufficiently well informed to provide valuable relevant information.
- The combination of stakeholder input gathered will, as a package, provide sufficient certainty about importance for the given decision-making context; that is, no other information will be required to supplement stakeholder input.

Whenever one or both of these conditions are shaky, the evaluation team would be well advised to consider alternative or additional options for determining importance.

Strategy 3: Using Evidence From the Literature

In some situations, the evaluand may be too complex and/or stakeholder knowledge may be insufficient to allow the determination of importance with the degree of precision needed in the particular decision-making context using either of the previous two methodologies. In such cases, it may be advisable to either replace or supplement stakeholder input regarding importance with evidence from the empirical literature. Useful sources of evidence include the following:

- Meta-analyses or literature reviews addressing the effectiveness of this type of evaluand, success factors, and/or common weaknesses
- Evaluations of similar evaluands, especially in similar contexts
- Research documenting the key drivers (or strongest predictors) of success or failure with this type of evaluand

It is easy to get sidetracked in the literature when using this method, so it is important to keep a focus on evidence pertaining to the importance of certain evaluand characteristics or components as opposed to the myriad details about evaluand functioning that may have been researched. For many evaluands, we can use the potential impact rule of thumb that we employed for gathering and interpreting stakeholder knowledge (Strategy 2). In some cases, this might need to have other considerations incorporated.

However importance is defined for the particular evaluand, it will be helpful to draw up a matrix or rubric to help guide importance determination and to document how this was done for potential readers of the evaluation report. A sample matrix is shown in Table 7.2.

Table 7.2   A Simple Matrix for Determining the Relative Importance of Criteria Based on Evidence From the Literature

		What evidence exists that it would be detrimental overall if the evaluand did *very poorly* on this component or criterion?		
		Little or No Evidence of a Potential Detrimental Impact	*Clear Evidence That Some Detrimental Impact Would Be Possible*	*Evidence That Unacceptably Detrimental Impact Would Be Possible*
What evidence exists that it would be beneficial overall if the evaluand did *very well* on this component or criterion?	*Clear Evidence That Some Beneficial Impact Would Be Possible*	Somewhat important	Important	Important (and set a bar)
	Clear Evidence of Substantial Beneficial Impact	Important	Very important	Very important (and set a bar)
	Consistently a Major Determinant of Evaluand Quality or Value	Very important	Extremely important	Extremely important (and set a bar)

NOTE: A *bar* is a defined minimum level of criterion or component performance below which the evaluand is considered completely unacceptable, regardless of performance on other dimensions or components.

The use of evidence from the empirical literature alone for determining the relative importance of evaluative criteria or components depends on the following assumptions or conditions:

- The volume and quality of the available research is sufficient to allow inferences about importance to be drawn.
- The context in which the other research was conducted is sufficiently similar to that of the evaluand that the findings can reasonably be assumed to apply in this case.

Because of the questionable comparability of context in nearly all cases, it is a good idea to supplement the evidence from the literature with other evidence such as stakeholder input, specialist judgment (which is covered next), evidence from the needs assessment, and any other evidence that can be applied economically. The particular mix that works best in a given evaluation will depend on the level of certainty required and the costs of obtaining the various kinds of evidence about importance.

Strategy 4. Using Specialist Judgment

Suppose that you are evaluating something relatively complex on a fairly tight timeline, do not have sufficient expertise among the stakeholders to provide solid enough evidence of importance, and are not able to locate enough in the way of really relevant literature within the time you have available. What options are available for a "fairly quick and fairly clean" assessment of the relative importance of various criteria?

One extremely useful strategy in a situation like this is to identify one or two well-known specialists who have spent many years evaluating or studying numerous examples of this type of evaluand in contexts that are at least partially similar to yours. These kinds of seasoned evaluation (and/or research) practitioners have seen numerous examples of successes and failures and have become attuned to the things that can make or break an evaluand such as yours.

As with all undertakings in evaluation, it is always risky to base any part of the evaluation on input from just one source or even on input from two very similar sources. For this reason, you should deliberately choose two or more specialists who have quite different theoretical perspectives or who have worked in somewhat different contexts. Their assessments of importance should, wherever possible, be supplemented with other evidence gathered by the evaluation team, preferably evidence that speaks to the applicability of the specialists' judgments to this particular evaluand and setting and to these particular recipients or consumers.

Strategy 5: Using Evidence From the Needs and Values Assessments

The first four importance determination methods just discussed draw on a combination of stakeholder and expert judgment and the existing empirical research. There are pros and cons to each of these. Stakeholders are more in touch with the context at hand (or at least a specific aspect of it), although they might sometimes be a little too deep into the forest to see the trees. However, they usually lack both specific content expertise and experience with similar evaluands in different contexts. The literature and content experts, on the other hand, can usually contribute more in-depth knowledge of content (i.e., subject matter expertise) as well as evidence from multiple contexts, but they have less familiarity with the current context.

Perhaps the most relevant and powerful method for importance determination is to use evidence directly from the needs assessment (and the assessment of other relevant values). The use of this method may vary somewhat depending on whether one is determining the importance of criteria (or dimensions) of merit or the importance of evaluand components.

Determining the Importance of Criteria

What kind of evidence would we draw from a needs and values assessment, and how could we make sure that the assessment was designed to capture the information needed to establish the importance of criteria? Let's take an example of a master's program in evaluation. Based on the methods described earlier, we can list a number of sources of evidence for identifying the relevant performance needs (Table 7.3).

The needs assessment outlined in Table 7.3 is designed to identify key knowledge, skills, and other capabilities that constitute an important set of outcome criteria for the evaluation. But how do we know which of the criteria identified are the most important? At a conceptual level, we can say that the most important outcomes will be those that are particularly pivotal for distinguishing top-notch graduates from those who do poorly when they move into evaluation careers. In other words, the most important skills, knowledge, and abilities are the ones that make a huge difference in how effective an evaluator someone is. Less important outcome criteria are those that are a plus if you have them but not a serious problem if you do not.

How can we obtain information about importance from a needs assessment? One strategy might be to go back over the information collected and identify the

Table 7.3   Strategies for Identifying Different Kinds of Performance Needs for Students in (or graduates of) a Master's Program in Evaluation

	Conscious Needs	*Unconscious Needs*
Met needs	Ask evaluators (especially high performers) what skills, knowledge, and experience they gained in graduate school have been most useful for helping them to succeed.	Ask employers and clients about the skills, knowledge, and other characteristics of the best evaluators with whom they have ever worked.
Unmet needs	Ask evaluators what skills, knowledge, and experience they really needed when they first started working after graduation but had not learned in graduate school. Ask evaluators about instances when they have seen other relatively new evaluators do poorly. What skills or knowledge were the new evaluators missing that were most problematic?	Ask employers and clients for examples of people they have hired who turned out to be incapable of doing the jobs they were hired to do. What was missing from these people's repertoires? Ask employers and clients what knowledge, skills, and abilities are hardest to find when they are looking for good evaluators.
General sources (all four types)	Identify the top evaluation contracting organizations and ask what knowledge, skills, and other capabilities have made them successful and what they seek out when hiring. Talk to top evaluation theorists, identify the elements of a high-quality evaluation, and map out the knowledge and skills required to complete each one. Do some "job shadowing"; that is, observe evaluators with different skill levels in action doing their jobs. Note areas of excellence and of problematic performance. Look at examples of evaluation reports produced by master's-trained evaluators. In what area(s) were they lacking? Apply one or more meta-evaluation checklists to identify weaknesses.	

characteristics that are most frequently mentioned when respondents talk about the best and worst evaluators with whom they have ever worked. Although this is a relatively straightforward way in which to start, when using this strategy, it is important to bear in mind its key underlying assumption, that is, that *more frequently mentioned = more important.* This is not necessarily true given that the frequently mentioned dimensions might simply be the ones on which there is greatest variation, and this is quite different from importance.

A second (and better) option is to look for the characteristics of poor-performing evaluators that cause the most serious problems and, conversely, the characteristics of top-notch evaluators that have dramatic impacts on success. This information might be collected in interviews or focus groups by asking people to identify critical incidents with very serious or highly beneficial consequences (e.g., when an entire evaluation was derailed, when an evaluation created breakthrough valuable knowledge). Critical incidents are mined for information using probing questions to find out what skill, knowledge, and ability deficits or advantages appeared to be the causes of those incidents.

Determining the Importance of Components

Now suppose that we are separately evaluating several different components (i.e., distinct parts) that make up a single evaluand. What makes one component more important than another, and what relevant evidence could we gather in a needs and values assessment?

One central consideration should certainly be the severity of the needs addressed by a particular component. Interventions or services that address serious and life-threatening needs are more important than those that alleviate inconvenience. In many cases, one should also take into account whether the component in question is the only viable means of meeting those needs. The logic here is that a service or an intervention that provides the only available relief from certain problems is more important than one that is merely an option within a range of viable alternatives. Of course, the hypothetical availability of alternatives is only one part of that equation. If consumers are unlikely to seek out those alternatives, this lessens their viability and increases the importance of the evaluand component in question.

This was precisely the logic behind the importance determination task in an evaluation of a multicomponent school-based intervention (Mersman, 1999), a project for which this methodology was originally developed by the evaluation contractor and the author. This U.S. inner-city school-based program was designed to address health, mental health, and social problems of students and parents. Seven different services (program components) were offered to students: nutrition education, education about reproductive anatomy and safer sex, mental health counseling, transportation to and from school, legal services, case management of pregnant and parenting teens, and direct health services delivered by a nurse.

The client in this case (the school principal) needed to know how well each of the seven components was meeting students' needs. Thus, this was a component evaluation with no need for an overall synthesis, that is, no need to combine the performances of all the components to draw an overall conclusion about the value of the program as a whole. However, it was important for the client to know which services were most important to allow effective prioritization of improvements and/or to know which services to retain in the event of budgetary cuts.

We began by clearly defining the determinants of component importance as follows:

- *Severity of dysfunction addressed (primary consideration):* the extent to which the component targets a serious need, that is, a source of potentially severe dysfunction and/or highly beneficial effective functioning
- *Scarcity of alternatives (secondary consideration):* the extent to which there are no alternative options for addressing the needs in question
- *Intent to seek out alternatives (secondary consideration):* the extent to which potential recipients would actually bother to seek out alternative options if the evaluand component in question did not exist

Next, we set up rubrics to clearly state how we would classify each of the components with respect to these considerations. Table 7.4 shows the rubric for rating each service (program component) on the severity of need that it addressed.

The second determinant of importance was the scarcity of alternative ways in which to meet the presenting need. In the evaluation of this multicomponent school-based intervention, this was determined by asking students whether they thought that they could receive the same services elsewhere for free (all services were free). The rubric for scarcity ratings is shown in Table 7.5.

Finally, each service was given a rating based on the intent or energy of the students to seek out any available alternatives if the services in question were not available. The more likely students were to bother seeking out an

available alternative if it existed, the more important the service was inferred
to be. Like the scarcity of alternatives, this too was a secondary consideration
in the determination of component importance. The rubric for determining
intent ratings is shown in Table 7.6.

Table 7.4   Description of the Ratings for Severity of Dysfunction

Level of Severity	Description of Dysfunction
Low (■)	Not integral for survival Minor inconvenience if service not received Can function effectively without receiving service
Moderate (Δ)	Substantial inconvenience from not receiving service Implications of not receiving service probably do not include death
Severe (●)	Addresses serious dysfunction in physical, mental, or emotional health In some cases, implications of not receiving service can include death

SOURCE: Modified version reprinted with permission from Mersman (1999).

Table 7.5   Description of Scarcity Ratings

Level of Scarcity	Percentage Reporting That They Could Not Receive the Services for Free Elsewhere
Low (– –)	0% to 30% (clear majority believe that services for free exist elsewhere)
Slight (–)	31% to 50% (most people believe that services for free exist elsewhere)
Moderate (+)	51% to 65% (most people believe that services for free dos not exist elsewhere)
High (++)	66% to 100% (clear majority believe that services for free do not exist elsewhere)

SOURCE: Modified version reprinted with permission from Mersman (1999).

Table 7.6   Description of Ratings for Intent to Use Alternatives

Level of Intent	*Percentage Reporting That They Would Bother to Get Services Elsewhere*
Low (– –)	0% to 25% (majority would not bother to get services elsewhere)
Slight (–)	26% to 50% (some would bother to get services elsewhere, but most would not)
Moderate (+)	51% to 75% (majority would bother to get services elsewhere)
Strong (++)	76% to 100% (vast majority would bother to get services elsewhere)

Note that the symbols used to depict low (– –) through high (++) intent to seek out alternatives (Table 7.6) mirror those used to rate the perceived scarcity of alternatives (Table 7.5), with both being secondary considerations in the determination of importance. These symbols differ from the ones used to depict the severity of dysfunction addressed (●, Δ, and ■ in Table 7.4). The two different kinds of symbols come into play when the three considerations are combined to determine the importance of each program component. The severity rating provides the initial anchor (●, Δ, or ■). Then the ratings for (a) availability of alternatives and (b) the likelihood of their being used (– –, –, +, and ++) are used to "adjust" the importance rating up or down slightly to yield an overall importance rating on the scale shown in Table 7.7.

To illustrate how this methodology was used to determine the importance of each component of the school-based intervention, a full working illustration is shown in Table 7.8.

The three criteria for determining importance of the components of the school-based intervention—severity of dysfunction addressed, scarcity of alternatives, and student intent or energy to seek out those alternatives—were designed to fit the particular evaluation in question. For other evaluations, there might be a need to identify a different or modified set of determinants. The intent here was to provide an illustrative example to show the thinking behind the use of needs assessment data to determine importance.

Table 7.7   Description of Component Importance Ratings

Severity + Scarcity + Intent	Level of Importance
●⁺	Critical
●	Extremely high
●⁻	High
Δ⁺	Moderately high
Δ	Moderate
Δ⁻	Moderately low
■⁺	Low
■	Very low
■⁻	Trivial

Strategy 6: Using Program Theory and Evidence of Causal Linkages

The use of information from the needs assessment to determine importance works fairly well in dimensional evaluation when the dimensions (or criteria) relate very directly to identified needs. For example, certain skills, knowledge, and abilities of evaluation master's program graduates can be linked very directly with good or poor performance as an evaluator. The same is true in component evaluation where each evaluand component clearly addresses a need whose severity can be determined quite clearly (as was the case with the components of the school-based intervention mentioned earlier).

There are some other cases, however, where the criteria or components in evaluations are linked to needs through a more complex logic chain. For example, although the importance of certain job-related skills (e.g., time management, technical know-how, communication skills) can be determined by direct reference to how they affect performance, the importance of "soft" skills and attributes (e.g., inspirational leadership, self-esteem, stress management) is much more difficult to determine. This is because these criteria are not valuable in their own right (i.e., they have no intrinsic value) but are valuable to the extent that they lead to something else that is verifiably valuable (i.e., they have "instrumental"[2] value).

Table 7.8   Determination of Importance of Various Student Services in the School Health Program

Program Component	Types of Dysfunction Addressed	Severity Rating[a]	Scarcity of Services	Scarcity Rating[b]	Intent/Energy to Obtain Available Alternatives	Intent/Energy Rating[b]	Overall Importance
Health education in nutrition	• Malnutrition • Weight problems • Illness	↑ ●	• Slight—most people (58%) believe that they could receive services elsewhere	↑ −	• Moderate—majority (59%) would bother to seek out available alternatives	↑ + ↑	● Extremely high
Case management of pregnant or parenting teens[c]	• Poor health for self or baby • Lack of parenting skills • Inability to plan academically and vocationally	↑ Δ/●	• Slight—most people (50%) believe that services exist elsewhere	↑ −	• Strong—mass majority (100%) would bother to seek out available alternatives	↑ ++ ↑↑	●[−] High
Transportation[c]	• Lack of access to child care, case management, and existing services • Economic hardship • Threatened safety if forced to walk	↑ ■/Δ	• High—clear majority (67%) report that they could not receive services elsewhere	↑ ++	• Moderate—majority (67%) would bother to seek out available alternatives	↑ + ↑	●[−] High
Mental health	• Suicide • Depression • Inability to focus on schoolwork • Absence from school • Lack of referrals (reduced access to other services)	↑ ●	• Slight—most people (60%) report that they could receive services elsewhere	↑ −	• Slight—most (60%) would not bother to seek out available alternatives	↑ − ↑	Δ[+] Moderately high

(Continued)

119

Table 7.8 (Continued)

Program Component	Types of Dysfunction Addressed	Severity Rating[a]	Scarcity of Services	Scarcity Rating[b]	Intent/Energy to Obtain Available Alternatives	Intent/Energy Rating[b]	Overall Importance
Health education in reproductive anatomy and safer sex	• Spread of sexually transmitted diseases and AIDS • Pregnancy • Absence from school	↑ Δ/●	• Slight—most people (60%) report that they could receive services elsewhere	↑ −	• Slight—most people (58%) would not bother to seek out available alternatives	↑ −	Δ Moderate
Legal services	• Economic hardship • Legal problems • Inattention to schoolwork	↑ ■	• High—vast majority (70%) report that they could not receive services elsewhere	↑ ++	• Slight—most people (57%) would not bother to seek out available alternatives	↑ −	■+ Low
Health clinic	• Lack/Delay of emergency care for minor illness • Inability to access care • Lack of referral system to other services	↑ Δ	• Slight—most people (54%) believe that services exist elsewhere	↑ −	• Slight—most people (58%) would not bother to seek out available alternatives	↑ −	■+ Low

NOTES:

a. ● = severe, Δ = moderate, ■ = low severity.

b. ++ = strong, + = moderate, − = slight, − − = low.

c. N < 10 (warrants caution in interpretation).

120

Another way in which to conceptualize these criteria with instrumental value is as "upstream variables" in a program logic model. To illustrate, Exhibit 7.4 shows an example of a logic model used in an evaluation of the learning capacity of a small biotechnology start-up company on the U.S. East Coast (Davidson, 2001).

Exhibit 7.4   Logic Model Linking Aspects of Organizational Learning Culture to Performance Needs at the Individual Level of Analysis

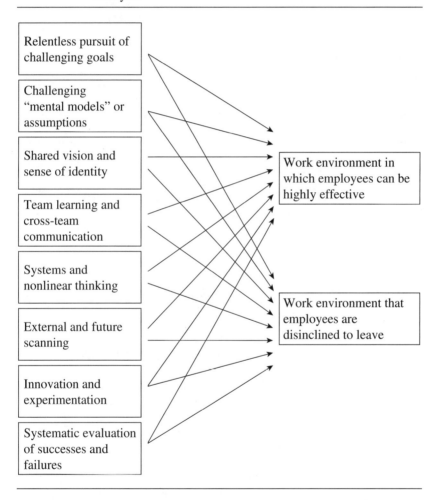

Eight dimensions of organizational culture had been identified from the literature as being the elements that distinguish "learning-enabled" organizations from "learning-impaired" organizations. The underlying logic was that if

these elements of the organizational culture were strong, this would create an environment where employees could be highly effective in their jobs while at the same time making them disinclined to leave the organization. The latter variables can be considered the *performance needs* of the organization at the individual level of analysis[3] (for a review of performance needs, refer back to Chapter 3).

The importance of these two criteria was determined using Strategy 2 (drawing on the knowledge of selected stakeholders). Based on an in-depth interview with the company's owner-manager, it was determined that it was somewhat more important for this organization to create an environment where employees could be highly effective (in this case, creative), given the innovation-intensive nature of the biotechnology industry, than it was to create an environment that would ensure employee retention (Table 7.9).

Table 7.9   Determining the Importance of Criteria Related to Performance Needs

Criterion	Potential Impacts of Excellent or Poor Performance on This Criterion	Importance
Individual performance	Quality/Productivity of the creative process (which drives product quality and, therefore, is central to organizational survival) is heavily dependent on each individual's ability to add maximum value in his or her position.	Extremely high
Employee retention (especially of top performers)	Continuity is important for the development of a particular product and is desirable across multiple projects due to cumulative learning effects. Employees have high levels of very specific expertise, are hard to replace, and carry significant organizational knowledge.	High

For this evaluation of organizational learning capacity, the goal was to produce a profile of organizational "learning-enabledness" on the eight dimensions of organizational culture. To help the organization prioritize any efforts to improve the organization's learning culture, it was also necessary to provide some indication of the relative importance of each dimension.

Although determining the importance of the downstream criteria was relatively simple, the challenge in this evaluation was determining the importance of the dimensions of organizational learning culture, that is, the upstream variables. The organizational stakeholders had little or no knowledge about organizational learning, which ruled out Strategy 1 (stakeholder vote) and Strategy 2 (using stakeholder input). In addition, because this was a relatively new area of study, the lack of relevant empirical evidence ruled out both Strategy 3 (using evidence from the literature) and Strategy 4 (using specialist judgment). In any case, it seemed likely that the importance of the eight dimensions of organizational learning culture would vary from organization to organization. Finally, because the organizational learning culture dimensions were not performance needs, Strategy 5 (using evidence from the needs assessment) was also inappropriate.

The challenge posed by this evaluation sparked the development of a new methodology for determining the importance of upstream variables. The underlying logic was as follows: The more important upstream variables are those that are most strongly causally linked to the most important downstream variables. Accordingly, the first task was to draw on the tools outlined in Chapter 5 to assess the strengths of the causal links between each of the organizational learning culture dimensions and the two performance needs-related criteria.

For this particular evaluation (which was conducted on a shoestring), all that was required was a broad-brush estimate of dimension importance rather than a high degree of accuracy. The causal analysis drew on several pieces of data to estimate the strengths of the links:

- Visual analysis of two-dimensional scatterplots
- Correlation coefficients (excluding outliers where appropriate)
- Employee responses to open-ended questions about the most important determinants of their ability to perform effectively and of their intent to stay with or leave the organization
- Owner/Manager accounts of the work environment variables that appear to affect employee performance and turnover

Based on this mix of information, the strengths of the links were added into the logic model, and the information was used to determine the importance of the organizational learning culture dimensions (Exhibit 7.5). Extremely important organizational learning culture dimensions were those that were strongly linked to the most important need and had at least a weak

Exhibit 7.5   Determination of the Importance of Upstream (learning
culture) Dimensions Using a Logic Model and Evidence of
Causal Links

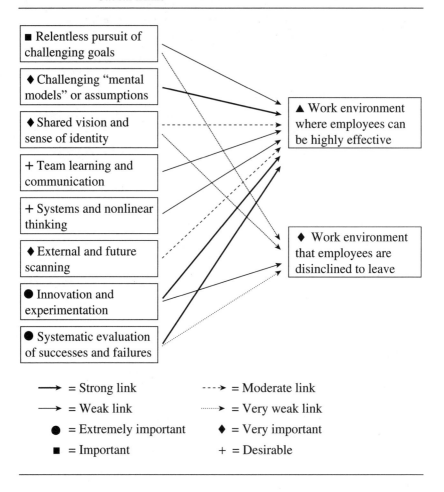

link to the other need. Very important dimensions had a strong or moderate
link to the most important need. Important dimensions had weak or very
weak links to both needs, whereas the least important (desirable) dimensions
had weak or very weak links to both needs.

Of course, it is always possible to argue for slightly different cutoffs when
classifying the dimensions into the four importance categories. Some debate
about this is healthy to ensure that the classification system is justifiable and
to help stakeholders understand how it works. However, it is important to bear

in mind the purpose of the exercise, that is, to provide a broad-brush assessment of dimension importance that will allow the client to identify priorities and make effective decisions more easily. This is illustrated in Exhibit 7.6, which shows the learning culture profile presented to the client in this case. Although many evaluations will require more accuracy than was used in this example, it is important not to obsess about achieving a far higher level of precision than what is really required.

Exhibit 7.6   Learning Culture Profile Arranged According to Importance Weightings

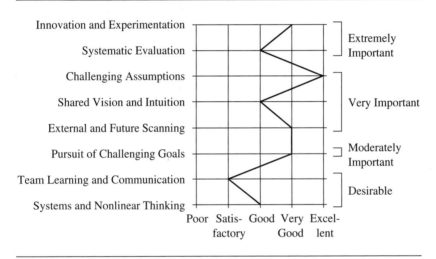

Strengths and Weaknesses of the Six Strategies

The six importance determination strategies outlined in this chapter vary considerably in their complexity and in the kinds of situations to which they are most applicable. Each has its own set of advantages and challenges, as outlined in Table 7.10. Often the best option is to employ the principles of critical multiplism (Shadish, 1994; Shadish, Cook, & Campbell, 2002) and to choose two or three complementary strategies with different weaknesses.

As noted in this chapter, one of the main uses of importance determination is to allow more illustrative profiling of findings for a client. However, there is another application: synthesizing mixed findings on several dimensions or components to draw an overall conclusion about evaluand quality or

Table 7.10   Advantages and Challenges of the Six Importance Determination Strategies

Strategy	Advantages	Challenges
1. Having stakeholders or consumers "vote" on importance	Is inclusive and democratic; maximizes buy-in to the evaluation process; requires relatively little expertise in importance determination on the part of the evaluation team	Assumes that all voters are equally well informed; assumes that *popularity* = *importance* (which weighs minority opinions more lightly); may be expensive if many opinions are sought; opens the "who chooses the voters?" can of worms
2. Drawing on the knowledge of selected stakeholders	Targets those stakeholders in the best position to know about importance; combines stakeholder expertise with evaluator expertise; relatively cost-effective compared with Strategy 1; gets buy-in from the top	Requires more skill on the part of the evaluation team; needs stakeholders to have sufficient defensible knowledge of importance; requires careful justification of the choice of stakeholder informants
3. Using evidence from the literature	Avoids reinventing the wheel; provides justification that is independent of those with a vested interest in the evaluand; is a good method to complement stakeholder input or other methods	Requires sufficient literature that addresses this issue (often not available for very innovative evaluands); can be time-consuming if literature is widely dispersed; can be seen as overly academic and undervaluing of local knowledge

Strategy	Advantages	Challenges
4. Using specialist judgment	Is considerably quicker than a literature search; does not rely on either stakeholder expertise or evaluation team expertise; can help with credibility (if the specialist has "brand recognition"); is a good method to complement stakeholder input or other methods	May yield information that represents just one line of thought in the body of knowledge on this topic; can be seen as undervaluing of local knowledge
5. Using evidence from the needs and values assessments	Provides independently verifiable evidence of importance that is directly related to this evaluand in this context	Requires expertise in needs and values assessments; works only for those criteria for which there is direct evidence of importance
6. Using program theory and evidence of causal linkages	Provides independently verifiable evidence of importance that is directly related to this evaluand in this context; can also determine importance of upstream outcomes where there is no direct evidence of "intrinsic" importance	Requires substantial expertise on the part of the evaluation team (or hiring an expert to help); requires a defensible program theory; can be time-consuming and expensive; may be difficult to explain to stakeholders and/or to use in participatory mode

value. We discuss this challenging task later in Chapter 11. But first, we need to tackle another explicitly evaluative task: merit determination.

NOTES

1. By far the greatest contributions in this area to date, especially with respect to conceptualizing what it is we do when we infer merit or worth, have been from Scriven (in particular, see Scriven, 1991). He certainly deserves credit for providing much of the conceptual "grist for the mill" that the author has used to develop these methodologies and put them into a form that we can all run with—and, hopefully, that he and others will help the author improve on.

2. Many thanks go to colleague Christopher Nelson for suggesting this terminology.

3. It is true that the organization has other performance needs at the group/team, business unit, and organizational levels of analysis. However, these are immaterial for the purposes of demonstrating this importance determination methodology.

ADDITIONAL READINGS

Entries in Scriven's (1991) *Evaluation Thesaurus:*
- Analytic/Analytical
- Component evaluation
- Dimensional evaluation
- Global
- Going native
- Incestuous relations
- Interactive evaluation
- Perspectival evaluation
- Stakeholder
- Technicism
- Therapeutic role
- Utilization

Davidson, E. J. (2002). Organizational evaluation: Issues and methods. In R. L. Lowman (Ed.), *Handbook of organizational consulting psychology* (pp. 344–369). San Francisco: Jossey-Bass.

Davidson, E. J. (2003). Linking organizational learning to the bottom line: Methodological issues, challenges, and suggestions. *Psychologist-Manager Journal, 6*(1), 54–67.

Fetterman, D. M. (2000). *Foundations of empowerment evaluation.* Thousand Oaks, CA: Sage.

Patton, M. Q. (1997). *Utilization-focused evaluation* (3rd ed.). Thousand Oaks, CA: Sage.

EXERCISES

1. In your own words, briefly define and explain the differences among (a) holistic evaluation, (b) component evaluation, and (c) dimensional evaluation. For each one, (i) give a real-world example of an evaluation in your profession for which you would choose one over the others and (ii) indicate why—for example, not just why (a) but also why not (b) or (c). The examples should not be taken from the texts, from one of your assignments, or from your project. (A suggested answer to this question is provided in the "Answers to Selected Exercises" section.)

2. What are the two main applications of importance determination as outlined in this chapter? Are there any other possible applications?

3. List and explain clearly in nontechnical terms the six different strategies for determining the importance of criteria of merit and/or evaluand components. For each one, describe a hypothetical evaluation in your field where that particular strategy would probably be the best option. Justify your choice in each case.

4. List the main criteria (under the headings of Process, Outcomes, and Cost) that you will be using to determine the quality or value of your evaluand. Outline at least two or three strategies that you would use to determine their relative importance and indicate how you would go about using them (e.g., If you use stakeholder input, exactly whose input would you seek and why?). Explain your choices, particularly why you did not use the other three or four importance determination options.

⊰ EIGHT ⊱

THE MERIT DETERMINATION STEP

———•◦•———

valuation is the systematic determination of the quality, value, or
importance of something (Scriven, 1991). That "something" can refer
to an entire evaluand (e.g., a program or product), or it can refer to aspects
(i.e., dimensions or criteria) or pieces (i.e., components) of an evaluand. The
previous chapter outlined several strategies for determining the *importance*
of evaluand components or dimensions. This chapter explores how to determine the *quality or value* of performance on these components or dimensions
(i.e., the merit determination step).

> **Merit determination** is the process of setting "standards" (definitions
> of what performance should constitute "satisfactory," "good," etc.) and
> applying those standards to descriptive data to draw explicitly evaluative
> conclusions about performance on a particular dimension or component.

The merit determination step is where we apply the contents of the Values
checkpoint to the descriptive data we gather to draw evaluative conclusions
under the Sub-evaluations checkpoints of the Key Evaluation Checklist (KEC)
(Exhibit 8.1). Note the explicitly evaluative questions under each checkpoint.

The "big picture" question of how we should determine the quality, value,
or importance of an evaluand overall is addressed later in Chapter 9, where
we talk about synthesizing all of our findings to draw an overall evaluative
conclusion.

131

Exhibit 8.1   The KEC Checkpoints Where the Merit Determination Step
                    Appears

6. Process Evaluation How good, valuable, or efficient is the evaluand's content (design) and implementation (delivery)?	7. Outcome Evaluation How good or valuable are the impacts (both intended and unintended) on immediate recipients and other impactees?	8 & 9. Comparative Cost-Effectiveness How costly is this evaluand to consumers, funders, staff, and so forth, compared with alternative uses of the available resources that might feasibly have achieved outcomes of similar or greater value? Are the costs excessive, quite high, just acceptable, or very reasonable?	10. Exportability What elements of the evaluand (e.g., innovative design, approach) might make it potentially valuable or a significant contribution or advance in another setting?

DETERMINING MERIT: WHAT AND WHY

Merit determination involves two steps: (a) defining what constitutes poor, adequate, good, very good, and excellent performances on a particular dimension (or for a particular component) and (b) using that definition to convert empirical evidence of evaluand performance (descriptive facts) into evaluative conclusions (i.e., saying something explicit about quality or value). Here we are applying a basic evaluation formula:

Descriptive Facts About Performance	+	Quality or Value Determination Guide	→	Evaluative Conclusions

Merit Determination Using a Single Quantitative Measure

In the special case where performance is being measured on a single quantitative dimension, the quality or value determination guide would simply be a set of cutoff scores (e.g., for a test, > 90% = A/excellent, 80%–89% = B/good, 70%–79% = C/adequate). In some cases, it might be just one cutoff, that is, the line between satisfactory and unsatisfactory performance.

The difficult issue when converting scores to grades is determining where the cutoff score should be placed.

Pop Quiz: Using Fixed Cutoffs to Ensure Consistency

In the United States, school and university exam and course grades are frequently determined using the following cutoff scores: > 90% = A, 80%–89% = B, 70%–79% = C, 60%–69% = D, < 60% = F. Many argue that mandating such cutoffs is one way in which to ensure objectivity and consistency of grading across courses. Is this true? If so, why? If not, why not?

In New Zealand, school and university exam and course grades are frequently determined using the following cutoff scores: > 80% = A, 65%–79% = B, 50%–64% = C, 35%–49% = D, < 35% = F. Does this mean that it is easier to get A's in New Zealand universities than in U.S. universities? If so, why? If not, why not? (Puzzled? Make contact with someone who has been to a university in New Zealand, or in a country that uses different cutoffs from those in your home country, and ask him or her about it.)

Merit Determination With Qualitative or Multiple Measures

As mentioned previously, the use of a single measure to assess performance on a particular dimension is not generally good practice. This means that for most evaluations, the evaluation team will be faced with a much more complex set of data (often a mix of qualitative and quantitative data) that must be converted to evaluative conclusions.

Many of us are trained in either the social sciences or the hard sciences, so breaking things down into their component parts comes fairly naturally. Once we have done that, we can go out and gather the data while applying our knowledge of research methodology. The tricky part comes when all of those data come in and we are left with a mass of information that needs to be

packed back together to find answers to the question of how well the evaluand
did on a particular dimension or component (Exhibit 8.2).

Exhibit 8.2   Synthesizing Multiple Data Sources to Draw Evaluative
Conclusions About Performance on Dimensions and
Subdimensions

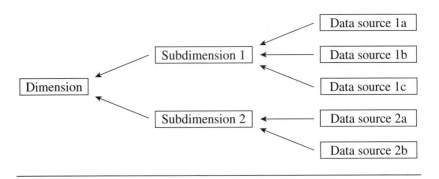

A more concrete example of what the problem looks like is provided
in Table 8.1. Here we have multiple sources of data pertaining to the performance of a hypothetical graduate program on just one dimension: job
placement. To assess the program's performance on job placement, four **subdimensions** have been defined: (a) speed and ease of placement, (b) level and
quality of jobs obtained, (c) prestige and desirability of organizations where
graduates find work, and (d) match of positions with graduates' interests and
aspirations. For each of the subdimensions, multiple measures and indicators
have been collected.

In the next section, we look at how to make sense of a mix of data such
as this. But first, let's tackle a couple of key points that are important to bear
in mind as we do this.

Merit Determination and the Futility of Seeking Precision

For each of the subdimensions pertaining to the quality of job placement in
our hypothetical graduate program, there are several sources of data (Table 8.1).
Some of these point in the same general direction, whereas others seem to partially contradict each other. Either way, we are in need of some strategy for figuring out whether the information we have obtained about, say, speed and ease
of placement (one of the subdimensions) should be considered "excellent,"
"very good," "good," "barely acceptable," "poor," or "completely unacceptable."

Table 8.1   Example Data on Subdimensions Related to Quality of Job
Placement

Speed or ease of placement	Three quarters (75%) of graduates who sought work found employment within 3 months of graduation (mean = 6 weeks).
	Nearly one third (30%) had job offers by the time they graduated.
	Only 15% were still unemployed, underemployed, or in jobs unrelated to their degrees 12 months after graduation.
	Most graduates (85%) complained that finding work was considerably more difficult than they had expected.
	The average graduate sent out 22 applications, was invited in for three or four interviews, and was offered one or two jobs.
Level or quality of jobs obtained	Most jobs obtained were entry level, with 10% of the class making it into "senior associate"-level positions (all of these people had 5 or more years of previous experience).
	The starting salary mean was $38,000 (range = $29,000–$84,000).
	Feedback from graduates indicated that jobs were generally moderately challenging relative to their skills.
Prestige or desirability of organizations where graduates find work	Among graduates in the for-profit sector, 12% found work in Fortune 500 companies.
	A small percentage (2%) found work in companies rated in the top 20 "best places to work" lists.
	Expert assessments showed that the reputations of most graduates' new organizations were moderate to weak, although one or two graduates found work in very highly regarded institutions and organizations.
Match of positions with graduates' interests and aspirations	Analysis of pregraduation areas of specialization against job and/or company type showed that 65% of graduates found work in desired areas of specialization, 20% were in appropriate industries but not appropriate job areas, and 15% were in jobs that were only marginally related to their areas of specialization.
	Most graduates expressed at least some disappointment regarding the degree of match between their jobs and their career aspirations and interests.

Of course, a particular evaluation might not require such fine gradations. This is just an example using a number of quality categories (six) that tends to be workable in most cases. In the author's experience, there is not much to be gained from trying for greater precision (e.g., 10 categories of merit) unless the evaluand really lends itself to that (this may be possible in some product evaluation tasks). Attempts to strive for high levels of precision in evaluation usually result in a lot of time-consuming debate about what should go where.

When it comes to the evaluation of programs, policies, and/or other things that involve people (this would include most evaluands), evaluation is sometimes a fairly blunt instrument. We can usually attain a reasonable broad-brush level of accuracy that is good enough to meet the informational needs of the client and other right-to-know audiences. But attempts to achieve a level of precision that outstrips the tools and knowledge at our disposal can do little but undermine credibility and increase accusations of arbitrariness.

Remember that just because we can measure something to four decimal places does not mean that we can rate its quality or value to the same level of precision. Performance on all dimensions or criteria of merit should be assessed using a mix of data, usually both qualitative and quantitative, plus a mix of information drawn from the needs assessment and other relevant considerations (e.g., professional standards). Rarely is this cut-and-dried. But neither is it a hopelessly impossible task so long as we can stay comfortable with a certain amount of fuzziness around the edges and we do not oversell the precision of our work.

The practical point to remember here is that it is usually impossible to obtain high levels of precision on the merit determination step. However, you should keep in mind the following:

• Providing a well-supported broad-brush answer to an important question is generally far more valuable to clients (and to other audiences) than is telling them that the answer is impossibly mired in subjectivity and so they will have to work it out for themselves.

• It is perfectly appropriate to give an answer that still has a certain amount of fuzziness or uncertainty associated with it. (As mentioned earlier in the discussion of causation, one does not always need a very high degree of certainty about the answer. In any case, it may be extremely helpful indeed to get even part of the way there, e.g., by dealing with the parts that are reasonably straightforward, narrowing the options, and clarifying the trade-offs surrounding any dangling issues.)

USING RUBRICS FOR DETERMINING "ABSOLUTE" MERIT

So, how are we going to convert a mix of quantitative and qualitative data into some rating of the quality or value of that attribute or level of performance? One tool that can be incredibly useful (and a good conversation starter with the evaluation team and stakeholders) is a rubric.

> A **rubric** is a tool that provides an evaluative description of what performance or quality "looks like" at each of two or more defined levels.
>
> A **grading rubric** is a rubric that is used to determine *absolute* quality or value, whereas a **ranking rubric** is used for questions of *relative* quality or value.
>
> (See Chapter 2 for a review of absolute versus relative quality or value.)

A generic example of a grading rubric that can provide a good starting point for the merit determination step is shown in Table 8.2. The rubric shown in the table is merely a starting point for rubric development. It does, of course, take a significant amount of additional work to define terms such as *exemplary performance* and *serious weakness*. This usually requires a combination of

Table 8.2   Generic Rubric for Converting Descriptive Data Into "Absolute" (rather than "relative") Determinations of Merit

Rating	*Explanation*
Excellent	Clear example of exemplary performance or best practice in this domain; no weaknesses
Very good	Very good or excellent performance on virtually all aspects; strong overall but not exemplary; no weaknesses of any real consequence
Good	Reasonably good performance overall; might have a few slight weaknesses but nothing serious
Barely adequate	Fair performance; some serious (but nonfatal) weaknesses on a few aspects
Poor	Clear evidence of unsatisfactory functioning; serious weaknesses across the board or on crucial aspects

background research and extensive discussions with experts and/or key stakeholders. (Two simple examples of this are provided later in the chapter.)

Developing Rubrics in a Participatory Evaluation

This process of defining "how good is good" can be an incredibly valuable exercise for helping all sorts of organizations to think through what they mean by *quality* or *value*. In a participatory evaluation, this part of the process forms an important part of the groundwork for the evaluation and doubles as an intervention that helps people to focus on what is really important about the work they do.

Whether the evaluation is being conducted in participatory mode or not, it is very important to talk to consumers at this point when developing a merit determination rubric. After all, the program, policy, or product is presumably designed to create value for them. This can help organizational staff to identify incorrect assumptions they might have been making about needs and other issues.

Sample Grading Rubric 1

To give an example of a more fully fleshed-out merit determination rubric, Table 8.3 shows what an early draft might look like for one of the subcriteria identified for a hypothetical master's program in evaluation. It is important to note that the example given in the table is merely a sample rubric that has not been subjected to discussion with key stakeholders or job placement experts. In nearly all cases, rubrics such as this need considerable refinement based not only on, for example, student or graduate expectations but also on expert (e.g., recruiter, job placement specialist, employer) input regarding the job market and what expectations would be reasonable for graduates with this particular mix of qualifications and experience.

Recall the data collected for our hypothetical master's program:

- Three quarters (75%) of graduates who sought work found employment within 3 months of graduation (mean = 6 weeks).
- Nearly one third (30%) had job offers by the time they graduated.
- Only 15% were still unemployed, underemployed, or in jobs unrelated to their degrees 12 months after graduation.
- Most graduates (85%) complained that finding work was considerably more difficult than they had expected.
- The average graduate sent out 22 applications, was invited in for three or four interviews, and was offered one or two jobs.

Table 8.3   Rubric for Determining the Merit of a Master's Program in Evaluation on the Subcriterion "Speed or Ease of Job Placement"

Rating	Description
Excellent	All students had evaluation-relevant job offers on graduation or soon after (within 2 months excluding those who were not actively seeking such employment), and several students had more than one strong job offer. Several high-profile organizations recruited on campus or sought recommendations through program faculty to identify the best recruits.
Very good	The vast majority of students (> 80%) had evaluation-relevant job offers on graduation or soon after (within 2 months excluding those who were not actively seeking such employment), and several students had more than one strong job offer. A small number of high-profile organizations recruited on campus or sought recommendations through program faculty to identify the best recruits. Most students had to be quite proactive about networking and applying for jobs.
Good	Most students (> 70%) had job offers on graduation or soon after (within 2 months excluding those who were not actively seeking such employment), although some of these were not directly related to evaluation, and some students had more than one reasonable job offer. Most students had to drive their own job-seeking agendas quite hard, although some assistance was provided. Those students without job offers tended to be those who were more passive about job seeking.
Barely adequate	Most students (> 70%) had at least one job offer within 3 or 4 months of graduation, although many of these were not related to evaluation. Job-seeking efforts had to be very intensive to obtain decent job offers. Many graduates reported that employers were not at all familiar with their university or the program.
Poor	With only a few exceptions (< 30%), most graduates of the program took up to 6 months to obtain placements (or promotions in their current jobs) that were only slightly better than what they had left to enroll in the program (or that were only slightly better than what bachelor's-level graduates were getting). Most positions were not related to evaluation but rather were related to the cognate areas.
Completely unacceptable	Graduates of the program found it difficult even to obtain positions equivalent to the ones they had left to enroll in the master's program.

Based on this information, the program in question seems to fit most closely with a rating of "good" on the rubric in Table 8.3. In a real evaluation, you might need to do some further digging to make sure that the rating is justified. For example, there might be a high proportion of graduates who have decided to go on to doctoral programs, in which case they should not be counted as having been unable to find full-time jobs.

Sample Grading Rubric 2

Here is another example of a grading rubric that draws on much more qualitative (i.e., nonnumerical) information to draw conclusions about merit. In this case, the rubric is used for performance appraisal; however, the logic is the same as for program evaluation. The rubric was designed for evaluating the performance of clerical staff in a small accounting office on their management of monthly accounts (one of several duties). It was developed in discussion with the two business owners/partners, who defined the expectations. The rubric starts with a description of the scope of duties, lists the main performance indicators, and then defines each level of performance—in this case, from "unacceptable" to "excellent" (Table 8.4).

Table 8.4   Performance Appraisal Rubric for a Specific Set of Tasks in a Small Accounting Firm

Monthly Support Packages (clerical)

Scope:
  • Preparing monthly financial reports
  • Responsible for data entry
  • Liaising with clients
  • Critically analyzing results
  • Systematically reviewing income tax liabilities
 	
Performance indicators:
  • Timeliness and efficiency
  • Accuracy
  • Clarity of communication, tact, and diplomacy
  • Use of Inland Revenue Department (IRD) or Internal Revenue Service (IRS) compliance knowledge
Instructions: Choose the description that best fits how well the objective has been met, and check the appropriate box.

Rating	Description
Totally unacceptable performance (score = 1)	Any one or more of the following: (a) inadequate checking and/or following up of queries or missing information, leading to serious inaccuracies in data entry and/or monthly reports; (b) failed to report one or more major problems or issues to partners; (c) inadequate documentation, making auditing extremely difficult or impossible; (d) frequently rude or abrupt with clients; (e) failed to inform clients of important obligations on one or more occasions
Mediocre (substandard) performance (score = 2)	Any one or more of the following: (a) inadequate use of communication skills, checking or following up of queries, or missing information, leading to minor inaccuracies in data entry and/or monthly reports; (b) failed to report one or more minor problems or issues to partners; (c) failed to inform clients of minor obligations on one or more occasions, causing inconvenience; (d) barely adequate documentation and/or auditing trails, making quality checking possible but somewhat difficult; (e) inadequate prioritizing of time, leading to one or more jobs being completed outside budgeted time frames (except when delay was out of the accounting firm's control)
Good performance (expected level) (score = 3)	Efficient checking of data entry, allowing preparation of accurate monthly reports supported by clear work papers and audit trails; clients always informed of their obligations and requirements; partners kept informed of any problems or issues as they came to light; time prioritized so that all jobs were completed within budgeted time frames unless delays were out of the organization's control; queries and missing information always documented and followed up quickly and efficiently to ensure that jobs were not held up; all clients handled professionally and courteously with excellent communication skills displayed; thorough documentation, allowing for rapid evaluation of clients' overall financial positions and internal record keeping and systems

(Continued)

Table 8.4 (Continued)

Rating	Description
Performance exceeded expectations (score = 4)	All of the above in addition to the following: excellent use of communication skills and time management, ensuring that clients had an excellent understanding of their financial situations and that statements were 100% accurate and consistently completed well within budgeted time frames; meticulously organized work papers and audit trails, allowing any staff member to quickly ascertain the current state of any work in progress and to check the accuracy of work completed; constantly worked to streamline procedures for both clients and the accounting firm
All-around excellent performance (score = 5)	All of the above in addition to the following: superb professional service to clients, enhancing the reputation of the accounting firm and resulting in positive feedback and/or new clients through word-of-mouth advertising; innovative approach to managing monthly support packages, resulting in a smooth-running and error-free system that allowed jobs to be completed significantly more efficiently than time frames budgeted for (levels to be agreed on between partners and employees)

USING RUBRICS FOR DETERMINING "RELATIVE" MERIT

In some cases, the evaluation team will need to determine the relative merit (rather than the absolute merit) of performance on a particular dimension. Relative merit evaluations (i.e., ranking) tell us little or nothing about how good the performance was in any absolute sense. They simply tell us how the person or program did relative to peers or competitors, respectively.

"Grading on the Curve"

Perhaps the simplest example of this is the practice called "grading on the curve." Although the term *grading* is used (and letter grades may even be given), the instructor is actually ranking rather than grading evaluees. Table 8.5 shows a hypothetical rubric that might be used to generate grades for student performance in a large class.

The main problem with grading on the curve is that the letter grades imply that there is some sense of absolute merit (e.g., A = excellent, B = good, C = satisfactory). But the reality is that this system forces the instructor to fail

Table 8.5   Hypothetical Rubric for "Grading on the Curve"
(actually ranking)

Score Falls in:	Grade Assigned
Top 10%	A
Next 25%	B
Next 50%	C
Next 15%	D
Bottom 5%	F

a certain proportion of the class, whether those students are performing at an unsatisfactory level or not. In addition, it forces the instructor to give A's to 10% of the students, regardless of whether their performance was truly excellent. In general, if ranking is being used, the terminology used to label the categories should make it clear that this is ranking (e.g., "top 10%" instead of "A").

Standardized Tests

Most standardized tests, such as the Scholastic Aptitude Test (SAT), the Graduate Record Examination (GRE), and the Graduate Management Admission Test (GMAT), also determine relative merit rather than absolute merit, expressing scores in percentile terms that indicate the test taker's percentile rank (i.e., what proportion of all test takers scored lower). One recently added exception is the analytical writing section of the GRE, which provides a numerical rating that corresponds to a description of absolute merit. Tests of intelligence quotient (IQ) are another example of tests that determine where someone falls relative to the population. Unlike the aforementioned standardized tests, IQ score ranges are assigned explicitly evaluative labels such as "gifted" (see Table 8.6 for the conversion rubric).

Relative Merit and Experimental and Quasi-Experimental Designs

Determination of the relative merit of outcomes is particularly important for experimental and quasi-experimental evaluation designs, that is, designs that incorporate the use of a control or comparison group. For example, student achievement scores for a particular school are often interpreted relative to state

Table 8.6   Rubric for Interpreting IQ Scores

Evaluative Intelligence Rating	IQ Score	z Score[a]	Percentage Below
Exceptionally gifted	160	+4	> 99%
Highly gifted	145	+3	99%
Very superior/gifted	130	+2	98%
High average	115	+1	84%
Average	100	0	50%
Low average	85	−1	16%
Borderline	70	−2	2%
Mild mental retardation	55	−3	1%
Moderate mental retardation	40	−4	< 1%

NOTE: a. A z score indicates how many standard deviations a score is above or below the mean.

SOURCES: www.psychologicaltesting.com/iqtest.htm and http://iq-test.learninginfo.org/iq04.htm

averages or by comparison with schools from areas with a similar demographic and socioeconomic makeup.

The usual approach of researchers using experimental and quasi-experimental designs is to assume that a statistically significant difference in the right direction is evidence of merit, whereas failing to attain statistical significance implies a nonmeritorious outcome. In evaluation, there is a need to look further than statistical significance—to practical significance.

> A **statistically significant** result tells us only that any observed difference (or statistical relationship) is unlikely to be due to chance (e.g., a fluke sample yielding unusual data).
>
> A **practically significant** result is one that translates to real impact on people's lives (e.g., the difference has a noticeable and nontrivial effect on functioning or performance).

When determining the merit of a particular outcome, it is important to take into consideration both its practical significance and its statistical significance (or the qualitative equivalent).

Using Comparisons to Determine Relative Merit

To determine the relative merit of a process, an outcome, or a cost criterion, it is important to identify useful comparisons. For example, the evaluation team might "benchmark" process, outcome, and cost criteria against what has been achieved elsewhere (e.g., by other evaluands of a similar scope).

Benchmarking is a systematic study of one or more other organizations' systems, processes, and outcomes to identify ideas for improving organizational effectiveness. It has been used in manufacturing for years and is now widely used throughout business and industry.

Benchmarking most commonly refers to a process of gathering comparison data about what organizations in similar or related industries are achieving. This approach to benchmarking focuses primarily on collecting quantitative data about process efficiency, outputs, outcomes, and costs.

Sometimes organizations undertake their own benchmarking studies. In such cases, two or more organizations (often doing business in different sectors) each agree to allow teams from the other organization(s) to come in and study their practices, compare results, and discuss how improvements were made. These studies are typically heavier on qualitative data gathering (e.g., observation of processes, interviews with key stakeholders), although they still look at specific quantitative data.

The following example, taken from an evaluation of a large-scale organizational change effort, illustrates the use of a simple rubric to determine the relative merit of evaluand components. In this case, the components were clusters of initiatives that formed part of the change effort. The rubric is designed to assess the relative cost-effectiveness of each cluster of change interventions (Table 8.7).

After drawing up the simple rubric, the next task was to rate each component (i.e., cluster of organizational change interventions) on the given scale. As an example, one of the components was a set of interventions intended to create a more strategic and constructive work environment. To this end, the organization had implemented a culture survey and a climate survey, that is, quantitative instruments sourced from separate providers that were to deliver periodic "snapshots" of the organizational culture and climate that managers would then reflect on before making changes in their business units.

Table 8.7   Rubric for Determining the Relative Merit of Organizational
                 Change Interventions

Relative Merit	Description
Superior practice	Clearly the most cost-effective of the available alternatives
Above average	Considerably more cost-effective than most alternatives
Average	Approximately as cost-effective as most of the alternatives
Below average	Considerably less cost-effective than most alternatives
Inferior practice	Clearly the least cost-effective of the available alternatives

Table 8.8 outlines the main costs and benefits of the two surveys and
provides a list of alternative options given the resources the organization had
at its disposal. By applying this information to the rubric in Table 8.7, this
component of the organizational change effort was rated "below average."

MAKING PRACTICAL USE OF
MERIT DETERMINATION RUBRICS

There you have it—the basics of rubric methodology for synthesizing
qualitative and/or quantitative data to draw conclusions about the merit of an
evaluand on a particular dimension, subdimension, or component. Naturally,
a lot of the finer points, such as how you might go about talking to various
informants (e.g., evaluation team members, experts, other stakeholders) about
the definitions of levels within the rubrics and resolving any differences of
opinion, had to be skipped over here. The main thing to remember is to keep
an open mind, draw in the views of all those who can help you to make
good sense of the data, and do not let any one group drive the agenda to the
exclusion of other points of view.

Table 8.8 Costs, Benefits, and Alternatives for Two Related Components of an Organizational Change Intervention

Component	Costs and Benefits	Alternatives
Improvement of work environment: 1. Culture survey 2. Climate survey	• Large financial outlay exists for each survey (several hundred thousand dollars each). • Culture and climate surveys are scheduled to alternate each year for several years. • Organization receives information with a lot of overlap. • Some managers believe that the information is interesting; only a few managers believe that it is useful and report having used it to make some changes. • Employees report seeing no substantial change arising from the surveys, which suffer from a poor response rate and widespread cynicism.	• Just one of the surveys would give sufficient information about the organization's climate or culture (there is a large overlap between organizational culture and organizational climate when both are assessed using quantitative methods). • A focused questionnaire would address only the issues that the organization faces (and those aspects of the climate that affect such issues) rather than provide a full cultural profile. This could be developed with managerial input and reported back in a session that generated ideas for improving problem areas. • One of the above could be combined with manager and employee focus groups and interviews. These would provide two different perspectives that could be integrated to provide a much more complete picture of the organization's underlying culture than two surveys ever could.

By now, you may find yourself in one of two camps. Either you are saying, "Well, that's not exactly rocket science," or you are holding your head in your hands and saying, "You go to all that trouble for just one teeny tiny subdimension? How on earth am I going to get an evaluation done in real time?" The methods described in this chapter are not intended to plunge you into paralysis by analysis. Sure, there will be times on very extensive evaluation projects where this level of analysis (right down to rubrics on each subdimension) is appropriate. But there will be other times when you simply cannot go into that level of detail.

The intent here was simply to present a tool that can be used when appropriate to find answers to evaluation questions or that can be used to help clearly explain the rationale behind your conclusions to a client or critic. The most important point is not to either (a) resort to "smoke and mirrors" in your interpretation of evaluative data (i.e., present determinations of merit as just your own judgments or impressions) or (b) throw your hands in the air and proclaim that it cannot be done. We use rubrics again in the next chapter, not only to determine merit for another example but also to blend multiple sources of data more systematically so as to draw evaluative conclusions about an entire evaluand or its components (i.e., the synthesis step).

ADDITIONAL READINGS

Entries in Scriven's (1991) *Evaluation Thesaurus:*
- Benchmarks, benchmarking
- Merit
- Rubric
- Worth

Camp, R. C. (1995). *Business process benchmarking: Finding and implementing best practices.* Milwaukee, WI: ASQC Quality Press.

EXERCISES

1. Recall the earlier example of a training program that you have been asked to evaluate. The program was designed to help young unemployed people to seek and obtain work effectively. Although the "proof of the pudding"

is whether the participants actually find jobs, one other important outcome (a little further upstream) is the extent to which they apply the skills they have learned when they hunt for jobs. One of these skills is effectively tailoring résumés for different job applications. Draw up a rubric to show how you would translate into a rating (e.g., "very good") evidence of how well the program recipients as a group did on tailoring their résumés to the specific jobs for which they applied (on half a page or less).

2. Choose the most important dimension of merit for your evaluand. Draw up a rubric that shows how you will interpret data from at least three different sources (including at least one qualitative source and one quantitative source) to determine the merit of your evaluand's performance on that dimension.

NINE

SYNTHESIS METHODOLOGY

---•◦•---

L ike merit determination, synthesis is another task that is very specific
to evaluation. It is the tool that allows us to draw overall evaluative
conclusions from multiple findings about a single evaluand.

> **Synthesis** is defined as "the process of combining a set of ratings or per-
> formances on several components or dimensions into an overall rating"
> (Scriven, 1991, p. 342).

Synthesis is most relevant to the Overall Significance checkpoint in the Key
Evaluation Checklist (KEC) (Exhibit 9.1). This is where the evaluation team needs
to combine all of the evaluative information gleaned from looking at Checkpoints
6 through 10 (Process Evaluation, Outcome Evaluation, Comparative Cost-
Effectiveness, and Exportability) to draw overall conclusions about the evaluand.

Exhibit 9.1   The KEC Checkpoints Where Synthesis Methodology Is Used

---

11. Overall Significance

Draw on all of the information in Checkpoints 6 through 10 to answer the
main evaluation questions such as the following. What are the main areas
where the evaluand is doing well, and where is it lacking? Is this the most
cost-effective use of the available resources to address the identified needs
without excessive adverse impact?

The form of synthesis covered in this chapter is not to be confused with meta-analysis or literature reviews. These involve summarizing or combining the findings of multiple research or evaluation studies (about different evaluands) to draw overall conclusions about the relationships among variables. Meta-analysis uses a very specific statistical technique to give a weighted average of effect sizes across multiple studies. As such, it can handle only quantitative studies. In contrast, a literature review uses the reviewer's judgment, rather than an explicit technique, to synthesize studies.

There is a substantial overlap between the merit determination and synthesis steps in an evaluation. Many readers likely noticed that the rubrics we used to combine a mix of data in the merit determination chapter are in fact a very simple synthesis methodology. In this chapter, we take that basic logic further with some more systematic methods that can handle more complex data.

SYNTHESIS: WHAT AND WHY

Nearly any evaluand has a range of strengths and weaknesses—some more important than others—that we need to consider when we draw evaluative conclusions about quality or value on a particular dimension or component or about the evaluand overall. After all, doing poorly on some aspect of minimal importance is less serious than doing poorly on something crucial. This is why we need synthesis methodology—to have a systematic way of taking into account the pluses and minuses uncovered when the evaluation team draws evaluative conclusions.

Erroneous Arguments Against Doing Synthesis at All

At this point, it is worth presenting again the typical argument against the use of synthesis:

> This book [*Assessing Organizational Change*] is largely silent on the issue of combining outcomes from different domains in order to reach an overall conclusion about the effectiveness of a change effort. This is by design. The decision was made early on to simply report how the organization had changed on a wide array of outcome measures. No common metric was developed, nor was a weighting system developed that argued that gains in some measures are more important than gains in others. The rationale for not doing this is simple and to us persuasive. It is that different constituents value outcomes

> differently, and thus it is best to let interested parties reach their own overall conclusions. There are also practical problems in trying to translate diverse outcomes to a common metric. (Lawler, Seashore, & Mirvis, 1983, p. 542)

Hopefully, the holes in Lawler and colleagues' (1983) argument are becoming more apparent to the reader as we progress through this book. In Chapter 6, we learned that the definition of "value" in a well-designed evaluation is derived from multiple defensible sources, including the needs of impactees, ethics, the law, and relevant professional standards. Therefore, the claim that "different constituents value outcomes differently" is much less problematic than it first appears because good evaluation does not rely on personal values.

In Chapter 7, we took this further and showed why the relative importance of certain dimensions of merit can and should be determined using much more than just the opinions of individual stakeholders. Certain outcomes, for example, can often be shown objectively to be of greater or lesser value (e.g., to the organization or the community) than certain other outcomes.

In Chapter 8, we learned a method for translating diverse outcomes to a "common metric," that is, merit ratings (excellent, very good, good, acceptable, or poor). In this chapter, we tackle the task of *combining* multiple ratings of merit in a way that takes their relative importance into account.

The Need for Synthesis at Multiple Points in the Evaluation

In the course of doing an evaluation, there are multiple points where some form of synthesis is required. One that we have already encountered in the chapter on merit determination is when multiple sources of data (often both qualitative and quantitative) are combined with quality or value "standards" (definitions of "how good is good") to provide an explicitly evaluative rating on a particular dimension. From that point, there may be another one or two steps (or perhaps more) required to generate quality or value ratings on broader dimensions, on components of the evaluand, and/or on the evaluand as a whole.

An important point to note is that some synthesis is always necessary, whether the evaluation is formative or summative in nature. If an overall conclusion about the quality or value of the entire evaluand is needed (this is always the case for summative evaluations and is quite often the case for formative evaluations), a full synthesis will be needed. If the evaluand's quality or value simply needs to be reported on several dimensions or components, synthesis will stop short of the final step. But however the evaluative conclusions are reported, there is still a need to combine multiple findings or sources of data to draw those conclusions.

The synthesis step involves one additional piece beyond combining the data we have collected about the current evaluand (process, outcomes, and cost). We also use comparisons in the synthesis step to help place the evaluand's performance in a wider context. This is where the Comparative Cost-Effectiveness checkpoint of the KEC comes into play.

THE ROLE OF COSTS AND COMPARISONS IN SYNTHESIS

Every evaluand requires resources to be created and maintained. And whenever resources are allocated to something, this is always at the expense of whatever else might have been done with the same resources (i.e., opportunity costs). Therefore, whether the evaluation is formative or summative, the question is not just "Did the value of the outcomes outweigh the value of the resources it took to achieve them?" Rather, it is always "Is/Was this evaluand the best possible use of available resources to achieve outcomes of the greatest possible value?"

For evaluations where the primary evaluation question is a "ranking" one (e.g., Which of these three innovative pilot programs best meets the needs in this community? Which job candidate should we hire?), the evaluation team needs to go into considerable detail on each alternative and make very explicit comparisons. We cover some methodologies for doing this when we look at synthesizing for "ranking" later.

In cases where the primary evaluation question is a "grading" one (e.g., Was this executive training program worth implementing?), the comparisons are used to put the evaluation findings in context to allow better interpretation of merit rather than to make explicit and detailed comparisons with all possible alternatives (in most cases, this would be "paralysis by analysis"). Several methodologies for doing this are covered in the next section on synthesizing for "grading."

In some cases, comparisons do not play a large part in the synthesis step, whereas in other cases, they are extremely important. For example, when selecting someone for a job from a short list of three persons, comparisons are central because this is a ranking task. In performance appraisal, an employee's performance can often be interpreted purely in terms of the value of his or her contributions to the organization without needing to compare these to what others have achieved.

For program evaluation, comparisons in some form are almost always necessary. They can either be worked into the synthesis steps very explicitly or be used to place the synthesized findings in a broader context for interpretation.

SYNTHESIZING FOR "GRADING"

Rubrics are one of the simplest methods for blending (or synthesizing) data. But in some cases, the nature of the data is a little more complex, making it difficult to use a rubric as the only tool. For example, the data about evaluand performance that are gathered might not all be equally important or reliable, and we might need to have some way of taking this into account when we use the rubric. In addition, there might be so many different sources of data with different nuances and combinations that it becomes extremely difficult to determine merit reliably using a rubric and the limited powers of the human brain.

As mentioned previously, there are several different options when it comes to synthesis methodology. Which one is used depends, first, on whether the main evaluation question is an "absolute" (grading) or a "relative" (ranking) one. (For a review of these terms, refer back to Chapter 2.) The second consideration when selecting the right synthesis methodology is whether a qualitative or quantitative synthesis method is to be employed. A quantitative synthesis methodology is one that uses numerical weights that are applied using multiplication. A qualitative synthesis methodology is one that uses qualitative labels that are applied without the use of multiplication. In the following sections, an example is given for four different evaluation tasks that answer a grading or ranking question using quantitative or qualitative methods.

When the primary evaluation question is one of absolute quality or value, we are seeking to answer questions such as the following:

- How well did the evaluand perform on this dimension?
- How effective, valuable, or meritorious is/was the evaluand overall?
- Is/Was this component worth the resources (e.g., time, money) put into it?

Quantitative (numerical) Weighting Example With "Bars"

The first example is drawn from **personnel evaluation** (specifically, performance appraisal). It uses a quantitative (numerical weighting) methodology with some twists to generate an overall performance rating for an employee for the review period. This overall rating is then used to determine performance-based rewards.

The setting is a small accounting firm. The process began with a clear definition of the main tasks performed by employees. For this particular organization, 13 separate tasks were defined (e.g., telephone and reception, data entry for particular types of client support packages, tax agency database management). Each employee typically had responsibility for approximately 4 to 6 of these tasks in any one quarter.

Next, each task was given an importance weighting using Strategy 2 (drawing on the knowledge of selected stakeholders) from Chapter 7. After an in-depth discussion, the business owners agreed on a definition of "importance" at four levels as follows:

1. Minor task (worth doing but not particularly important for the success of the business)

2. Normal-priority task

3. High-priority task (very important for the success of the business)

4. Extremely high-priority task (crucial for the success of the business)

Note the small number of levels of importance here. In general, it is best to define approximately three to five levels. Anything more fine-grained than that makes it extremely difficult to get good agreement on importance. With a 10-point scale, for example, it is possible to waste hours arguing whether a particular task should be weighted 6 or 7. In reality, there is seldom any need for this level of precision, so for practical reasons, the three- to five-level rule works well in most cases.

Having established importance weightings, the next step was to draw up rubrics for each of the 13 tasks. Here, approximately four to six levels were usually sufficiently fine-grained to capture the variation in performance without wasting a lot of time deciding which category should apply in a particular case. An example of one of those rubrics was shown in Table 8.4 in the previous chapter.

Each employee was rated on four to six tasks (depending on which ones fell within the employee's job responsibilities), receiving a score from the following scale:

1. Totally unacceptable performance

2. Mediocre (substandard) performance

3. Good performance (expected level)

4. Performance that exceeded expectations

5. All-around excellent performance

Each task had an importance weighting ranging from 1 (minor task) to 4 (extremely high-priority task), as outlined earlier.

The synthesis methodology used to generate an overall performance rating for each employee incorporated both a numerical weighting strategy (weighted average of performance ratings) and bars (i.e., minimum acceptable levels of performance, in this case, on each task). A rating of 1 on any task was defined as totally unacceptable performance regardless of how well the person did on his or her other tasks. Any more than one rating of 2 was also defined as unacceptable. The synthesis algorithm is shown in Exhibit 9.2.

Qualitative (nonnumerical) Weighting Example 1 (with no "bars")

A quantitative weighting strategy works well in simple cases provided that bars are included to ensure that very poor performance on a particular dimension is not inappropriately masked by better performance on other dimensions. But numerical weighting systems often lead to conclusions that have the evaluation team staring at a conclusion that seems not to be quite right, thereby leading to the temptation of juggling the weights until the answer looks right. Such cases call for a qualitative (i.e., nonnumerical) weighting strategy.

The qualitative synthesis strategy presented in this section is a simple, step-by-step method for synthesizing mixed evaluation information that was developed by the author and a colleague for an evaluation of a school-based health program (Mersman, 1999; Mersman & Davidson, 1999). Those readers who are used to working with large-scale evaluations might find this example somewhat unimpressive. This was a real shoestring evaluation—short timeline, low budget, and little access to data. We too were amazed to find that even the

Exhibit 9.2   Synthesis Algorithm for a Performance Appraisal and
Rewards System in a Small Accounting Firm

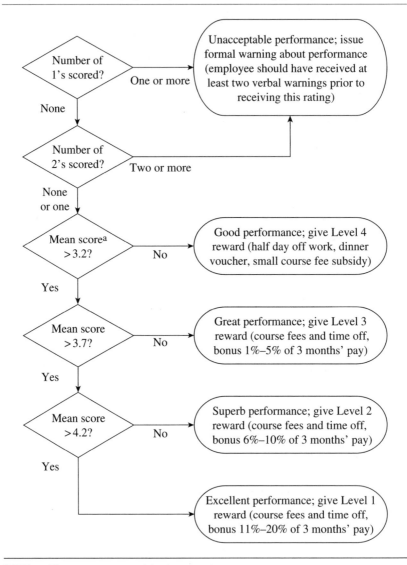

NOTE: a. All mean scores are weighted means.

relatively simple data generated by such a small-scale evaluation project
presented a synthesis problem that we found could not be solved satisfactorily
using any existing methodology. The good news is that once we developed the
methodology, it was clear that it could be applied even to situations where
there were many more criteria. So, the intent here is to provide a small simple

example that is easy enough to grasp as well as to deliver some principles and methods that could be applied to a more elaborate evaluation.

The evaluand in this case was a school-based health program with approximately nine different components that were aimed specifically at students: nutrition education, mental health services, case management for pregnant and parenting teens, safer sex, legal services, and several others. The client needed very quick and approximate answers to the question of how well each of these components was meeting important needs of the students and their families.

As just mentioned, this was the proverbial shoestring evaluation. Because of time and budgetary constraints, apart from limited observation and one or two interviews, the main data collection device was a short survey of students who had used the services. The survey was devised in both Spanish and English and was filled out in class in the presence of a bilingual teacher who explained each question in Spanish after the lead evaluator had explained it in English. Three questions about each program component were asked: two quantitative (using 4-point response scales) and one open-ended. Students were asked, "How useful was the [nutrition education] program to you?" "How satisfied were you with the program?" and "What other changes or events, good or bad, have happened to you or someone you know because of [receiving the service]?" A brief summary of the responses for the nutrition education component of the program is shown in Table 9.1.

The content of both the open-ended answers and the first quantitative item addressed the extent to which the program met student *needs,* which is a more important consideration than **satisfaction,** the other quantitative item (which deals with *wants*). Therefore, we had two sources of information about needs and one about satisfaction. Of the needs-related information, the open-ended responses contained rich information, but we obtained responses from only a third as many people as completed the quantitative items. The question was, How could we combine the results systematically in a way that took account of both the centrality to the needs issue (which was the main evaluation question) and the fact that some of the data were more representative of the users of the program due to the higher rate of response?[1]

Taking into account both of these considerations (and after much debate between us), we prioritized the three different sources of data as follows (1 = strongest data, 3 = weakest data):

1. Ratings of usefulness (directly related to needs and reasonably representative of the students who used the program)

Table 9.1   Summary of Responses to Questions About the Nutrition
Component of a School-Based Health Program

How useful was the program to you?	Not at all useful 1.6%	Somewhat useful 23.8%	Useful 57.7%	Very useful 15.9%	
How satisfied were you with the program?	Not at all satisfied 1.6%	Somewhat satisfied 11.3%	Satisfied 69.4%	Very satisfied 17.7%	*N* = 63
What other changes or events, good or bad, have happened to you or someone you know because of [receiving the service]?	"I have lost weight and I am more healthy, I believe." "When I was pregnant, I was avoiding junk food and eating more nutritious food." "I found that I am anemic and got all my shots." "Now when I eat something from a bag, I check the nutrition. It helped me a lot." "My sister is taking it seriously and losing weight. I am too." "First I was trying to eat healthy, but then I didn't care anymore and went back to junk food."				*N* = 20

2. Responses to open-ended question about effects of the program (directly related to needs, rich and descriptive data, but weaker on repesentativeness)

3. Satisfaction ratings (useful information to add to the mix, strong on representativeness, but addresses met wants or satisfaction rather than needs, which were more important)

Having identified which criteria were to be considered primary, our next task was to come up with a way in which to convert each of these three pieces of raw data into explicit determinations of merit. For example, should the usefulness ratings for the nutrition program be considered satisfactory, good, or excellent? What should we make of the mix of positive and negative statements collected in the open-ended responses?

The greater challenge was presented by the quantitative data because they lacked the richness of evaluative content in the open-ended comments. What spread of ratings on the usefulness question should be considered poor, marginal, satisfactory, good, or excellent? Obviously, this is by no means a precise science, but we needed to have at least some sort of broad-brush evaluative rating to be able to clearly answer the client's questions.

To convert the usefulness ratings into determinations of merit, we used two strategies. The first was to look across the ratings for the nine different program components and to see how the distribution of scores stacked up against the others. As we looked across the different ratings of usefulness, there seemed to be some natural splits. The lowest-rated program component had only 57% of students rating it as useful or very useful, the highest-rated programs were close to 90% or higher, and the other program components were bunched in the middle between 70% and 80%.

To work out how we should characterize the performance of programs that fell into each of these three "clumps," we went back to the qualitative data to see what sorts of comments were associated with these categories. It was clear from this that the kinds of outcomes being produced by even the lowest-rated services were by no means indicative of dismal performance. On the other hand, having only approximately half of the respondents consider a service useful meant that this could not rightly be called a good outcome either; this judgment was based purely on what we believed was reasonable common sense. Balancing these considerations, we labeled the bottom category "adequate" (or, in shorthand form, we called it a "C"). At the other end of the scale, the comments associated with some of the services with very high usefulness ratings (90% or higher) were clearly indicative of extremely valuable outcomes for the students. Accordingly, we labeled the top category "excellent" (or shorthand "A") and the middle category "good" (or shorthand "B"). Based on similar logic (and due to similar rating distributions), we used the same rubric for the satisfaction ratings (Table 9.2).

Table 9.2   Rubric for Converting Quantitative Data to Determinations of Merit

Merit Rating	*Evidence*
Excellent (A)	Approximately 90% or more of respondents rated the service as useful or very useful (or said that they were satisfied or very satisfied)
Good (B)	Approximately 70% to 90% of respondents rated the service as useful or very useful (or said that they were satisfied or very satisfied)
Adequate (C)	Approximately 50% to 70% rated the service as useful or very useful (or said that they were satisfied or very satisfied)

When the usefulness ratings were converted to merit ratings, we used the preceding categories as broad guides but applied grade adjustments depending on where the evidence fell within the defined range. For example, approximately 74% of students rated the nutrition component as useful or very useful, so this component was assigned a rating of B/B– on usefulness.

Note that this is an extremely simple example due to the broad-brush information needs in this particular evaluation. For evaluations that require more factors to be taken into account, it is advisable to create a more sophisticated rubric. In the next chapter, we discuss an example of a synthesis rubric used for another project where the author took many more factors into account. But for now, let's stick with the simple example and follow it through.

Next, we had to convert the qualitative responses to explicit determinations of merit. Using the fundamental principles underlying the basic rubric in Table 8.2 in the previous chapter, we created a rubric of our own to convert the qualitative data into merit ratings (Table 9.3). The ratings were defined in terms of both the strength of the evidence and the magnitude of the impact described in the responses.

Note that the top end of the merit scale includes not only requirements for the magnitude and volume of positive comments but also some limitation on the magnitude and volume of negative comments. Including guidelines for both positive and negative elements is often essential for creating a good merit determination rubric.

The rubrics in Tables 9.2 and 9.3 allowed us to convert the three types of data into explicit determinations of merit. The next step was to take these three determinations of merit and combine them to draw an overall conclusion about the nutrition component (and then other components) of the school health program (Exhibit 9.3).

To combine these three sources of data (now all converted to determinations of merit), we used a step-by-step process that began with the strongest source of data (usefulness ratings) to provide us with what we called a "working grade." We then blended in the data from the open-ended comments that would influence the working grade by up to half a grade depending on how incongruous they were with the quantitative usefulness ratings. For example, the usefulness ratings for the mental health component were low (C), but the open-ended comments showed a strong positive impact. Therefore, the working grade for the mental health component was adjusted up to B/C. Finally, the satisfaction ratings were taken into account. These could influence the working grade by up to a third of a grade. The full working for this step-by-step merit determination process is shown in Table 9.4.

Table 9.3   Rubric Used for Converting Data From the Open-Ended
Responses Into Merit Ratings for the Nutrition Component of
the Health Program

Merit Rating	Evidence
Excellent	*Evidence of a strong positive impact:* very positive comments, with a substantial number that indicated a very strong impact; few if any neutral or negative comments
Good	*Evidence of a noticeable positive impact:* a good number of positive comments (few neutral or negative), clearly showing that the program had made a noticeable positive effect on students
Satisfactory	*Evidence of some positive impact:* a mix of positive and negative comments, skewed somewhat toward the positive; evidence pointing in the right direction but not to a very noticeable impact
Marginal	*Little or no impact either way:* a real mix of comments; no clear skew in either the positive or negative direction
Poor[a]	*Evidence of some negative impact:* a mix of positive and negative comments, skewed somewhat toward the negative; not enough evidence to call this a really noticeable negative impact

NOTE:

a. Categories lower than "poor" (e.g., "completely unacceptable") were not defined because none of the program components was performing that poorly. (There was no point in doing unnecessary work.)

Exhibit 9.3   Synthesizing Three Data Sources to Draw Evaluative
Conclusions About the Merit of the Nutrition Component of
the School-Based Health Program

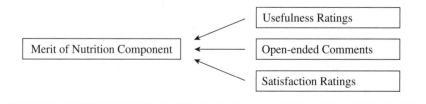

Table 9.4   Step-by-Step Determination of Program Component Merit for a School-Based Nutrition Program

Program Component	Working Grade		Type of Effects From Responses to Open-Ended Questions[a]		Adjusted Working Grade	Satisfaction Level		Final Grade	Overall Component Rating
Transportation	A	→	Some negative (need more of service) and noticeable positive	→	A−	Low to moderate	→	A/B[b]	Extremely good
Legal	A	→	None	→	A	Low to moderate	→	A/A−	Close to excellent
Case management for pregnant or parenting teens	A/B	→	Little to some negative[c]	→	B	High	→	B+	Very good
Anatomy	B/B+	→	No open-ended question asked	→	B/B+	Moderate to high	→	B/B+	Good to very good
Safer sex	B	→	Noticeable positive	→	B+	Moderate to high	→	B+	Very good
Nutrition	B/B−	→	Noticeable positive	→	B+	High	→	A−	Extremely good to excellent

Program Component	Working Grade		Type of Effects From Responses to Open-Ended Questions[a]		Adjusted Working Grade	Satisfaction Level		Final Grade	Overall Component Rating
Health educator or clinic nurse	B/B−	↑	Some negative as well as noticeable positive	↑	B−	Moderate	↑	B−	Good to adequate
Siblings pregnancy prevention	B−	↑	Little to some negative[c]	↑	B/C	High	↑	B/B−	Close to good
Mental health	C	↑	Very noticeable positive	↑	B/C	Low	↑	C+	Adequate to good

NOTES:

a. Comments from students and staff.

b. The negative comments conveyed a need for more of the service since it was discontinued.

c. The negative comments conveyed that high turnover had led to a lack of continuity in these services.

The process described here for synthesizing multiple determinations of merit to rate program components might seem like overkill for a small program like this. That may well be true given the miniscule size of the evaluation budget. The main reasons for doing this were (a) clarification and improvement of the evaluator's logic in synthesizing a mix of data, (b) making that logic clear and transparent for the client and other interested parties, and (c) as an opportunity for learning and methodology development that could be applied to other projects. Hopefully, it will now be useful for others to apply or develop.

Qualitative (nonnumerical) Weighting Example 2 (with "hurdles")

The third synthesis example also uses a qualitative (nonnumerical) weighting system. It also uses a variation on bars called "soft hurdles" and "hard hurdles." Soft and hard hurdles were developed specifically for an evaluation of an organization's learning capacity (Davidson, 2001), which is the example used here.

A **bar** is a minimum level of performance on a *specific dimension,* performance below which cannot be compensated for by much better performance on other dimensions, for example, a rating of 1 (totally unacceptable performance) in the small accounting firm's performance appraisal system described earlier.

A **hard hurdle** (Davidson, 2001) is an *overall passing requirement* for an evaluand as a whole, for example, no more than one rating of 2 (mediocre [substandard] performance) in the small accounting firm's performance appraisal system described earlier. If the evaluand or evaluee fails to meet the requirement, he, she, or it fails overall. Hard hurdles are referred to elsewhere as "global bars" (Scriven, 1991).

A **soft hurdle** is an overall requirement for entry into a high rating category (Davidson, 2001). Unlike a bar, it does not automatically classify an evaluand as "failed" (i.e., it is nonfatal); rather, it places a *limit* on the maximum rating that can be achieved if the evaluand does not clear a particular soft hurdle (e.g., to get an overall A for a course, none of the assignments completed during the semester can be lower than a B–).

The specific example to be used here was an evaluation of the learning capacity of a small biotechnology start-up company in the United States referred to here as "Biosleep." Biosleep's performance was rated on 27 subdimensions of organizational learning capacity (Table 9.5). This performance profile was derived from survey and interview data, a merit determination rubric similar to Table 8.2 in the previous chapter, and importance determination Strategy 6 (using program theory and evidence of causal linkages) from Chapter 7. The comparative element, in this case with other organizations, was built directly into the merit determination rubric.

The synthesis in this case required two steps. First, the performance ratings on the subdimensions needed to be packed together to make determinations of merit on the eight main dimensions. From there, the final step was to combine the performances on the eight dimensions to draw an overall conclusion about the organization's learning capacity.

Subdimensions → Dimensions

Using the hurdle principle, an algorithm was created to guide the way in which conclusions at the dimensional level could be derived from different combinations of subdimension ratings. A synthesis algorithm that included soft hurdles was used (Table 9.6). Because there was no compelling evidence to suggest that any of the subdimensions should be given greater consideration (or weight) than any of the others, each subdimension was treated equally in the synthesis.

For each organizational learning dimension, the median rating on the relevant subdimensions (of which there were between two and five) was the initial criterion used to determine the probable overall rating. The reason for this was twofold. First, it ensured that extreme ratings on one subdimension did not have a disproportionate effect on results. Second, it avoided making the erroneous assumption that the rating categories represented an interval scale (as would have been required if a "mean" rating had been computed).

Based on the algorithm in Table 9.6, a more condensed organizational learning capacity profile for Biosleep that summarized its performance on the eight main dimensions was generated (Exhibit 9.4).

Dimensions → Overall Evaluation

Having profiled Biosleep on the eight learning culture dimensions, the final task was to synthesize this information one step further to draw overall

Table 9.5   Subdimensional Learning Culture Profile for Biosleep

Dimension	*Subdimensions*	*Performance Rating*				
		P	S	G	VG	Ex
Experimentation (extremely important)	Support for risk taking					
	Diversity of practice or methods					
	Marketplace for ideas					
	Continuous improvement					
Practicing excellent evaluation (extremely important)	Tapping true value in personnel evaluation					
	Flexible use of goals					
	Multiple evaluative perspectives					
	Customer needs focus					
	Benchmarking and comparisons					
Mental models (very important)	Valuing diversity of thought					
	No "sacred cows"					
	Open communication and trust					
Shared vision (very important)	Shared vision and purpose					
	Shared sense of identity					
	Using own good judgment					
External or future scanning (very important)	External or market scanning					
	Future and scenario scanning					
	Openness to change					
Personal mastery (moderately important)	Striving for excellence					
	Seeking out criticism					
	Seeing the performance gap					
Team learning (desirable)	Team synergy or intelligence					
	Dialogue and debate					
	Cross-project communication					
Systems thinking (desirable)	Understanding interdependence					
	Seeing systemic causes					

NOTE: P = poor; S = satisfactory; G = good; VG = very good; Ex = excellent.

Table 9.6   Guidelines for Synthesizing Subdimensions Into Dimensions

Dimensional Rating	Median Subdimension Rating	Subdimensions Below "Good"	Subdimensions Below "Satisfactory"
Excellent	Excellent	0	0
Very good	Very good (or better)	0	0
Good	Good (or better)	< 35%	0
Satisfactory	Satisfactory (or better)	(No restrictions)	< 35%
Poor	(No restrictions)	(No restrictions)	(No restrictions)

NOTE: Conditions in all three columns must be met to receive the corresponding rating.

Exhibit 9.4   "Dimension" Learning Culture Profile for Biosleep

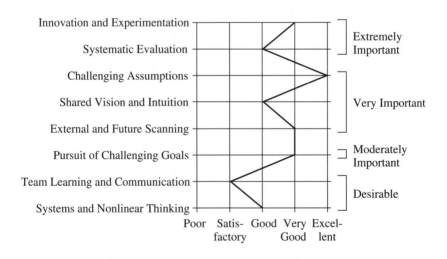

conclusions about the organization's learning capacity. Using similar logic to the dimensional synthesis step, an algorithm was constructed to combine performance on both the outcome dimensions and the eight dimensions of the learning culture to yield an overall evaluative conclusion about each organization's learning capacity (Table 9.7). Using these guidelines, Biosleep was rated as having a *high* organizational learning capacity.

Table 9.7   Guidelines for Determining Overall Organizational Learning
            Capacity

Organizational Learning Capacity Rating	Conditions for Learning Culture Dimensions[a]		
	All Learning Culture Dimensions	Extremely Important and Very Important Dimensions	Moderately Important and Desirable Dimensions
Extremely high learning capacity	• No ratings below good • At least six excellent ratings	• All extremely or very important dimensions rated very good or higher	• Maximum one dimension rated good; all others rated very good or excellent
Very high learning capacity	• No poor ratings • At least six ratings in the very good to excellent range	• Maximum one dimension rated good; all others rated very good or excellent	• Maximum two dimensions rated satisfactory; all others rated good or higher
Biosleep High learning capacity	• At least six ratings of good or better	• Maximum one dimension rated satisfactory; all others rated good or higher	• No more than one poor rating
Moderate learning capacity	• No more than two poor ratings	• No poor ratings	• (No restrictions)
Learning impaired	• One or more poor ratings on extremely or very important dimensions *or* more than two poor ratings overall		

NOTE:

a. Conditions in all three columns must be met to receive the corresponding rating except
   where noted otherwise.

Note that the logic here is more complex than simple averaging. To receive a high overall rating for its organizational learning capacity, an organization must have several dimensions of organizational learning capacity in the highest performance categories, with very few dimensions in the lowest performance categories. In line with the logic underlying hurdles, stricter limitations were placed on those dimensions classified as extremely important or very important.

The criteria in each cell (e.g., requiring at least six dimensional ratings of excellent or higher for an extremely high overall learning capacity rating) were based on the author's own judgment and a careful read of the literature on organizational learning. The rationale was that to receive the top rating, an organization should have a clear majority of its learning culture dimensions rated as excellent. Given that there were eight dimensions altogether, six was seen as a "clear majority."

As with any attempt to make such cutoff criteria very explicit, there might well be room for debate and revision of these cutoffs. For example, if future research finds that organizations with only five learning culture dimensions rated excellent consistently outperform virtually all competitors in terms of adaptiveness, survival, and financial performance, this would provide a solid rationale for revising the cutoff down to five. In the absence of such a body of evidence, the intent here was to propose a viable working methodology that would be subject to constant refinement and improvement as the relationship between organizational learning and effectiveness or survival is better understood.

SYNTHESIZING FOR "RANKING"

Chapter 2 explained why, for some evaluations, the evaluation team needs to determine the quality or value of something relative to one or more other evaluands. Examples might include published rankings of graduate programs, comparative evaluation of several different pilot programs or interventions, evaluation of job candidates for hire or promotion, and rankings of consumer products (e.g., in *Consumer Reports,* in computer magazines, in car magazines).

When the primary evaluative task is ranking, there is a need for a much more explicit treatment of the Comparisons checkpoint in the KEC. Rather than simply using information about "critical competitors" to place performance data in context for evaluative interpretation, a ranking evaluation requires much more detail about the critical competitors and much more in-depth comparison.

Once again, there is a choice to be made regarding the use of numerical synthesis methods or nonnumerical synthesis methods: numerical weight and sum (NWS) versus qualitative weight and sum (QWS).

Numerical Weight and Sum

Numerical weight and sum is a quantitative synthesis methodology (i.e., one that uses numerical importance weights and merit scores) for summing evaluand performance across multiple criteria.

NWS involves ascribing numerical importance weights and a numerical performance score to each evaluative dimension, multiplying weights by performance scores, and then summing these products. The resulting sum represents the overall merit of the evaluand.

NWS works adequately for ranking provided that (a) there are only a small number of criteria, (b) there is some other mechanism for taking bars into account, and (c) there is a defensible needs-based strategy for ascribing weights. Perhaps the most important thing to understand about NWS is some of the problems that can occur when the first two of these three conditions are not met. These are illustrated in the following hypothetical example.

Suppose that you had been asked to conduct a comparative evaluation of three different interventions for training managers: (a) a mountain retreat featuring interactive sessions with multiple world-class management gurus, (b) an in-house training and mentoring program run by human resources, and (c) a set of videos and the latest book on management from management guru Peter Drucker.

We start with a brainstorming session to identify the main dimensions of merit (under the headings of Process, Outcomes, and Cost) and follow this up with a needs assessment to make sure that we understand the nature and extent of the needs and the relative importance of the various dimensions of merit. This leads us to generate a list of the main dimensions to examine when comparing the three interventions (Table 9.8).

The next step is to collect relevant data about each of the three evaluands on these dimensions and to rate their performance using any one of five ratings: excellent, very good, good, fair, or poor (for hypothetical ratings, see Table 9.9).

Table 9.8   List of Dimensions for the Evaluation of Management
                  Training Interventions

Dimension of Merit		*Importance*
	Content matches needs of participants	Important
	State-of-the-art management content	Desirable
	Tailored to organization's strategic needs	Desirable
	Professionally presented	Desirable
Process dimensions	Interesting for participants	Desirable
	Useful materials for later referral	Desirable
	Built-in follow-up for transfer of training	Important
	Networking opportunities	Desirable
	Quality of facilities provided	Desirable
	Quality of refreshments	Desirable
Cost dimensions	Time costs for participants (away from job)	Extremely important
	Financial cost of training (to organization)	Important
Outcome dimensions	Impact on effective management of people	Extremely important
	Impact on communication and persuasion	Important
	Impact on organizational skills	Desirable

The next step is to convert the importance weights and performance
ratings into numerical form so that we can complete the NWS. In Table 9.10,
the weight "extremely important" was given a 3, "important" was given a 2,
and "desirable" was given a 1.[2] For the performance ratings, numerical scores
of 5, 4, 3, 2, and 1 were used to represent the ratings of excellent (5) through
poor (1). The dimensions have also been ordered by importance to make it
easier to comprehend the main differences among the evaluands.

The final step is the final synthesis step. Here we take each performance
rating and multiply it by the importance weight. Then all of these products are
summed and the evaluands are compared (Table 9.11).

Table 9.9   Evaluation of Management Training Interventions on All
                   Dimensions

Dimension of Merit	Ratings for:		
	Retreat	In-House	Video
Content matches needs of participants	Good	Very good	Fair
State-of-the-art management content	Excellent	Fair	Very good
Tailored to organization's strategic needs	Excellent	Good	Fair
Professionally presented	Excellent	Fair	Very good
Interesting for participants	Excellent	Fair	Fair
Useful materials for later referral	Excellent	Fair	Good
Built-in follow-up for transfer of training	Poor	Very good	Fair
Networking opportunities	Excellent	Good	Poor
Quality of facilities provided	Excellent	Fair	Poor
Quality of refreshments	Excellent	Fair	Poor
Time costs for participants (away from job)	Poor	Good	Excellent
Financial cost of training (to organization)	Poor	Good	Excellent
Impact on effective management of people	Good	Very good	Good
Impact on communication and persuasion	Very good	Fair	Poor
Impact on organizational skills	Poor	Fair	Good

Two important points should be apparent from Table 9.11. First, the mountain retreat option won largely because it did extremely well on nearly all of the "trivia" (aspects of the evaluand that are desirable if good but not important),

Table 9.10 Numerical Importance Weights and Performance Ratings for All Three Management Training Interventions

Dimension of Merit	Importance Weight	Performance (unweighted)		
		Retreat	*In-House*	*Video*
Impact on effective management of people	3	3	4	3
Time costs for participants (away from job)	3	1	3	5
Built-in follow-up for transfer of training	2	1	4	2
Content matches needs of participants	2	3	4	2
Financial cost of training (to organization)	2	1	3	5
Impact on communication and persuasion	2	4	2	1
State-of-the-art management content	1	5	2	4
Tailored to organization's strategic needs	1	5	3	3
Professionally presented	1	5	1	4
Interesting for participants	1	5	2	2
Useful materials for later referral	1	5	2	3
Networking opportunities	1	5	3	1
Quality of facilities provided	1	5	2	1
Quality of refreshments	1	5	2	1
Impact on organizational skills	1	2	2	3

even though it did poorly on many of the important dimensions. In more complex evaluations where the number of criteria is often extremely large, it is common for minor considerations to "swamp" the major ones in this way. Increasing the numerical size of the importance weightings can correct this problem, but this also drives "tie-breaker" considerations so far into the background that they can hardly influence the conclusion at all.

Table 9.11   Numerical Weight and Sum Synthesis for Three Management
             Training Interventions

Dimension of Merit	Importance Weight	Importance × Performance		
		Retreat	In-House	Video
Impact on effective management of people	3	9	12	9
Time costs for participants (away from job)	3	3	9	15
Built-in follow-up for transfer of training	2	2	8	4
Content matches needs of participants	2	6	8	4
Financial cost of training (to organization)	2	2	6	10
Impact on communication and persuasion	2	8	4	2
State-of-the-art management content	1	5	2	4
Tailored to organization's strategic needs	1	5	3	3
Professionally presented	1	5	1	4
Interesting for participants	1	5	2	2
Useful materials for later referral	1	5	2	3
Networking opportunities	1	5	3	1
Quality of facilities provided	1	5	2	1
Quality of refreshments	1	5	2	1
Impact on organizational skills	1	2	2	3
Sum of Importance × Performance		72	66	66

The second important point is that the mountain retreat was by far the most expensive option in terms of both time and money costs, being rated as poor on both. In many organizational contexts, it is likely that one or both of these costs could simply be too high. This means that the retreat should not have been rated as the top intervention because it was not cost-feasible. In other words, there needed to be a bar on one or both cost criteria. This may also have been true for some of the other dimensions besides cost.

The reality is that although NWS seems simple and intuitive, it can often leave the evaluation team looking at a conclusion that does not seem quite right. The temptation at that point is often to fiddle with the numbers to see whether the right answer can be coaxed out of the data. An alternative is to work with a synthesis strategy that incorporates the key elements of how the human brain naturally weights considerations, making them explicit so that they can be applied to larger numbers of dimensions. Qualitative Weight and Sum is such a strategy.

Qualitative Weight and Sum

Qualitative weight and sum (QWS) is a non-numerical synthesis methodology devised by Scriven (1991) for summing the performances of an evaluand on multiple criteria to determine overall merit or worth. QWS is a ranking methodology for determining the relative merit of two or more evaluands or evaluees. Typical applications include **personnel selection,** comparisons of experimental or pilot programs to decide which to roll out elsewhere, and selection among competing products, services, or proposals. QWS is not suitable for grading (i.e., determining absolute merit).

Step 1: Determine Importance in Terms of Maximum Possible Value

The first step is to assign each criterion a qualitative importance rating by determining whether the maximum possible value of excellent performance on that criterion should be considered extremely valuable, valuable, or marginally valuable. Importance ratings should be determined using the appropriate combination of strategies from Chapter 7.

To each importance label, assign the appropriate symbol from the list provided in Table 9.12.

Table 9.12   Maximum Possible Value of Excellent Performance on Each
Dimension of Merit for Management Training Interventions

Dimension of Merit	Maximum Possible Value	Symbol
Content matches needs of participants	Valuable	▲
State-of-the-art management content	Marginally valuable	✦
Tailored to organization's strategic needs	Marginally valuable	✦
Professionally presented	Marginally valuable	✦
Interesting for participants	Marginally valuable	✦
Useful materials for later referral	Marginally valuable	✦
Built-in follow-up for transfer of training	Valuable	▲
Networking opportunities	Marginally valuable	✦
Quality of facilities provided	Marginally valuable	✦
Quality of refreshments	Marginally valuable	✦
Time costs for participants (away from job)	Extremely valuable	★
Financial cost of training (to organization)	Valuable	▲
Impact on effective management of people	Extremely valuable	★
Impact on communication and persuasion	Valuable	▲
Impact on organizational skills	Marginally valuable	✦

Step 2: Set Bars

For each criterion, regardless of importance, determine whether there is
any completely unacceptable level of performance, that is, performance so
poor that even excellence on all other criteria would not compensate (e.g., a
price so high that consumers or funders simply could not afford it even if

the project is highly meritorious in other respects). This cut point between acceptable and unacceptable is called the bar. For each criterion that has a bar, describe what "completely unacceptable" performance would look like.

For example, if the participants in the training must spend 2 weeks or more away from their jobs, that might be considered an unacceptable time cost. Similarly, financial costs of more than $5,000 per participant might be considered too high for a particular organization. Based on the needs assessment, the evaluation team might also specify some minimum level of match between the training content and the individuals' needs.

Step 3: Create Value Determination Rubrics

This step is basically equivalent to creating a merit determination rubric (see Chapter 8) except that with the focus on value levels, it is more accurately referred to as a value determination rubric. It is best to start with the simplest rubrics and work your way up.

Start with the dimensions you have weighted as "marginally valuable." Define or describe what performance on each dimension would look like at two levels: marginally valuable and no noticeable value. (If the dimension also has a bar, you will have definitions for three possible levels of performance: marginally valuable, no value, and completely unacceptable.) Each definition should describe in evaluative terms (preferably referring to a mix of required qualitative and quantitative evidence) what performance would look like at each level. A simple example for rating the training in terms of networking opportunities for participants is shown in Table 9.13.

Table 9.13   Rubric for Rating Management Training Interventions on Networking Opportunities

Value Level	Symbol	Description
Marginally valuable	**+**	Sufficient opportunity for networking so that participants could develop business relationships
No noticeable value	(Blank)	Little or no opportunity for networking with other participants

Now take any dimensions you have weighted as valuable. Define or describe what performance on each dimension would look like at three levels: valuable, marginally valuable, and no noticeable value. Again, there will be a fourth level of performance if you have defined a bar, as in the example shown in Table 9.14, a rubric for rating the financial cost of training.

Table 9.14   Rubric for Rating Management Training Interventions on Financial Cost of Training

Value Level	Symbol	Description
Valuable	▲	Extremely cheap (money cost less than $400 per participant)
Marginally valuable	✚	Moderately priced (money cost between $400 and $1,500 per participant)
No noticeable value	(Blank)	Quite expensive (money cost between $1,500 and $5,000 per participant)
Unacceptable	✗	Excessively expensive (money cost in excess of $5,000 per participant)

Repeat the step for any criteria weighted as extremely valuable, this time defining four possible levels of performance (from extremely valuable to no value) as well as defining below the bar if there is a bar. Table 9.15 gives an example rubric for one of the most important dimensions, that is, impact on effective management of people.

Step 4: Check Equivalence of Value Levels Across Dimensions

The validity of the QWS method is highly dependent on ensuring that the value levels defined for each dimension are roughly equivalent. To check this, look across your criteria at the evaluative definitions you have created for each level of value and consider what they convey about equivalent value or trade-offs. One way in which to do this (especially when you are just starting with QWS) is to put the information into a matrix such as the one in Table 9.16.

Table 9.15   Rubric for Rating Management Training Interventions on
Impact on Effective Management of People

Value Level	Symbol	Description
Extremely valuable	★	Very substantial impact[a] on participants' effective use of people management strategies on the job
Valuable	▲	Significant (but not substantial) impact on effective use of people management strategies on the job
Marginally valuable	✚	Just noticeable (but not significant) impact on effective use of people management strategies on the job
No noticeable value	(Blank)	No noticeable impact on effective use of people management strategies on the job
Unacceptable	✗	Noticeable detrimental impact on people management strategies used on the job

NOTE:

a. Evidence used included (a) interviews with participants 3 months after
completing the program, (b) "360-degree" feedback (i.e., performance ratings
gathered from direct reports, peers, and senior managers), and (c) employee
turnover rate in the business unit.

Looking across the rows in Table 9.16, the evaluation team should consider whether each defined level of performance has a sufficiently similar
value or whether it is more similar in value to entries in the rows above
or below. One way in which to think about this is in terms of trade-offs by
taking diagonal pairs. For example, according to the matrix in this table, a
very cheap training program (< $400 per participant) that has a just notice-
able impact on people management performance should be about as valuable to the organization as a moderately priced one (say, $1,000 per
participant) that has a significant (but not substantial) impact on the same
outcome. If one of the two also offered good networking opportunities, that
would be the "tie-breaker" that would lead to the choice of that program.

The other thing to check is where the levels of maximum possible value
have been set. Note that the impact on people management has a highest

Table 9.16   Comparison Matrix for Assessing the Equivalence of Value
Levels Across Dimensions

Maximum Value	Impact on People Management	Financial Cost per Participant	Networking Opportunities
★	Very substantial impact on participants' effective use of people management strategies on the job		
▲	Significant (but not substantial) impact on effective use of people management strategies on the job	Extremely cheap (money cost less than $400 per participant)	
✚	Just noticeable (but not significant) impact on effective use of people management strategies on the job	Moderately priced (money cost between $400 and $1,500 per participant)	Sufficient opportunity for networking so that participants could develop business relationships
(Blank)	No noticeable impact on effective use of people management strategies on the job	Quite expensive (money cost between $1,500 and $5,000 per participant)	Little or no opportunity for networking with other participants
✗	Noticeable detrimental impact on people management strategies on the job	Excessively expensive (money cost in excess of $5,000 per participant)	

possible rating of extremely valuable, whereas the other two dimensions have lower maximum values. This means that if one training program produced a very substantial impact on people management performance and was moderately priced (say, $1,000 per participant), an alternative program that produced a significant (but not substantial) impact could not beat it *no matter how low the cost* (assuming that ratings on all other dimensions were equal).

These trade-off comparisons, which may be made in collaboration with stakeholders, are essential for testing the validity of the value determination rubric. This phase of QWS often requires some adjustment of the bars and/or rubric categories.

Step 5: Rate Value of Actual Performance on Each Dimension

For each evaluand (there must be more than one evaluand because this is a ranking exercise), use the value determination rubric to ascribe a value rating (e.g., valuable, marginally valuable) to its performance on each dimension (Table 9.17).[3] Note that the rating on any criterion cannot be higher than the maximum possible value weighting you have assigned to that criterion.

Step 6: Tally the Number of Ratings at Each Level and Look for a Clear Winner (if evident)

Sum the number of ratings of each type separately (extremely valuable, very valuable, valuable, marginally valuable, no value, and completely unacceptable) for each evaluand (see the bottom rows of Table 9.17). Throw out any evaluands with unacceptable ratings (✘). Then look to see whether there is a clear winner.

For the two training programs still in the running, the difference is one ▲ versus three ✚. Because there is no fixed formula for how many ✚ are equivalent to one ▲, there is not yet a clear winner between the two. This is a key difference between QWS and NWS. In NWS the numbers make up your mind for you, whereas in QWS you are forced to stop and think explicitly about the trade-offs.

Step 7: Refocus

In the refocus step (Table 9.18), we drop the columns of evaluands that did not make the first cut (i.e., the mountain retreat). We also delete the rows on which the remaining evaluands score the same (i.e., the extent to which the training was tailored to the organization's strategic needs).

Table 9.17 Initial Value Ratings on Each Dimension for All Three Management Training Interventions (QWS)

Dimension of Merit	Maximum Value	Actual Value		
		Retreat	In-House	Video
Impact on effective management of people	★	▲	★	▲
Time costs for participants (away from job)	★	✘	▲	★
Built-in follow-up for transfer of training	▲		▲	✚
Content matches needs of participants	▲	✚	▲	✚
Financial cost of training (to organization)	▲	✘	▲	▲
Impact on communication and persuasion	▲	▲	✚	
State-of-the-art management content	✚	✚		✚
Tailored to organization's strategic needs	✚	✚	✚	✚
Professionally presented	✚	✚		✚
Interesting for participants	✚	✚		
Useful materials for later referral	✚	✚		✚
Networking opportunities	✚	✚	✚	
Quality of facilities provided	✚	✚		
Quality of refreshments	✚	✚		
Impact on organizational skills	✚			✚
Totals		—	—	—
★			1	1
▲		2	3	2
✚		9	4	7
✘		2		

Table 9.18   Refocus Step for Remaining Two Management Training Interventions (QWS)

Dimension of Merit	Maximum Value	Actual Value	
		In-House	Video
Impact on effective management of people	★	★	▲
Time costs for participants (away from job)	★	▲	★
Built-in follow-up for transfer of training	▲	▲	✦
Content matches needs of participants	▲	▲	✦
Financial cost of training (to organization)	▲	✦	▲
Impact on communication and persuasion	▲	✦	
State-of-the-art management content	✦		✦
Professionally presented	✦		✦
Interesting for participants	✦		
Useful materials for later referral	✦		✦
Networking opportunities	✦	✦	
Quality of facilities provided	✦		
Quality of refreshments	✦		
Impact on organizational skills	✦		✦
Totals		—	—
★		1	1
▲		3	2
✦		3	6

At this point, the evaluation team members need to examine exactly where the differences lie so that they can work out whether the three additional marginally valuable elements offered by the video instructional program outweigh the one valuable element from the in-house training. The team may also consider reweighting the dimensions in light of the smaller range of values between the two remaining evaluands. For example, if the video training costs $350 per participant and the in-house training costs $800, it might be true for this organization that financial cost is now a relatively minor matter and should be weighted as a tie-breaker (✚) instead of a more important dimension (▲).

NOTES

1. Unfortunately, no information was available regarding how many students had actually attended the nutrition education program. Therefore, all we knew about the representativeness of the data was that it was higher for the quantitative items.

2. Clearly, there is a need to put considerably more thought into what the exact numerical weightings should be if NWS is to be used effectively. These values were chosen to maximize the illustrative value of the example.

3. In this case, I have derived these from the original performance ratings in Table 9.10. This would not usually be necessary, however, because when using QWS, the evaluands should be rated directly on each dimension using the value determination rubrics outlined earlier instead of being rated first on an excellent-to-poor scale and then converted.

ADDITIONAL READINGS

Entries in Scriven's (1991) *Evaluation Thesaurus:*
- Apples and oranges
- Linear combination approach
- Meta-analysis
- Numerical weight and sum
- Qualitative weight and sum
- Synthesis (in evaluation)
- Synthesis (of research studies)
- Unconsummated evaluation

Scriven, M. (1994). The final synthesis. *Evaluation Practice, 15,* 367–382.

EXERCISES

1. Design a quantitative synthesis algorithm to draw an evaluative conclusion about the overall grade for an evaluand of your choice. Make sure that

you explain what the evaluand is and clearly lay out what the dimensions of merit are. If you can find actual data for the evaluand, use them to try out the algorithm.

2. Find a copy of *Consumer Reports* and identify a product you might consider buying in the future and that the magazine has rated on several dimensions. Identify three or four products to compare. Supplement this information with additional information (e.g., from the Internet) if necessary. Do a QWS to determine which you should buy. The QWS should involve at least one refocus step.

TEN

PUTTING IT ALL TOGETHER

———•◦•———

A t the beginning of the book, it was mentioned that the overarching
framework used here is Scriven's (2003) Key Evaluation Checklist
(KEC).[1] In the preceding chapters, we have worked through nearly all of the
checkpoints. This chapter reviews the parts that go into the report and how
they fit together. This is intended as a step-by-step guide for writing up a report
using the KEC as a framework.

The KEC is intended to be an iterative checklist. In other words, it is not
a list that you just go through mechanistically once and you are done. The
KEC needs to be applied thoughtfully, revisiting most of the checkpoints
several times as more of the evaluation is fleshed out. This chapter goes
through each of the checkpoints to clarify what content should feed into it
from previous chapters. The most important links among the checkpoints are
noted to help readers with the iterative aspects of using the KEC.

When using this book to teach an introductory course in evaluation, the
author usually has the students write an evaluation plan in the form of a skeleton report. The report follows the KEC format and includes actual information
about the evaluand (usually a program) for many of the early checkpoints to
the extent that it is available. For the later checkpoints, especially under the
Sub-evaluations and Conclusions sections, students write an outline of what
information is to be collected and how it will be interpreted.

The main rationale behind having people write a skeleton report (as
opposed to a typical proposal) is that it forces them to think very hard about
exactly how each piece of information is going to be used to draw evaluative
conclusions. Without a skeleton report, we tend to end up with long lists of

"wouldn't it be interesting to know" indicators but no clear conceptualization of how they should be interpreted and fitted together systematically to answer the "big picture" evaluation question.

THE KEC PRELIMINARY CHECKPOINTS

The KEC starts with three elements that should be put right at the beginning of an evaluation report (called Preliminaries in the KEC). Their purpose is to orient readers to the basics of what the evaluand is, why the evaluation was done, and what the main approach was. These checkpoints, like the rest of the report, should be written or presented so that someone not familiar with the project (e.g., someone looking through archived reports in 10 years' time) could understand what was going on and why.

I. Executive Summary

The Executive Summary should be a very quick (one- to two-page) overview of what was evaluated and what the main findings were. It is often useful to include the following elements in the executive summary:

- A very short description of the program, context, and big picture evaluation questions from Chapter 2 (this part should be approximately one quarter to half a page, with bullet points making it more "skimmable")
- The "bottom line," that is, an overall conclusion about the quality or value of the evaluand (based on its current state of development, e.g., relatively new, mid-stage, fully mature) in either absolute or relative terms, as appropriate (for a reminder about the different types of evaluation questions, see Chapter 2)
- A graphical profile of the evaluand's performance on 7 ± 2^2 dimensions or components, indicating the relative importance of those dimensions or components (for examples, see Chapter 7)
- Two bullet point lists (no more than seven items each) of the most important strengths and weaknesses, respectively

Tip for Students

If you are writing an evaluation plan rather than writing up actual results, the Executive Summary should cover the first bulleted item completely, should skip the second item, should give a hypothetical profile for the third item to show what it would look like, and (instead of the fourth item) should just describe briefly what mix of evidence should lead the evaluation team to draw an overall conclusion about the evaluand as being excellent versus just acceptable versus poor.

II. Preface

The Preface answers a few basic questions about the evaluation:

- Who asked for this evaluation and why?
- What are the main big picture evaluation questions?
- Is this a formative evaluation, a summative evaluation, or both? If both, which purpose is the primary one?
- Who are the main audiences for the evaluation report? (In general, this list of the *main* potential readers should not be more than two or three key stakeholder groups, so try not to list everyone who might possibly be interested.)

The "Big Picture" Evaluation Questions

An important point to note is that the list of big picture evaluation questions under the second bulleted item should *not* be at the variable level of analysis (e.g., What effect did the program have on Outcome X?). We will get to this more detailed part later. Instead, you should be drawing on your work in Chapter 2 where you identified whether the primary purpose of the evaluation was to determine absolute or relative quality or value. Do not just pick one of these. Instead, explain how you came to the conclusion that this was the main question.

III. Methodology

The Methodology checkpoint provides readers with an overview of what approach or model and what main methodologies were used in the evaluation design as well as the rationale for these choices. In other words, what was the overall design of the evaluation (e.g., experimental, quasi-experimental, or case study; goal oriented or goal free; participatory or independent) and why (briefly)?

In each case, the *why* part of the answer should make it clear why you chose one option and not the other. The point here is to demonstrate that you have not simply applied your "favorite" evaluation approach for no particular reason but rather have chosen a blend of design features that are appropriate under the particular conditions and in the context where the evaluation will take place. Explain how the chosen methodology addresses the causation issue (Chapter 5). Your methodology should be demonstrably strong enough to make causal inferences at the level of certainty needed for the client to make decisions.

The next two sections of the KEC, Foundations and Sub-evaluations, give us the ingredients required to draw a well-informed evaluative conclusion about the evaluand. These elements, with some more detail about how they are interlinked, are shown in Exhibit 10.1.

THE KEC FOUNDATIONS CHECKPOINTS

The Foundations section of the KEC (Checkpoints 1–5) represents all of the initial ingredients we need before starting to get into explicitly evaluative tasks. Here we cover the background and context of the evaluand, a description of what it is and whom it serves, the nature and limitations of any resources on which it could draw, and a description of where the values come from for the evaluation.

1. Background and Context

The depth and breadth of coverage within this checkpoint will depend on the nature of the evaluand and its context. Without going into a full, detailed history of the evaluand, the evaluation team should include just enough information here for readers to be able to understand the basic rationale for the program and the context that constrains or enables its performance. At a minimum, this checkpoint should answer the following questions:

- Why did this program or product come into existence in the first place? Who saw the initial need for it, and what did they see exactly? (Compare this later with the assessed needs found under the Values checkpoint.)

- How is/was the evaluand supposed to address the original need, problem, or issue in the minds of the original designers? What was their original

Exhibit 10.1 The Core Elements of the Key Evaluation Checklist (modified from Scriven's 2003 version)

1. Background and Context	2. Descriptions and Definitions	3. Consumers	4. Resources	5. Values
Why did this program or product come into existence in the first place? How is/was it supposed to address the original need, problem, or issue? (Compare this with the assessed needs found under the Values checkpoint; later links to Process Evaluation checkpoint.)	Describe the evaluand in enough detail so that anyone can understand what it is and what it does. Do not just use brochures or Web sites to find out what it is supposed to be like; describe it as it really is. (Later links to Process Evaluation checkpoint.)	Who are the actual or potential recipients of the program (e.g., demographics)? Who else could potentially be affected by the program (e.g., families, friends, community)? (These are the people you consider when you do the Outcome Evaluation checkpoint.)	What resources are/were available to create, maintain, and help the program or policy succeed? (Information about resources help you determine which comparisons are fair to make under the Comparative Cost-Effectiveness checkpoint.)	On what basis will you determine whether the evaluand is of high quality or valuable? Where will you get the criteria (e.g., needs of recipients, needs of the organization, relevant laws, professional standards, ethical considerations)? How will you determine "how good is good"? (Links to all five Subevaluation checkpoints [6–10].)

Foundations

(Continued)

Exhibit 10.1 (Continued)

	6. Process Evaluation	**7. Outcome Evaluation**	**8 & 9. Comparative Cost-Effectiveness**	**10. Exportability**
Sub-evaluations	How good, valuable, or efficient was the content and implementation? (Links back to Descriptions and Definitions and Values checkpoints; also consider any influence of context that facilitated or hindered effectiveness.)	What impacts did the evaluand have on immediate recipients and other impactees (check through your list under Consumers), and how good, bad, or valuable were those impacts? (Links back to Values checkpoint.) This includes causal analysis; are observed changes due to the evaluand?	(A blend of Scriven's Costs and Comparisons checkpoints) How costly was this evaluand to consumers, funders, staff, and so forth, compared with alternative uses of the available resources that might feasibly have achieved outcomes of similar or greater value? Include money costs, time costs, opportunity costs, and so forth. Be explicitly evaluative. Compared with the alternatives, are the costs excessive, high, acceptable, or extremely reasonable? (Links back to Values checkpoint.)	(Originally Generalizability in KEC) Regardless of the impact achieved by the evaluand in this context and for these consumers, are there any elements of the evaluand (e.g., innovative design or approach) that make it potentially valuable or significant in another setting? (Is the concept exportable? Does it have value or utility elsewhere?)

11. Overall Significance

<table>
<tr><td rowspan="1">Conclusions</td><td>Draw on all of the information in Checkpoints 6 through 10 to answer the main evaluation questions such as the following. What are the main areas where the evaluand is doing well, and where is it lacking? Is this the most cost-effective use of the available resources to address the identified needs without excessive adverse impact? (Links back to the big picture evaluation questions outlined in the Preface.)</td></tr>
</table>

program theory or logic (if there was one and if it is important to know)? (This part later links to the Process Evaluation and Outcome Evaluation checkpoints.)

- What aspects of the evaluand's context (e.g., physical, economic, political, legal, structural) constrain or facilitate its potential to operate effectively? (This information is essential for later interpretation of the merit of outcomes and the evaluand's internal functioning under the Process Evaluation checkpoint. Watch the overlap between context and resources. You do not want to repeat the same information under each checkpoint.)

2. Descriptions and Definitions

Under this checkpoint, your task is to describe the evaluand in enough detail so that readers who are not familiar with the evaluand can understand what it is and what it does. An important point here is not to just use brochures or Web sites to find out what the evaluand is *supposed* to be like; instead, here you should describe the evaluand as it *really* is. You should have already completed most of this groundwork in the exercises at the end of Chapter 1.

A useful tool to include in the Descriptions and Definitions checkpoint is a simple logic model of how the evaluand *actually* works (see Chapter 3). This is in contrast to the designer's program theory that you might have laid out under the Background and Context checkpoint. In some cases, it is useful to be able to contrast the two theories; for most evaluations, the actual program theory alone will suffice. Depending on the audience for each version of the report, the logic model could be relatively simple or somewhat complex.

Also included under this checkpoint should be an explanation of any of the terms or concepts that are used in the organization or community or that are relevant to the evaluation. This is particularly important for evaluands that are based on a specialized theory (e.g., cognitive–behavioral interventions for the treatment of violent offenders). The same is true for evaluands based on cultural concepts (e.g., culturally based programs for indigenous communities).

The Descriptions and Definitions checkpoint later links to the Process Evaluation checkpoint, where we evaluate (rather than just describe) the content and implementation of the evaluand. The logic model (i.e., a diagram showing likely and possible effects) feeds into the Outcome Evaluation checkpoint, where the value of the evaluand's actual effects is determined.

3. Consumers

To assess needs and identify potential outcomes accurately, it is extremely important to clearly identify the actual and potential recipients or users of the evaluand along with any other impactees (see Chapter 3). They are often divided into similar subgroups based on demographic or other variables (much like "target markets," to use marketing terminology). In this checkpoint, you should describe who the consumers are in terms of their geographic location, demographics, and any other information that is important to know. Do not forget to include any important downstream impactees (e.g., colleagues, families, or clients of the direct recipients).

The Consumers checkpoint links to the Values checkpoint because the consumers' needs are central to the definition of what makes a "valuable" program or other evaluand. It is the consumers whose needs are identified in the needs assessment. There is also a strong link between the Consumers checkpoint and the Outcome Evaluation checkpoint. Outcomes are things that happen to the impactees (consumers) as a result of their interaction with the evaluand. Therefore, all of the consumers you list here should also appear under the Outcome Evaluation checkpoint when you look at the effects of the evaluand on all potential impactees.

4. Resources

Any evaluand is constrained by what it can achieve with the resources at its disposal. It makes sense that a "shoestring" community program is not expected to achieve results of the same magnitude as is a very well-funded, large-scale intervention that has access to numerous resources. That is why it is important to give readers a sense of those resources to which the evaluand had access.

In this checkpoint, the evaluation team members should convey whatever they and the readers would need to know about resource availability and constraints to interpret the evaluand's achievements and disappointments fairly. In addition to listing what was used, list anything important that could have been tapped into but was not. Also, note any areas where important resources were needed (or would have been advantageous) but were not available. Resources to consider might include the following:

- Funds/Budget
- Physical space (including the quality of its location)

- Expertise
- Networks (e.g., community, business, professional)

The Resources checkpoint provides important background information for the Outcome Evaluation checkpoint to allow fair interpretation of the evaluand's achievements. It also links to (and differs from) the Comparative Cost-Effectiveness checkpoint in the following way. Under Resources, the evaluation team lists in descriptive terms what was available in the way of budget, time, and so forth. Under Comparative Cost-Effectiveness, the task is explicitly evaluative. There, we ask the following questions: "How reasonable/excessive was the cost (i.e., total resources used) overall?" and "Was this the most cost-effective use of available resources given the possible alternative uses of those resources?"

5. Values

The purpose of the Values checkpoint is to convey to the audience how the evaluation team determined what should be considered "valuable" or "high quality" for the evaluand. Here you should document your needs assessment and the other sources that you used to define "value." (Do not just repeat the list from Chapter 6. Explain which sources were relevant and how they applied.) In most cases, a brief summary will suffice for this section, and interested readers should be referred to an appendix for more detail.

Sometimes in an evaluation, you run into situations where the values conflict. If this happened, explain briefly how you dealt with this and how it affects the report.

A well-written Values checkpoint should clearly demonstrate that the evaluation team has reflected carefully on the difficult tasks of determining "How good is good?" and "How do we know what is most important?" For this reason, the Values checkpoint needs to go beyond simply listing what sources of value are applied in the evaluation and should also carefully justify the reasons for those choices. Make your reasoning as easy to follow as possible so that readers have enough information to judge its validity.

THE KEC SUB-EVALUATIONS CHECKPOINTS

The Sub-evaluations section of the KEC is where we get explicitly evaluative. We are no longer just describing "what's so"; we are drawing conclusions about "so what." If you find yourself repeating earlier reported information too much in this section, check to ensure that you are making the transition from description to evaluation.

6. Process Evaluation

The Process Evaluation checkpoint usually addresses the issues of evaluand content and implementation, although there may be other elements in a particular case (for a review, see Chapter 4).

It is important to be clear about the distinction between this checkpoint and Descriptions and Definitions (Checkpoint 2). Whereas the Descriptions and Definitions checkpoint *describes* the program's content and (to some extent) implementation, under Process Evaluation we apply the Values checkpoint so that we can say something explicit about how *good* the content and implementation are (i.e., the merit determination step outlined in Chapter 8).

Some of the sources of value that typically apply to the Process Evaluation checkpoint are as follows:

- Ethics, including the principles of equity and fairness
- Consistency with relevant professional and scientific standards
- Efficiency (i.e., minimal wasted effort or resources)
- Needs of consumers (e.g., timeliness, match with learning style and/or current level of knowledge)
- Needs of staff (e.g., dovetails well with other tasks and activities, match between the task and the person assigned to it)

When writing up the Process Evaluation checkpoint, it is a good idea to start by listing the main dimensions of merit that apply. If you have not yet explained in much detail how you arrived at this list of dimensions (e.g., under the Values checkpoint), it is worth mentioning that here. You should also provide some indication of the relative importance of each of the criteria and define any relevant "bars" (i.e., minimum levels of acceptable performance). Be extremely clear about how importance was determined, referring readers to an appendix for detail about the strategies you used (for a review of importance determination strategies, see Chapter 7).

Next, take each process dimension and rate the evaluand on it (e.g., excellent, very good, adequate). For each rating, show clearly what standards you used (a merit determination rubric could be helpful here) and detail the specific evidence that led you to assign the particular rating (for a review of merit determination methods, see Chapter 8). If this part seems too detailed for the client audience, insert a short summary (just the ratings and a brief explanation) and then refer interested readers to an appendix where they can see all of the details.

7. Outcome Evaluation

Most people find the Outcome Evaluation checkpoint to be the most intuitive one. Outcomes are all of the things that have happened to the consumers primarily as a result of coming into contact with the evaluand. Note the link to the Consumers checkpoint; you need to check back and ensure that you have included effects on all of the important impactees you listed under the Consumers checkpoint. The outcomes should include intended and unintended effects as well as short-term and long-term effects (if information is available).

As with the other Subevaluation checkpoints, it is important that the Outcome Evaluation checkpoint be explicitly evaluative in content. In other words, simply reporting outcomes is insufficient. Again, the Values checkpoint must be applied (e.g., with a merit determination rubric based on the needs assessment) so that the evaluation team can rate the evaluand on all of the key outcome dimensions.

As with the Process Evaluation checkpoint, a good way in which to write up the Outcome Evaluation checkpoint is to first list the main outcome dimensions with a brief explanation of how the list was generated. Rate each dimension on importance and explain the method(s) used to arrive at these importance ratings (see Chapter 7). Next, give the evaluand a quality or value rating on each outcome dimension (see Chapter 8). Finally, explain the standards used (e.g., using a rubric) and the evidence that led you to assign each rating.

8 & 9. Comparative Cost-Effectiveness

All programs, policies, products, and systems consume resources that might have been put to some other use. Therefore, one of the important questions in any evaluation is whether the evaluand represents the best possible use of available resources to achieve outcomes of maximum value. This is the question of comparative cost-effectiveness.

To address the Comparative Cost-Effectiveness checkpoint, we need a list of comparisons (or "critical competitors") and some information about their relative costs. Recall from Chapter 4 that useful comparisons usually include the "Rolls Royce" (an exemplary intervention), the "Shoestring" (a creative low-budget option), "A Little More" (an option that has slightly more resources allocated to it), and "A Little Less" (a slightly more streamlined or economical version of the evaluand).

Information about the relative costs of the evaluand and each of the comparisons does not usually need to be extremely detailed. In general, you should provide an overview of your comparative cost-effectiveness analysis under this checkpoint and refer readers to an appendix for your full working.

10. Exportability

Checkpoints 6 through 9 document the value of the evaluand in its current context. However, an evaluand (or some of its features) could also have value outside its current context. For example, suppose that you are evaluating a treatment program for long-term drug addicts with a highly innovative approach that is found to be substantially more effective than any other strategy tried previously. Not only does the program have value for the actual impactees in this setting, but the idea could potentially be applied in other contexts as well, perhaps completely revolutionizing drug rehabilitation around the world.

The Exportability[3] checkpoint often pertains to the significance of the evaluand as an advancement in the field (see Chapter 4). Note that it is not always the case that the evaluand has significant value outside its current context. However, it is always worth considering the possibility under this checkpoint, skipping it in the final report if there is nothing worth noting.

THE KEC CONCLUSIONS CHECKPOINTS

The final section of the KEC, Conclusions, is where all of the Sub-evaluations (Checkpoints 6–10) are combined to draw an overall conclusion about the evaluand. The Conclusions section should also include (if applicable) a list of recommendations, an analysis of the reasons for successes and failures, attribution of responsibility for these reasons, details about reporting and follow-up, and a critique or meta-evaluation of the evaluation itself.

11. Overall Significance

Under this checkpoint, the evaluation team should provide a succinct summary and synthesis of all the evaluative elements covered under Checkpoints 6 through 10, drawing on the appropriate synthesis methodology from Chapter 9. The final conclusions may be represented usefully as a condensed performance profile of the evaluand on 7 ± 2 major dimensions or components, often with an overall conclusion about the evaluand's quality or value given its performance on those dimensions.

In addition, the Overall Significance checkpoint should summarize the main strengths and weaknesses of the evaluand, highlighting which ones are most important and why. These may or may not be used in Checkpoint 12 to generate recommendations for improvement.

12. Recommendations and Explanations (possible)

This checkpoint, which may or may not be completed depending on the scope of the evaluation, provides a more in-depth analysis of why or how things went right or wrong. It may also provide some recommendations for improvement provided that you have sufficient knowledge of the budgetary and political constraints under which the organization operates and you can be confident that your recommendations (if implemented correctly) will produce the needed improvements.

To generate good recommendations, it is important to diagnose the causes of suboptimal performance and/or negative effects. This frequently requires the use of program theory, which can be used to show, for example, whether (and where) there were any breaks in the causal chain that prevented the evaluand from achieving worthwhile impacts. Also useful for explaining effects and diagnosing problems is the identification of causal loops that impede or accelerate change, points where there is a delay between causes and effects, unintended consequences that emerged spontaneously, and important interactions between the evaluand and its environment.[4]

13. Responsibilities (possible)

Occasionally, the evaluation team may be asked to provide a more in-depth analysis of exactly who (or what unit or organization) was responsible for good or bad results. This type of analysis is extremely difficult, and it is usually not prudent to enter this territory unless you are highly skilled.

14. Report and Support

It is important to note who got (or who will get) copies of the evaluation report and in what form (e.g., written, oral, detailed versions, executive summary only). Here you should link back to the Preface to make sure that you have covered your main audiences and addressed what they needed to know.

Also under this checkpoint, you should note any follow-up done (or planned) by the evaluation team to ensure that the findings are used. This phase, which should be written into the evaluation contract,[5] is extremely important to help the evaluation team assess the utility of its work, reflect on what might have been done to increase use, and document any learnings for the Meta-evaluation checkpoint.

15. Meta-evaluation

An extremely important phase in any evaluation is to take the time to critically review the quality of the evaluation itself. Evaluations should be judged on (a) the validity of their conclusions, (b) their utility to relevant stakeholders, (c) the way in which they were conducted, (d) credibility, and (e) cost.

At a bare minimum, the meta-evaluation should involve a critical and reflective assessment by the evaluation team of the strengths and weaknesses of the work. Ideally, this should be complemented with an independent assessment from an evaluation specialist. Several strategies may be employed for the review:

- Check back to see how well each of the KEC checkpoints was covered. This is the best method for checking the thoroughness of the evaluation's coverage and the validity of its conclusions. Accordingly, it should be supplemented with a separate assessment of utility and credibility.
- Use the Program Evaluation standards (with other tools such as follow-up surveys, as appropriate) to assess the evaluation's overall utility accuracy/validity, feasibility, and propriety.
- Use a specialized meta-evaluation checklist.
- Have an independent meta-evaluator gather firsthand information to cross-check key data and conclusions.

- Have an independent meta-evaluation team conduct a full evaluation using the same or a similar evaluation approach. Identify and investigate any differences in findings.

More detailed information about meta-evaluation methods is provided in Chapter 11.

NOTES

1. The original version of the KEC is accessible online (http://evaluation .wmich.edu/checklists) as part of the Western Michigan University Evaluation Center's checklist project.

2. Psychological research shows that the human short-term memory can hold only 7 ± 2 pieces of information. In general, it is best to err on the side of fewer items.

3. Scriven refers to this checkpoint as Generalizability. In the author's experience, this tends to make people think that it refers only to the likelihood that the evaluation report's *findings* would also be true for similar evaluands in other contexts. Although that is certainly part of this checkpoint, the author believes that the term Exportability allows for a broader definition that includes the exportability of good ideas and design features and not just the complete evaluand.

4. For more information on using systems approaches in evaluation, see the EVAL-SYS listserv (accessible at http://evaluation.wmich.edu/lists/archives.html).

5. Many thanks to Michael Quinn Patton for this idea, which he shared during a session on reflective evaluation practice at the American Evaluation Association meeting in 2003.

ADDITIONAL READING

Scriven, M. (1991). *Evaluation thesaurus.* Thousand Oaks, CA: Sage.

⊰ ELEVEN ⊱

META-EVALUATION

————•◦•————

So far, we have learned how to put together a solid evaluation using the Key Evaluation Checklist (KEC) as a framework. But suppose that you were asked to review an evaluation done by someone else. How would you know whether it was a good one? How would you evaluate an evaluation?

> **Meta-evaluation** is the evaluation of an evaluation (Scriven, 1991). In other words, it is a determination of the quality and/or value of an evaluation.

The Meta-evaluation checkpoint in the KEC is where the evaluation itself receives a critical assessment of its strengths and weaknesses (Exhibit 11.1). This chapter outlines several strategies for addressing the Meta-evaluation checkpoint.

THE FIVE CRITERIA FOR EVALUATING EVALUATIONS

Evaluations should be evaluated on five core dimensions of merit: validity, utility, conduct, credibility, and costs. In other words, evaluations should produce valid and justifiable conclusions; be useful to the client and other relevant audiences; be conducted in an ethical, legal, professional, and otherwise appropriate manner; be credible to relevant audiences; and be as economical, quick, and unobtrusive as possible.

Exhibit 11.1   The Meta-evaluation Checkpoint of the KEC

Meta-evaluation

A critical assessment of the strengths and weaknesses of the evaluation itself (e.g., How well were all of the KEC checkpoints covered?) and conclusions about its overall utility accuracy/validity, feasibility, and propriety (for details, see the *Program Evaluation Standards* [Joint Committee on Standards for Educational Evaluation, 1994])

When evaluating an evaluation report rather than an entire evaluation process, the conduct criterion would usually be omitted from the preceding list. Information needed to evaluate how professionally the evaluation was conducted is seldom included in an evaluation report. Even if it were included, input from other stakeholders (besides the report authors) would be essential to complete a fair meta-evaluation on this criterion.

Validity

A meta-evaluation should always check the extent to which conclusions reached by the evaluation team are justified. Recall that evaluative conclusions come from both descriptive facts (i.e., the data) and relevant values. The relevant values can tell us which criteria to include, which criteria are the most important, and how strong a performance should be considered satisfactory, good, and/or excellent. Therefore, in a meta-evaluation, it is important to check very carefully the sources and uses of both descriptive facts and relevant values.

One of the most important rules in meta-evaluation is *not* to simply check to see whether the evaluation team did what it said it was going to do (e.g., in a proposal) or whether the evaluation team's conclusions follow from the assumptions it took as given. As with all evaluation tasks, the meta-evaluators' job is to *question everything*. Did they even ask the right questions in the first place? Did they scope the evaluation appropriately? What was left out that might have been included and vice versa?

Of course, every evaluation team is usually operating within at least some constraints imposed by management, funders, and/or others. These must be taken into consideration in a meta-evaluation. These constraints often relate to budget and/or timeline, but occasionally the client may restrict access to information or insist on the use of a certain methodology or approach. If the evaluation team was required to use a suboptimal evaluation approach or method, this should be pointed out so that the evaluation team is not unfairly blamed for these decisions. At the same time, if the constraints were so severe that valid conclusions would be impossible to draw, this raises ethical questions as to whether the evaluation contract should have been accepted in the first place.

What tools or guidelines are available for looking at evaluation validity? The KEC (Scriven, 2003) is one of the most useful tools available for evaluating the validity of an evaluation. Even for an evaluation that has not been written up using the KEC as a guide, it is helpful to determine which checkpoints were covered in the evaluation report, which were not, and whether any omissions were serious enough to compromise the validity of the evaluation. As mentioned previously, it is not always essential that every checkpoint is covered, but there certainly needs to be a good reason for omitting any of them.

The following rating scale could be used alongside the KEC to rate an evaluation on its coverage of each checkpoint:

A = Hits *all* of the main aspects of this checkpoint (to the extent possible in a report of this length) and expresses them clearly and concisely

B = Hits *most* of the aspects covered under this checkpoint but misses one or two fairly important (but not absolutely crucial) points or has all of the right ingredients but is not 100% clear

C = Goes some of the way toward addressing this checkpoint but misses something crucial, misses or misstates several important points, or is quite unclear or disorganized

D = Has one or two elements that seem to implicitly speak to this checkpoint but really does a poor job on this checkpoint

F = Totally misses this checkpoint

When using a scale like this, it is important to note that the overall quality of the evaluation does not simply correspond to an average of its ratings on all of the checkpoints. Some checkpoints are more important than others and so should be weighted more heavily. For example, omitting information about background and context would merely make it difficult for readers to fully grasp the realities surrounding the evaluand. Failing to evaluate on outcomes (or missing several important ones) is much more serious because this would almost certainly result in invalid conclusions.

Another useful meta-evaluation tool is a copy of any relevant standards that apply to your evaluand. Perhaps the best-known tools are the *Program Evaluation Standards,* the *Personnel Evaluation Standards,* and the *Student Evaluation Standards,* all publications of the Joint Committee on Standards for Educational Evaluation (1988, 1994, 2003). Short summaries of each of these sets of standards are available online (www.wmich.edu/evalctr/jc/).

The standards cover four broad categories of criteria (or dimensions) for evaluating evaluations: utility, propriety, feasibility, and accuracy. The accuracy category addresses the issue of validity and provides many useful items for consideration. However, it is considerably less specific than the KEC with regard to what should be included in a high-quality evaluation, so it should be used as a supplement to the KEC rather than as a replacement for it. As will be seen later in this chapter, the standards really come into their own when we look at some of the other meta-evaluation criteria.

For particular meta-evaluations, there may be other standards that are highly relevant in a particular case. For example, if the evaluation contains (or should contain) a heavy financial audit component, the relevant auditing standards will apply. Government-based evaluation units may have specific legislative requirements for what should be included in an evaluation. Specific funding organizations may also have specific requirements for evaluations that should be applied in a meta-evaluation.

Drawing on both the KEC and the Joint Committee standards, the following is a short sample list of "big picture" criteria to consider when assessing the validity of an evaluation. This is not intended to be an exhaustive list, and not all of the questions will apply in a particular case. But it may well be useful as a tool to guide a team that is relatively new to meta-evaluation.

- Covers all relevant sources of value (e.g., needs, relevant standards, commonsense definitions of value)
- Comprehensively covers process, outcome, and cost
- Includes no irrelevant or illicit criteria
- Data used directly address the criteria
- Includes analyses (both qualitative and quantitative) that are appropriate for the data

- Clearly states how data are interpreted
- Is clear about where evaluative conclusions come from (no logical leaps or "smoke and mirrors")
- Includes valid recommendations (if any) (i.e., there are sufficient grounds for making them, and it is known that they are likely to work if implemented)

Utility

Evaluations are always conducted with a particular audience in mind, and a good evaluation must be useful to that audience. At a bare minimum, the evaluation and its findings should be (a) relevant to the questions or decisions being faced by the audience, (b) timely so that the findings are available when people need to make decisions, and (c) clearly communicated using appropriate language, media, and communication channels.

Participatory evaluations can earn extra "points" on utility when the evaluation process (and not just the product or output) leaves behind new skills or know-how for the people who participated in conducting the evaluation. Increased learning capacity can be thought of as an outcome of the evaluation itself and is sometimes the most important way in which the evaluation can be useful to the organization, its stakeholders, and/or the community.

An important part of evaluating the utility of an evaluation is to examine the extent to which the findings and/or know-how were eventually used or (if it is still too early to tell) the extent to which it is likely they will be used. Although a considerable part of the responsibility for use or nonuse rests with the client organization and its stakeholders, a good diagnostic meta-evaluation can help to uncover reasons that might have been related to the focus or conduct of the evaluation or to the communication of its findings. This can help the evaluation team to improve the utility of its next evaluation.

Many theorists and practitioners argue against the consideration of actual use as a criterion for meta-evaluation on the grounds that actual use is outside the control of the evaluator (e.g., Scriven, 1991). This may be viewed as similar to the argument that teachers should be evaluated only on how well they deliver the course material rather than on how much their students actually learn or that sales representatives should be evaluated on the quality of their sales pitches rather than on the dollar amounts of their sales. In fact, one could argue that nearly all outcomes are outside the immediate control of the persons, programs, or evaluation teams being evaluated.

Conduct

Evaluating the way in which an evaluation was conducted is a large part of the Process checkpoint for meta-evaluation. Some of the relevant values that apply here include legal, ethical, and professional standards; cultural appropriateness; and unobtrusiveness.

The application of legal standards might include ensuring that the evaluation complied with all relevant national, international, and local laws while conducting the evaluation. Ethical standards encompass the usual research ethics considerations such as not endangering participants, gaining consent, and protecting confidentiality. Relevant professional standards include the American Evaluation Association's *Guiding Principles for Evaluators,* equivalent guidelines published by other professional associations (with regard to evaluation and in the relevant content area for the evaluation), and the relevant evaluation standards (Joint Committee on Standards for Educational Evaluation, 1988, 1994, 2003).

Cultural appropriateness may be evaluated using any relevant guidelines pertinent to the particular cultural context. Some good example source documents include the following:

- *Guidelines for Ethical Research in Indigenous Studies* (Australian Institute of Aboriginal and Torres Strait Islander Studies, 2000)
- *Native Hawaiian Guidelines for Culturally Responsible Evaluation and Research* (Kamehameha Schools, 2003)
- *Principles for the Conduct of Research in the Arctic* (U.S. Interagency Arctic Research Policy Committee, n.d.)

One sticky issue to be aware of when assessing the cultural appropriateness of an evaluation is that some sets of guidelines advocate very substantial involvement of community members in the design and conduct of the evaluation and in the interpretation of the data. In general, some involvement of the local community is a very good idea to ensure that the evaluation team has a clear understanding of the context. On the other hand, the considerable time commitment required of community members who participate on the evaluation team might make this particular mode of involvement unfeasible. A good alternative in such cases might be to set up a community advisory panel that is asked to provide input on the evaluation at multiple stages throughout the process.

Unobtrusiveness refers to the extent to which the evaluation was conducted in a way that was minimally disruptive to the evaluand, its recipients, and its staff. When assessing the evaluation on this dimension, it is important to bear in mind the possible trade-offs with validity, utility, and cultural appropriateness. An extremely unobtrusive evaluation might be neglecting to tap into important sources of data from the staff or consumers, thereby jeopardizing the validity of the evaluation. Similarly, a highly participatory evaluation might often be extremely obtrusive, but the payoffs in learning, utility, and cultural appropriateness might far outweigh the downside of disrupting regular activities.

Credibility

Bearing in mind the extent to which the evaluation was conducted for accountability or internal learning, to what extent are the findings likely to be well received given their source? The three most important elements of credibility are (a) familiarity with the context; (b) independence, impartiality, and/or lack of conflict of interest; and (c) expertise in evaluation and in the subject matter under investigation.

Familiarity with the context includes having knowledge of a particular organization or program (e.g., politics, organizational culture, structure) or with the community or society that the evaluand serves (e.g., history, culture, infrastructure, access to resources). Familiarity with context is particularly important when reporting to internal audiences and to the community.

Independence and impartiality tend to be more important if the evaluation team is reporting to external audiences or to stakeholders whose interests or viewpoints conflict with those who commissioned the evaluation. Even the appearance of a specific agenda or some conflict of interest can seriously compromise credibility. If credibility is compromised, the findings are far less likely to be used.

Expertise in evaluation and in the subject matter under investigation tends to be more important for credibility in some settings than in others. In general, evaluation audiences tend to pay more attention to content expertise than to evaluation expertise, mostly because few laypeople understand the kinds of skills and knowledge required to be a competent evaluator. In extreme cases, stakeholders place excessive emphasis on content expertise, usually dismissing the importance of evaluation expertise altogether. The reality is that content expertise can sometimes get in the way of good evaluation (especially if all key evaluation team members are content experts) because it often comes with biases toward certain approaches or styles that might not be related to evaluand quality or value. Scriven (1991) refers to this error as the "fallacy of irrelevant expertise." The key point to remember here is that what the stakeholders see as credible might not be the best combination of expertise for maximizing validity. Furthermore, various stakeholder groups (e.g., funders, program staff, consumers) might find different combinations of expertise to be credible. For this reason, an evaluation's credibility is usually best assessed by ensuring that credibility has not been problematically compromised with any particular stakeholder group and that excessive pandering to stakeholder perceptions has not compromised validity.

Costs

When evaluating how reasonable the costs of an evaluation were, it is important to take into account the main kinds of costs that can be incurred by the different kinds of stakeholders. The most obvious of these are money costs, that is, the fee paid to the evaluation team plus any relevant expenses. Less obvious costs include opportunity costs on the part of internal staff who might have been taken away from their regular work duties (or given up some duties) to contribute to the evaluation, space or facilities, and other resources. Also important here are the time costs; that is, how long did the organization have to wait for information, especially when compared with the likely time frame of an alternative evaluation?

As in an evaluation, the point here is not simply to document or even add up all of the costs incurred. That would be a purely descriptive exercise rather than an evaluative one. The point is to answer the question of whether the costs were *reasonable* given the benefits reaped by the organization and/or community (e.g., gained knowledge, improved learning capacity).

KEY POINTS TO
REMEMBER IN META-EVALUATION

In all elements of the meta-evaluation, it is important to bear in mind the overarching purposes of the evaluation (e.g., building learning capacity, finding areas for improvement, accountability) and the constraints under which it operates (e.g., budget, timeline, access to information) when applying the relevant standards or guidelines. For example, a small-budget evaluation on a tight timeline is necessarily less comprehensive in its coverage of criteria, and this might appear to fall short on validity. For such an evaluation, the question is not whether the evaluation gets an "A+" on validity but rather whether it yielded the most valid conclusion possible given the resources available.

Similarly, it must be remembered that all evaluation design decisions involve trade-offs. For example, the kind of heavy stakeholder involvement that can maximize the evaluation's utility comes with a nontrivial opportunity cost when participants are taken away from their regular duties to participate on the evaluation team. It might also compromise credibility to outside audiences if evaluation team members were involved in the design and/or implementation of the evaluand or if they have had very little training in evaluation. In many cases, these drawbacks are minor in comparison with the substantial gains in organizational learning capacity that are gleaned from a well-conducted participatory evaluation. But in other cases, the drawbacks are serious enough that the evaluation falls "under the bar" (i.e., below minimum acceptable levels) on one or more of the other criteria.

In the end, the big picture meta-evaluation question is much the same as the overarching question that we usually ask in an evaluation: Is/Was this the best possible use of available resources to design and conduct an evaluation of the greatest possible value (for the organization, for society, for the community, etc.)? To answer this question, it is important to understand the nature and extent of the needs of the relevant audiences. How important was learning capacity compared with credibility, cost, and validity? Was utility so low that the value of a high-validity evaluation was effectively canceled out (e.g., because findings were not delivered in time for important decisions to be made)?

OTHER OPTIONS FOR
CONDUCTING A META-EVALUATION

The approach to meta-evaluation outlined in this chapter so far is just one of several options available. One alternative is to systematically assess the extent to which the evaluation meets the *Program Evaluation Standards* (Joint Committee on Standards for Educational Evaluation, 1994). A detailed meta-evaluation checklist has been created for this purpose and is listed at the end of this chapter under Additional Readings. This option is particularly useful when there is a strong need to focus on the propriety, feasibility, and utility of the evaluation. The standards provide much less guidance on the accuracy standard, particularly with regard to what should be included in an evaluation.

A second option for meta-evaluation is the "second opinion" approach, which is much the same as having one's health evaluated by a second specialist. In this approach, a different evaluation team conducts an independent evaluation of the same evaluand, and the reports are compared to see whether the same conclusions were reached. If the conclusions differ, further investigation will be necessary to find out why and whether one set of conclusions or the other is incorrect.

A third, less expensive option is a hybrid approach. In this approach, the meta-evaluator assesses the evaluation as it is but is asked to cross-check any findings that could be questionable. For example, some of the "questionable" aspects of the original evaluation might be identified by stakeholders who disagree with the findings.

FORMATIVE META-EVALUATION

The options outlined heretofore focus primarily on evaluating an evaluation that is already completed, usually for the purpose of accountability (i.e., summative meta-evaluation). But another, often ignored approach is to use meta-evaluation in a formative way, that is, to improve an evaluation that is still in progress.

There are many strategies available for formative meta-evaluation. At the simplest end, the evaluation team might solicit the advice of an evaluation specialist to comment on the design and conduct of the evaluation and to help the team solve any problems it encounters. A variation on this idea is to use an advisory panel consisting of an evaluation specialist, members of the organization where the evaluation is being conducted, and (perhaps) subject matter experts. This not only provides a rich source of ideas and information about content, context, and design but also maximizes buy-in to the evaluation due to the involvement of key organizational members.

The second possible approach to formative meta-evaluation is to have a meta-evaluator review drafts of evaluation progress reports before they are submitted to the client. If any gaps or problems are identified, the evaluation team still has the opportunity to gather additional data, hone its evaluative conclusions, and improve the way in which its work is communicated to the various audiences. It is also good practice to include organizational stakeholders in a round of reviews before any report is made final. This often works best if the preliminary findings are presented orally and participants are given various options for providing input (e.g., a group discussion, written feedback, a later conversation with the evaluation team).

SHOULD I USE META-EVALUATION MYSELF?

This question is similar to a dentist asking whether he or she should brush, floss, and get regular dental checkups. Quite simply, all individuals who practice evaluation as a substantial part of their jobs have a professional imperative to "practice what they preach" and subject their own work to the same level of criticism that they regularly mete out to others.

At a bare minimum, meta-evaluation should involve checking in regularly with clients to see how useful, valid, credible, cost-effective, and appropriately conducted the evaluations have been to them. Also helpful for self-directed meta-evaluation is the exercise of running through one or more evaluation or meta-evaluation checklists to see how well each of the relevant checkpoints or standards has been addressed. The meta-evaluation checkpoint in this case should consist of an honest critique of the strengths and limitations of the evaluation and what can and cannot be inferred from it.

For high-stakes evaluations, especially where credibility is essential, it is a good idea to hire an independent meta-evaluator to critique your evaluation before the final report is submitted.

For evaluations where utility is a primary concern, one suggestion is to build into the evaluation contract a follow-up visit to the organization to see whether and how findings and know-how are being used.[1] If use is different from what was anticipated (i.e., better, worse, or just qualitatively different), it is important to delve into any reasons for this and to document them carefully so that they are useful for later reflection and improvement of future evaluations. By including this feedback cycle in the evaluation contract from the start, stakeholders can be reassured that the evaluation team will not just "drop the bomb" and then disappear, never to be seen again. Rather, the evaluation team is presenting itself as willingly accountable for the quality of its work.

Building some form of serious meta-evaluation into evaluation practice conveys a very important value, that is, that the evaluation team is serious about quality, accountability, and improvement. If this is not true of the evaluators themselves, we can hardly expect clients to take our profession seriously.

NOTE

1. Many thanks go to Michael Quinn Patton for this idea, which he shared during a session on reflective evaluation practice at the American Evaluation Association meeting in 2003.

ADDITIONAL READINGS

Entries from Scriven's (1991) *Evaluation Thesaurus:*
- Demurrer
- Fallacy of irrelevant expertise
- Meta-evaluation
- Technicism

Guba, E. G., & Lincoln, Y. S. (2001). *Guidelines and checklist for constructivist (a.k.a. fourth generation) evaluation.* Available online: http://evaluation.wmich .edu/checklists/

House, E. R., & Howe, K. R. (2000). *Deliberative Democratic Evaluation Checklist.* Available online: http://evaluation.wmich.edu/checklists/

Patton, M. Q. (2002). *Utilization-focused Evaluation Checklist.* Available online: http://evaluation.wmich.edu/checklists/

Patton, M. Q. (2003). *Qualitative Evaluation Checklist.* Available online: http://evaluation .wmich.edu/checklists/

Scriven, M. (1969). An introduction to meta-evaluation. *Educational Product Report, 2,* 36–38.

Stufflebeam, D. L. (1999). *Program Evaluations Meta-evaluation Checklist.* Available online: http://evaluation.wmich.edu/checklists/

Stufflebeam, D. L. (2001a). *AEA Guiding Principles Checklist.* Available online: http://evaluation.wmich.edu/checklists/

Stufflebeam, D. L. (2001b). The meta-evaluation imperative. *American Journal of Evaluation, 22,* 183–210.

Stufflebeam, D. L. (2002). *CIPP Evaluation Model Checklist.* Available online: http://evaluation.wmich.edu/checklists/

EXERCISES

1. Devise a short interview protocol (maximum of six questions) that you would use as part of a follow-up on an evaluation completed by yourself 3 months earlier. Make sure that it covers all five meta-evaluation criteria.

2. Using the KEC checkpoints in Table 11.1, rate the outcome assessment of the U.S. Fulbright Scholar Program (http://exchanges.state .gov/education/evaluations/execsummaries/usscholar_fulbright.pdf) on the following scales, bearing in mind the level of detail it is possible to present in a six-page executive summary:

   A = Hits *all* of the main aspects of this checkpoint (to the extent possible in a short report) and expresses them clearly and concisely

   B = Hits *most* of the aspects covered under this checkpoint but misses one or two fairly important (but not absolutely crucial) points or has all of the right ingredients but is really not 100% clear

   C = Goes some of the way toward addressing this checkpoint but misses something crucial, misses or misstates several important points, or is pretty unclear or disorganized

   D = Has one or two elements that seem to implicitly speak to this checkpoint but really does a poor job on this checkpoint

   F = Totally misses this checkpoint

Table 11.1 KEC-Based Meta-evaluation Rating Table

	Checkpoint	Rating (A–F)	Justification for Rating
Preliminaries	I. Executive Summary		
	II. Preface		
	III. Methodology		
Foundations	1. Background and Context		
	2. Descriptions and Definitions		
	3. Consumers		
	4. Resources		
	5. Values		

	Checkpoint	Rating (A–F)	Justification for Rating
Sub-evaluation	6. Process Evaluation		
	7. Outcome Evaluation		
	8. Costs		
	9. Comparisons		
Conclusion	10. Exportability		
	11. Overall Significance		
	12. Recommendations and Explanations		
	13. Responsibilities		
	14. Reporting and Follow-up		
	15. Meta-evaluation		

Given how you have rated this evaluation on the checkpoints in Table 11.1, what rating would you give the evaluation overall? (circle just *one* letter grade)

A+   A   A–   B+   B   B–   C+   C   C–   D   F

Excellent   *Good*   *Barely adequate*   *Poor*

Explain *briefly* (in approximately four lines) how you came to this conclusion. (What logic did you use? Did you decide that some aspects were more important? If so, how?) (A suggested answer to this question is provided in the "Answers to Selected Exercises" section.)

ANSWERS TO
SELECTED EXERCISES

This section contains suggested answers to selected exercises from the ends of the chapters. In addition to these, a set of practice exam questions with answers is provided in the section following this.

CHAPTER 2, EXERCISE 1

Comment on the following statement: "Formative evaluation (i.e., evaluation designed to inform decisions about *improving* a program or another evaluand) looks at design and implementation issues rather than at outcomes. Summative evaluation is when you look at outcomes." Is this (a) always true, (b) sometimes true (if so, when?), or (c) never true? Explain.

This is never true, with perhaps very few exceptions. Both formative evaluation and summative evaluation should look at both process (design and implementation) and outcomes. (This is key point—and you need to hit it straight between the eyes).

It is true that design and implementation may be more important or central in a formative evaluation and that it will be too early to look at some of the more downstream outcomes, but a good evaluation would always look at preliminary outcomes.

In summative evaluation, it is crucial to get at pretty much all important outcomes. But process issues are also important, so that we can check to see whether the evaluand had good content and delivery and was implemented ethically, efficiently, legally, and so forth. Process evaluation can also help to give clues about reasons for poor results (e.g., inconsistent implementation).

CHAPTER 3, EXERCISE 1

(a) What is the purpose of doing a needs assessment as part of an evaluation of a mature program? What is it for? How does it fit into the evaluation? (b) Are there any evaluations for which a needs assessment might not be necessary? If so, describe them. If not, why not?

(a) Needs assessment identifies outcomes (or impacts) that we should look for in consumers (both intended and unintended impactees). So, it is a substantial part of determining what we should look at under the Outcome Evaluation checkpoint of the Key Evaluation Checklist (KEC). Needs assessment can also help us to identify the relative importance of various outcomes (e.g., based on extent and severity of need).

(b) A needs assessment might not be necessary if there was already a very solid one done when the program was created in the first place. But in most cases, it would be a good idea to look and see whether the nature and/or extent of the needs have changed over time.

CHAPTER 6, EXERCISE 1

Suppose that a client does not like the findings of your evaluation and says, "Well, that's just *your* opinion about the program. Evaluations are always just so subjective." How would you respond?

There are certainly some elements of the evaluation that involve using judgment rather than just measurement, so it certainly has that element of subjectivity (i.e., use of judgment). But if you mean, as I think you do, that the conclusions drawn were based merely on my arbitrary preferences rather than on fact, I would invite you to show me where you believe this has occurred so that I can correct it. The criteria were determined using a systematic needs assessment, data were gathered from multiple sources to ensure that we were getting a complete picture, and the results were benchmarked against the main alternative interventions. Now, was there something in there that should not have been included? Did I miss something important?

Help me out here. (Note: Diplomacy is key when you respond to something like this.)

CHAPTER 7, EXERCISE 1

> In your own words, briefly define and explain the differences among (a) holistic evaluation, (b) component evaluation, and (c) dimensional evaluation. For each one, (i) give a real-world example of an evaluation in your profession for which you would choose one over the others and (ii) indicate why—for example, not just why (a) but also why not (b) or (c). The examples should not be taken from the texts, from one of your assignments, or from your project.

(a) Holistic evaluation is determining the quality or value of an evaluand as a whole without explicitly first breaking it down into dimensions or components. (i) The example must clearly be something that is reasonably manageable to evaluate in this way (i.e., a large or complex program or system will not do it) and whose quality or value is experienced by consumers as a package. (ii) Good reasons include the fact that the quality or value of the evaluand is experienced by consumers as a package, the evaluand could reasonably be evaluated holistically by an expert, and the evaluation would likely have a very small budget (so that holistic would probably be the way to go).

(b) Component evaluation is determining the quality or value of an evaluand by first breaking it down into several component parts (i.e., pieces of the evaluand) and evaluating those separately. (i) The example should be a multicomponent program whose elements are experienced more or less separately by consumers. (ii) Good reasons include the fact that elements of the program are experienced more or less separately by consumers, elements of the program are too complex to evaluate holistically, and dimensions do not really apply to all components.

(c) Dimensional evaluation is determining the quality or value of an evaluand by first identifying the dimensions (or aspects of it) that distinguish good quality or value from poor quality or value. (i) There is very little restriction on the example here except that it should not be a multicomponent program whose elements are clearly experienced quite separately by consumers. (ii) Good reasons include the fact that the quality or value of the evaluand is experienced by consumers as a package and the client might need more detail than a holistic evaluation would provide.

CHAPTER 11, EXERCISE 2

Using the KEC checkpoints in the Answers to Selected Exercises Table 1, rate the outcome assessment of the U.S. Fulbright Scholar Program (http://exchanges.state.gov/education/evaluations/execsummaries/usscholar_ful bright.pdf) on the following scales, bearing in mind the level of detail it is possible to present in a six-page executive summary:

A = Hits *all* of the main aspects of this checkpoint and expresses them clearly and concisely

B = Hits *most* of the aspects covered under this checkpoint but misses one or two fairly important (but not absolutely crucial) points or has all of the right ingredients but is not 100% clear

C = Goes some of the way toward addressing this checkpoint but misses something crucial, misses or misstates several important points, or is pretty unclear or disorganized

D = Has one or two elements that seem to implicitly speak to this checkpoint but really does a poor job on this checkpoint

F = Totally misses this checkpoint

Answers are shown in Table 1 on next page.

Given how you have rated this evaluation on the KEC checkpoints in the table, what rating would you give the evaluation overall? (circle just *one* letter grade):

A+   A   A–   B+   B   B–   C+   C   C–   D   F

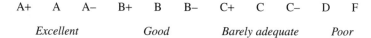

Explain *briefly* (in approximately four lines) how you came to this conclusion. (What logic did you use? Did you decide that some aspects were more important? If so, how?)

C. The report clearly met the client's political needs, that is, to create a glowing publicity document for justifying the continuation of the program. But in terms of figuring out whether this is a justifiable use of (taxpayer?) dollars and other resources to achieve these outcomes, it is weak given that many very serious weaknesses occurred at critical checkpoints (Values, Process, Costs, Comparisons, and Overall Significance).

Answers to Selected Exercises Table 1 KEC-Driven Meta-evaluation of the U.S. Fulbright Scholar Program Evaluation Report

	Checkpoint	Rating	Justification for Rating (type within the space provided)
Preliminaries	I. Executive Summary	C	Fine, the Overview of Outcomes (page 1) summed up the main points. However, the evaluation itself was somewhat lacking, so this was reflected in the summary.
	II. Preface	C	The source and nature of request were covered well on page 1. However, there is no clue as to what the purpose of the evaluation is (publicity?). There is no mention of other relevant audiences and how their information needs might be addressed by the evaluation.
	III. Methodology	D	This is covered concisely on page 1. There is okay coverage but weak methodology. No justification is given for the single-informant method (scholars only), which has a definite positive bias (obviously, the Fulbright scholars are keen to be funded again for an enjoyable trip).
Foundation	1. Background and Context	B	There is very good coverage of the program's original purpose, but there is no mention of its increased importance (if any) due to recent events (e.g., the events of 9/11). There is no mention of whether it has been evaluated before.
	2. Descriptions and Definitions	B	There is good coverage of this (mostly pages 1 and 3), but it is not clear how people and host institutions are selected for the program.
	3. Consumers	B	Most actual recipients (page 3) were identified, and other impactees were well identified in the context of outcomes. But what were the characteristics of those accepted compared with others?
	4. Resources	F	It is not clear at all either what was available or what was actually poured into the program. Who funds this program—the taxpayers?
	5. Values	D	This was mostly goal achievement. Other criteria identified were intuitive, but it is not clear how they were decided (apart from that the client requested them). It is pretty weak on this all-important checkpoint.

(Continued)

Answers to Selected Exercises Table 1 (Continued)

	Checkpoint	Rating	Justification for Rating (type within the space provided)
Sub-evaluations	6. Process Evaluation	D	There is some implicitly evaluative mention of activities performed by scholars (page 3), but there is no *evaluation* of how well the program was designed, implemented, or managed.
	7. Outcome Evaluation	B	There is good coverage of direct effects and ripple effects, but is it supposed to be intuitively obvious that these results are good? This checkpoint is weakened by weak coverage of values.
	8. Costs	F	There is zero coverage of costs.
	9. Comparisons	F	There is zero coverage of comparisons. In particular, it would be useful to know whether this program has a more cost-effective positive impact than do student exchanges.
	10. Exportability	F	There is zero coverage. Are there any ideas here that might be applied in industry, for example? How about in government? There might be some good potential here that the evaluation omits.
Conclusions	11. Overall Significance	C	Very positive conclusions are drawn, but these are really little more than reported evaluations done by someone else (i.e., a summary of what the scholars thought).
	12. Recommendations and Explanations	F (or N/A)	This was not requested and not given. (This was an optional checkpoint, so N/A might actually be more appropriate than an F grade here.)
	13. Justification and Responsibility	F (or N/A)	This was not requested and not given. (This was an optional checkpoint, so N/A might actually be more appropriate than an F grade here.)
	14. Report and Support	B	This executive summary was produced, as was a longer report (not that you were expected to know this). It is not clear how follow-up questions might be handled.
	15. Meta-evaluation	F	There is no critique of weaknesses, especially of the single-informant method, that is, asking people who got a free trip whether that was a good idea or not. Of course they think it was.

NOTE: N/A = not applicable.

226

SAMPLE EXAM QUESTIONS

———•◦•———

T he following questions are taken from exams used in graduate-level classes in evaluation that follow an approach similar to that outlined in this book. Not all of the issues in these questions have been explicitly covered in this book, but they should nevertheless provide interesting "stretch" exercises for class discussion.

TIPS FOR STUDENTS
ANSWERING THESE EXAM QUESTIONS

- Your answers will be graded on validity, clarity, conciseness, and insightfulness.
- Read the question *at least twice* before you start to answer it. Then read it again. Some of the questions have more than one issue embedded in them.
- Perhaps you disagree with some of what you have been taught in this class. That is fine. Your first priority, however, should be to demonstrate clearly that you have *understood* the point discussed in class. *Then* you may agree or disagree with it (and indicate why).
- When listing points or making arguments, list the most important points first. This shows that you know which elements are central and which are peripheral.
- It is okay to answer using bullet point lists and/or diagrams (not narrative) so long as your answer is not so brief as to be cryptic. You will get no credit for things you implied "between the lines" or meant to say or for answering a question other than exactly what was asked.

- Some questions give no hint as to how they should be approached. Part of your job as an evaluator is to identify issues or assumptions that are not made explicit and to create clarity out of confusion. These are "stretch" questions designed to enhance your ability to do this with clients and/or other evaluation team members or evaluator colleagues.

THE QUESTIONS

1. Clearly explain the *purpose* (not just the content) of the Consumers checkpoint in the Key Evaluation Checklist (KEC). What information does it give us that is essential for drawing valid conclusions about the quality, value, or effectiveness of the program (or another evaluand)? What mistakes (i.e., invalid conclusions) are likely if the Consumers checkpoint is skipped or used sloppily? Limit your answer to approximately half a page.

2. An applied social scientist tells you that incidents of domestic violence dropped by 0.7 standard deviation among a group of violent offenders who attended a "cognitive–behavioral" workshop (an intervention that focuses on changing people's thinking patterns to influence their behavior). What else would you need to know to conclude that this was the most cost-effective intervention for this type of offender?

3. Suppose that the person initially called in to evaluate the intervention mentioned in the preceding question was a well-known expert in criminal psychology who had published widely on the merits of cognitive-behavioral approaches for treating violent offenders.
   a. Is this person "biased"? Circle *one* of the following: (i) yes, definitely; (ii) no, definitely not; (iii) possibly, but we need to know more first
   b. Assuming that this person is a competent evaluator, but bearing in mind the issue just raised about bias, should this person be hired to do the evaluation? Circle *one* of the following: (i) yes, hire him or her; (ii) no, do not hire him or her; (iii) find out more and then decide

      c. Explain your answer. (Hint: Be very clear about the meaning(s) of the term *biased,* and state clearly what evidence supports your answer or what else you need to know if you chose option (iii). If the term *biased* does not fit the issue, suggest a better way in which to explain it.)

4. Are there any good reasons for having an evaluator on the team that designs a program? Are there any problems with this idea?

5. Comment on the following assertion made by Patton (1997):

> Scriven's goal-free model eliminates only one group from the game: local project staff. He directs data in only one clear direction—away from the stated concerns of the people who run the program. . . . The standards he applies are none other than his very own preferences about what program effects are appropriate and morally defensible. . . . Goal-free evaluation carries the danger of substituting the evaluator's own goals for those of the project. (p. 182)

6. Suppose that you have been asked to review an evaluation of a program where the conclusions are somewhat unfavorable. The stakeholders are accusing the evaluator of conducting a "totally subjective evaluation" and of being "biased against the program." Outline a step-by-step strategy to explain how you would go about investigating these claims to see whether they are true or not.

7. Compose any other question that does not overlap substantially with anything else on this exam and answer that question. The importance and difficulty of your question will determine its weight (5–20 points, as compared with 10 points for the average preceding question), and the quality of your answer will determine your grade on that question.

A RUBRIC FOR GRADING
ASSIGNMENT AND EXAM QUESTIONS

The following is a very general guide that the author uses to grade assignment and exam questions (see Sample Exam Table 1). Naturally, the "main points" differ from question to question, but the levels in the rubric remain the same.

Sample Exam Table 1 Rubric for Grading Assignment and Exam Answers

Grade	Quality of Answer
A+	Same as for A, but truly *exceptional* in terms of clarity and coverage
A	Hits all (or a large proportion of) the points and expresses them clearly and concisely; no irrelevant or invalid points included
A−	Same as for A, but may have missed (or misexpressed) some minor points or may have been slightly less clear than needed for an A answer
A/B	Between A− and B+
B+	Hits a good number of points and expresses them reasonably clearly and concisely, although there may be some room for improvement in clarity; may have one or two irrelevant points but no invalid ones
B	Hits most of the points but misses several and may have some irrelevant points listed; may be somewhat unclear but is still a pretty good effort
B−	Same as for B, but some serious holes in the answer; may have several irrelevant or invalid points
B/C	Between B− and C+
C+	Decent shot at the assignment and certainly fishing in the right waters; not clear or systematic enough to make a good answer, although passable; may have several irrelevant or invalid points
C	Same as for C+ but really quite vague or difficult to understand what points are being made
D	Made some attempt but really missed the mark; most points invalid, irrelevant, or trivial
F	Completely missed the point of the assignment

SUGGESTED ANSWERS TO PRACTICE EXAM QUESTIONS

Question 1: Clearly explain the *purpose* (not just the content) of the Consumers checkpoint in the KEC. What information does it give us that is essential for drawing valid conclusions about the quality, value, or effectiveness of the program (or another evaluand)? What mistakes (i.e., invalid conclusions) are likely if the Consumers checkpoint is skipped or used sloppily? Limit your answer to approximately half a page.

"Consumers" are the people who could or should be affected by the program. (Note that *should* is not the same as *intended.* Some people talk about intended consumers as being key; for example, did the program reach who it was intended to reach? But your job is also to check whether those intentions were well founded; for example, did the program reach who it should have reached regardless of whether all impactees were intended or not?)

Clearly identifying both intended and unintended actual and potential impactees helps us to achieve the following:

- Correctly identify who the needs assessment should be focused on (we use the needs assessment to identify outcome dimensions for the evaluation).
- Make sure that we consider who the program reached (or affected) and who it did not reach but should have reached.
- Identify where (i.e., for whom) we should look for outcomes (including **side impacts** and ripple effects).

Question 2: An applied social scientist tells you that incidents of domestic violence dropped by 0.7 standard deviation among a group of violent offenders who attended a "cognitive–behavioral" workshop (an intervention that focuses on changing people's thinking patterns to influence their behavior). What else would you need to know to conclude that this was the most cost-effective intervention for this type of offender?

The following is a crucial point (you must get this):

- Actual size and practical significance of a decrease of 0.7 standard deviation (including how it was measured)

The following are very important:

- Whether the content of the workshop was legally, ethically, and logically justifiable (e.g., Were men told that it is okay to feel angry, even just because dinner is late?)

- How this improvement compares with what has been achieved by other interventions that address domestic violence
- The cost of the workshop (including length of time), especially compared with alternatives
- Any other impacts of the workshop on the attendees, their families, their friends, and so forth

The following are also useful (i.e., good ideas) but are not the most important kinds of information:

- Characteristics of the attendees: age, ethnicity, severity of behavior, socioeconomic status, and so forth (the purpose is to get some ideas of who this worked best for)
- Resources needed to implement the program (especially relative to what is usually available in the country where the program is implemented)
- Any issue with attrition rates (Did all participants complete? Who did not and why not?)
- Whether it was court mandated or voluntary (important for assessing exportability)
- Whether there was any control or comparison group
- Whether a decrease in incidents persisted over time
- What experts think of the design, results, and so forth

(Note that you did not have to get *all* points to get an "A" but that you did need to get the most important ones. There may well be other good points apart from those listed above.)

Question 3: Suppose that the person initially called in to evaluate the intervention mentioned in the preceding question was a well-known expert in criminal psychology who had published widely on the merits of cognitive behavioral approaches for treating violent offenders.

(a) Is this person "biased"? Circle *one* of the following: (i) yes, definitely; (ii) no, definitely not; (iii) possibly, but we need to know more first

(b) Assuming that this person is a competent evaluator, but bearing in mind the issue just raised about bias, should this person be hired to do the evaluation? Circle *one* of the following: (i) yes, hire him or her; (ii) no, do not hire him or her; (iii) find out more and then decide

(c) Explain your answer. (Hint: Be very clear about the meaning(s) of the term *biased,* and state clearly what evidence supports your answer or what else you need to know if you chose option (iii). If the term *biased* does not fit the issue, suggest a better way in which to explain it.)

Answer to (a): (iii) possibly, but we need to know more first. *Explanation:* The person clearly has an *opinion* in favor of cognitive–behavioral interventions that may be based on good evidence. Merely having an opinion is not the same as being biased. The person is "biased" only if this belief is so strong that he or she would ignore evidence of ineffectiveness. (It is likely, though not certain, that the person will look *harder* for evidence of effectiveness and not notice counterevidence, and this would be good evidence of at least *some* bias.)

Answer to (b): (iii) find out more and then decide. *Explanation:* It is quite possible that anyone with a clue about treating violent offenders knows that cognitive–behavioral interventions have the best track record. As such, to exclude from the evaluation team all who favor such treatment would be to rule out all who have a clue. If the bias is serious enough to blind the person's objectivity, or if the person has a conflict of interest (e.g., he or she invested in or designed the workshop), do not hire this person. If it is not clear whether bias is a problem, add a meta-evaluator who either is not a criminology specialist or has experience with the success of alternative interventions but is open to the possibility that cognitive–behavioral interventions might work.

Question 4: Are there any good reasons for having an evaluator on the team that designs a program? Are there any problems with this idea?

There are lots of good reasons, including the following:

- The evaluator can lead a high-quality needs assessment that informs program design.
- The needs assessment can double as baseline data that will help with the evaluation later.
- The evaluator can help the team to draw up a program theory, think critically about the program logic, and make sure that the program designed makes excellent sense and has maximum likelihood of succeeding.
- The evaluator can also help with designing a database and data collection system so that evaluation data could be collected as a seamless part of program activities.
- The evaluator can also help the team to choose a good external evaluator.

There is a potential problem with this idea:

- If the same evaluator ends up doing the evaluation of the program later, the evaluator would have a conflict of interest because he or she would have a vested interest in the success of the program, having been one of the designers.

Question 5: Comment on the following assertion made by Patton (1997):

> Scriven's goal-free model eliminates only one group from the game: local project staff. He directs data in only one clear direction—away from the stated concerns of the people who run the program. . . . The standards he applies are none other than his very own preferences about what program effects are appropriate and morally defensible. . . . Goal-free evaluation carries the danger of substituting the evaluator's own goals for those of the project. (p. 182)

It is true that evaluations need to be designed and conducted in ways that address the information needs of program staff and other upstream stakeholders. However, the primary reason why any program or project is put into place is to meet the needs of a particular group of potential program recipients. Therefore, their needs and concerns are paramount, whereas those of the program staff are not. A good evaluation will, in any case, meet the information needs of the program staff; these may well be different from what the staff's wants and/or concerns might be. Nevertheless, Patton's caution is a fair one (i.e., staff information needs should not be ignored in an evaluation).

As for the contention that goal-free evaluation involves applying the evaluator's personal preferences to the program, this would be true only if the evaluation were not being conducted competently. Another term for goal-free evaluation is needs-based evaluation. So, the standards used to determine program quality or value should be mostly the actual documented needs of consumers (along with several other relevant sources of value) and *not* the "personal preferences" of the evaluator. Of course, the evaluator needs to make sure that the sources of values used for the evaluation are valid and defensible ones. But replacing those with the preferences of program staff is not a great solution.

Question 6: Suppose that you have been asked to review an evaluation of a program for which the conclusions are somewhat unfavorable. The stakeholders are accusing the evaluator of conducting a "totally subjective evaluation" and of being "biased against the program." Outline a step-by-step strategy to explain how you would go about investigating these claims to see whether they are true or not.

First, speak with the stakeholders who are making the complaint. Identify exactly those conclusions or actions with which they have a problem, where they see that any information was erroneously omitted or wrongly included, what incorrect assumptions were being made, and so forth.

Second, systematically review the evaluation report and interview stakeholders to determine whether you can find any inappropriate use of personal preferences (here you are dealing with the "totally subjective" accusation). Be sure to distinguish such instances from the appropriate use of professional judgment. In cases where judgment has been used with little concrete supporting evidence, determine whether such conclusions were justified. Ask the evaluator to be more explicit about how he or she came to these conclusions, that is, based on what exactly. If inadequate explanation is forthcoming, this could be a red flag.

Third, to address the accusation of bias, identify any important preexisting beliefs or preferences that the evaluator might have had coming into the evaluation, particularly those that relate to the complaints from program staff. Check the evaluation report to see whether evidence that ran counter to those beliefs was either underinvestigated or ignored.

Fourth, presumably the program staff can highlight something that they believe was either ignored or given too much weight. Check to see whether this or something important was in fact ignored or given too much weight. Note that the ignored or overweighted evidence must have been serious or substantial enough to change the conclusion of the evaluation and not just a slight difference in perspective.

Fifth, if some evidence might have been over- or underweighted, use an appropriate importance determination strategy to double-check this. (Usually, the accusation will be that program staff views were given less consideration than they should have been given. This might well be the case and needs to be checked.)

GLOSSARY

———•◦•———

The following is intended to be a brief guide to the main terms used within this book. It is not intended to be an exhaustive listing of all terms used in evaluation. Readers are strongly advised to obtain a copy of Scriven's latest *Evaluation Thesaurus* as a companion guide to be used along with this book.

Absolute merit. The quality or value of something in "absolute" terms (i.e., not just in comparison with something else). See also *grading, quality, ranking,* and *relative merit.*

Analytical evaluation. The usual approach to evaluation, whereby the evaluand is first broken down into dimensions and/or components that are then evaluated separately before being combined to draw final conclusions. Analytical evaluation is distinguished from holistic evaluation (which involves considering the evaluand as a whole rather than breaking it down for analysis). See also *component evaluation, dimensional evaluation,* and *holistic evaluation.*

Assessment. A simile for evaluation. This term is usually used in a sense that implies formative evaluation (i.e., evaluation done for the purpose of finding areas for improvement). Assessment is usually analytical in nature with no synthesis step (i.e., it involves pointing out the strengths and weaknesses of something without adding up all of these to draw an overall conclusion).

Bar. A minimum level of performance on a specific dimension, performance below which cannot be compensated for by much better performance on other dimensions. See also *hard hurdle* and *soft hurdle.*

Baseline data. Information gathered about the performance or functioning of an organization, program, or community prior to (or at the introduction of) an evaluand. Baseline performance is compared with performance after the evaluand has been introduced so as to determine whether change has taken place.

Benchmarking. A systematic study of one or more other organizations' systems, processes, and outcomes to identify ideas for improving organizational effectiveness. This is often an information exchange, whereby two or more organizations agree to provide access to certain information for the purpose of mutual learning. Benchmarking has been used in manufacturing for years and is being used increasingly throughout business and industry.

Causation/Causality. "The relation between mosquitoes and mosquito bites. Easily understood by both parties but never satisfactorily defined by philosophers or scientists" (Scriven, 1991, p. 77). In evaluation, changes cannot correctly be referred to as outcomes unless they are caused by (i.e., substantially but usually not solely produced by) the evaluand. See also *outcome.*

Client. The person who commissioned and is paying for an evaluation. This term is also used in many professions to refer to patients or customers, so to avoid confusion in this book, we usually refer to these people as recipients, impactees, or consumers. See also *recipients, consumers,* and *impactees.*

Collaborative evaluation. An evaluation conducted in collaboration with (i.e., with substantial involvement from and power sharing with) program staff or (sometimes) consumers, impactees, and/or community members. In collaborative evaluation, staff or consumers participate with (usually external) evaluators in the design and conduct of the evaluation, including the interpretation and presentation of findings, and have a "vote" on all major decisions made as the evaluation progresses.

Comparative cost-effectiveness. The extent to which the evaluand represents the best possible use of available resources to achieve outcomes of maximum value in comparison with the available alternatives.

Competitors. Organizations producing a product or providing a service that meets a similar need in the same community or target market.

Component evaluation. A form of analytical evaluation in which the quality or value of the evaluand is determined by evaluating each of the evaluand's components (or parts) separately and then (usually) synthesizing these findings to draw conclusions about the evaluand as a whole. Each component is usually evaluated on several dimensions of merit that pertain specifically to that component rather than to the evaluand as a whole. See also *dimensional evaluation* and *holistic evaluation.*

Connoisseurial evaluation. An evaluation that is conducted drawing solely or heavily on the judgment of an expert or connoisseur. Connoisseurial evaluations are often faster and much less analytic than nonconnoisseurial evaluations. See also *analytical evaluation* and *holistic evaluation.*

Conscious needs. Needs (met or unmet) that are known to the person who has them. See also *needs* and *unconscious needs.*

Constructivist/Interpretivist paradigm. The belief that there is no such thing as "reality." Rather, there are always multiple realities, all of which are socially constructed. "Truth" is simply "the best informed . . . and most sophisticated . . . construction on which there is consensus" (Guba & Lincoln, 1989, p. 84).

Consumers. Actual or potential users or recipients of the evaluand. Consumers are individuals for whom something changes or could change as a result of the evaluand. They are actual and potential impactees. See also *customers, impactees,* and *recipients.*

Criterion/Criteria. Dimension/Dimensions of merit. These are the aspects of an evaluand that define whether it is good or bad and whether it is valuable or not valuable.

Customers. Consumers. The term *customers* is used more often in the for-profit sector to indicate people who buy (and perhaps also use) products and/or services.

Dimensional evaluation. A form of analytical evaluation in which the quality or value of the evaluand is determined by looking at its performance on multiple dimensions of merit (also called criteria of merit) that pertain to the evaluand as a whole rather than separately to its parts. See also *component evaluation* and *holistic evaluation.*

Dimensions of merit. Criteria of merit. These are the aspects of an evaluand that define whether it is good or bad and whether it is valuable or not valuable. See also *dimensional evaluation.*

Direct recipient. Someone who uses a product, receives a service, participates in a program, or is directly affected by a policy. See also *immediate recipient.*

Downstream consumers. Impactees who are not direct recipients or users of the evaluand but who are affected indirectly through direct recipients.

Effect. Outcome or impact. An effect is a change or (sometimes) a lack of change caused by the evaluand.

Evaluand. That which is being evaluated (e.g., program, policy, project, product, service, organization). In personnel evaluation the term is *evaluee.*

Evaluation. The determination of something's quality, value, or importance or the product of such a determination (e.g., a report).

Evaluation-specific logic and methodology. A set of principles (logic) and procedures (methodology) that directly tackle the issue of how one blends descriptive data with relevant values to draw explicitly evaluative conclusions.

Evaluative conclusions. Conclusions or findings that are explicitly evaluative in nature, that is, that say how good, valuable, or important something is rather than just describing what it is like or what happened when something was implemented or used.

Evaluee. A person whose performance or attributes are being evaluated. See also *evaluand.*

Experimental designs. Evaluation designs in which potential recipients are randomly assigned to either a "treatment" group (receive the evaluand) or a "control" group (receive either nothing or an alternative intervention). Provided that sampling is done carefully and that sample sizes are large enough, randomization helps to make sure that there are no systematic differences between the evaluand recipients and nonrecipients so that any observed differences can be causally attributed to the evaluand. See also *causation* and *quasi-experimental designs.*

External evaluator. An evaluator who is not an employee of the organization that designed or implemented/distributed the evaluand. This is an independent evaluation contractor.

Formative evaluation. An evaluation conducted for the purpose of finding areas for improving an existing evaluand.

Goal-free evaluation. An evaluation in which the evaluation team deliberately avoids learning what the goals are or were so as to avoid being overly focused on intended outcomes. The rationale behind this approach is that both intended and unintended effects are important to include in an evaluation. Therefore, it is important to find all effects, and it is of little consequence whether the identified effect happened to be intended or unintended. Goal-free evaluation is sometimes called needs-based evaluation because needs assessment is one of the primary tools used to identify what effects (both positive and negative) should be investigated.

Grading. Placing evaluands or evaluees into categories of absolute (i.e., not just relative) merit. See also *ranking.*

Grading rubric. A guide for classifying evaluands or evaluees into categories that represent their absolute (i.e., not just relative) quality or value. See also *ranking rubric.*

Hard hurdle. An overall passing requirement for an evaluand as a whole. If the evaluand (or evaluee) fails to meet the requirement, the evaluand fails overall. Hard hurdles are referred to by Scriven (1991) as "global bars." See also *bar* and *soft hurdle.*

Holistic evaluation. An approach to evaluation that is either not analytical or not explicitly so in which the quality or value of the evaluand is determined at the whole evaluand level without explicit analytical consideration of separate evaluand components or dimensions of merit. See also *component evaluation* and *dimensional evaluation.*

Immediate recipient. Someone who uses a product, receives a service, participates in a program, or is directly affected by a policy. See also *direct recipient.*

Impact. Change or (sometimes) lack of change caused by the evaluand. This term is similar in meaning to the terms *outcome* and *effect.* The term *impact* is often used to refer to long-term outcomes.

Impactees. Individuals for whom something changes as a result of the evaluand. Impactees include direct recipients, downstream impactees, and side impactees.

Importance determination. The process of assigning labels to dimensions or components to indicate their importance.

Importance weighting. See *importance determination.*

Independent evaluation. An evaluation conducted by an individual or a team with no substantial connections with the evaluand, its designers, or its implementers and without any participation in the evaluation process of organizational or program staff.

Instrumental need. An intervention, a product, or a substance that is required to attain a satisfactory level of functioning in a particular context. See also *performance needs.*

Internal evaluator. An evaluator who is on the payroll as an employee of the organization that designed, produced, and/or implemented the evaluand.

Learning organization. An organization that acquires, creates, evaluates, and disseminates knowledge—and uses that knowledge to improve itself—more effectively than do most organizations.

Logic model. A diagram that illustrates the cause-and-effect mechanism(s) by which an evaluand meets (or is supposed to meet) certain needs or produces (or is supposed to produce) certain effects. See also *program logic* and *program theory.*

Management-by-objectives. A goal-based performance evaluation system first proposed by Drucker (1954). Organizational goals are used as a basis for creating goals for different business units and subunits, which are then broken down further to create performance objectives for individuals against which their performance is evaluated.

Merit. Quality, usually considered independent of context and cost. See also *worth* and *value.*

Merit determination. The step in an evaluation that involves the combination of descriptive facts with relevant values to draw evaluative conclusions about performance on particular dimensions or components. See also *analytical evaluation.*

Met need. A dimension on which a satisfactory level of functioning has been achieved. See also *performance need.*

Meta-evaluation. The evaluation of evaluations. Evaluations should be evaluated on five core dimensions of merit: validity, utility, conduct, credibility, and costs. In other words, evaluations should produce valid justifiable conclusions;

be useful to the client and other relevant audiences; be conducted in an ethical, legal, professional, and otherwise appropriate manner; be credible to relevant audiences; and be as economical, quick, and unobtrusive as possible.

Needs. Things without which unsatisfactory functioning occurs. See also *wants, performance need,* and *instrumental need.*

Needs assessment. A systematic process for identifying the dimensions on which impactees need to achieve or maintain satisfactory functioning. See also *performance need.*

Needs-based evaluation. An evaluation in which the criteria of merit are identified using a needs assessment (and other sources of value as appropriate). A needs-based evaluation may or may not be a goal-free evaluation.

Nonparticipatory evaluation. An evaluation conducted without any participation in the evaluation process by organizational or program staff.

Numerical weight and sum. A quantitative synthesis methodology (i.e., one that uses numerical importance weights and merit scores) for summing evaluand performance across multiple criteria. Numerical weight and sum involves ascribing numerical importance weights and a numerical performance score to each evaluative dimension, multiplying weights by performance scores, and then summing these products. The resulting sum represents the overall merit of the evaluand. See also *qualitative weight and sum.*

Objective. An adjective meaning free of inappropriate personal or cultural preferences or biases.

Objectives. Specific measurable goals. Many people use the phrase *goals and objectives* in which broad-brush goals are broken down into specific measurable objectives. However, the term *objective* is also used in a broader sense in many contexts.

Opportunity costs. The activities that might have taken place if certain resources had not been devoted to the program.

Organizational learning. The purposeful acquisition, creation, evaluation, and dissemination of important knowledge about organizational effectiveness and the use of that knowledge to improve it.

Organizational learning capacity. The extent to which an organization has an organizational culture that allows it to effectively engage in organizational learning. Essential elements of a learning culture include systems, policies, practices, values, and expertise that favor and support organizational learning.

Outcome. Change or (sometimes) lack of change caused by the evaluand. It is similar in meaning to the term *impact.*

Outcome evaluation. The part of an evaluation that focuses on the changes (or lack of change) caused by an evaluand. It can also be an evaluation that focuses primarily or exclusively on outcomes, usually (and not prudently) omitting process evaluation, consideration of cost, and so forth.

Participatory evaluations. Evaluations conducted with participation in the evaluation process of organizational or program staff. Staff have input into decisions about the evaluation but may or may not be in a genuine power-sharing situation on the evaluation team. See also *collaborative evaluation.*

Performance appraisal. The formal evaluation of individual or team performance for both formative (e.g., feedback for improvement) and summative (e.g., promotion, performance bonus allocation) purposes.

Performance need. A state of existence or level of performance required for satisfactory functioning in a particular context. Roughly, it is a "need to do" something, a "need to be" something, or a "need to be able to do" something. See also *instrumental need.*

Personnel evaluation. See *performance appraisal* or *personnel selection.*

Personnel selection. The evaluation of individual abilities, attributes, and experience for the purpose of deciding who to hire.

Policy. A written statement intended to guide action and decision making under a particular set of circumstances. A policy broadly outlines an agreed position, point of principle, or preferred response to a particular issue or activity. [SOURCE: Adapted from http://www.newera.org.uk/pdf/policy_framework. pdf]

Policy analysis. Policy evaluation that is usually preformative in nature (i.e., it is conducted for the purpose of estimating the likely costs and effects of implementing a particular policy). Policy analysis is occasionally conducted for formative purposes (i.e., improving an existing policy). See also *policy evaluation.*

Policy evaluation. The determination of the value of a policy. Policy evaluation is often conducted in preformative or formative mode, but summative policy evaluations (e.g., of policies implemented elsewhere) are sometimes conducted. See also *policy analysis.*

Policy instrument. An intervention or a program implemented to turn a public policy into reality.

Potential impactee. Someone in whom something might change (or could have changed) as a result of the evaluand. Potential impactees include any individuals in the pool from which direct recipients, downstream impactees, and side impactees might be drawn.

Practically significant. A result that translates to real impact on people's lives (e.g., the difference has a noticeable and nontrivial effect on functioning or performance).

Process. The content and implementation of an evaluand. Often includes its outputs. A process can also be a particular type of evaluand (e.g., a manufacturing process).

Process evaluation. The part of an evaluation that focuses on the content, implementation, and outputs of an evaluand. It can also be an evaluation that focuses primarily or exclusively on process, usually (and not prudently) omitting outcome evaluation, consideration of cost, and so forth.

Products. Tangible items that can be identified and described and that are designed to meet a particular set of needs and/or wants.

Program. A set of coordinated activities designed to achieve beneficial outcomes for recipients and/or other impactees.

Program logic. Program theory. The term *program logic* is often used in cases where the program theory is very simple or straightforward.

Program theory. A description of the mechanism by which the program is expected to achieve its effects. A program theory can be expressed in a narrative or a picture, or it can be depicted in a simple logic model (i.e., a visual representation of the program theory). See also *logic model* and *program logic.*

Project. A temporary endeavor, with a finite beginning and end, that consists of a set of activities and tasks undertaken to produce a specific product or service, usually within a relatively short time frame.

Qualitative weight and sum. A nonnumerical synthesis methodology devised by Scriven (1991) for summing the performances of an evaluand on multiple criteria to determine overall merit or worth. It is a ranking methodology for determining the relative merit of two or more evaluands or evaluees. See also *numerical weight and sum.*

Quality. Merit or the extent to which an evaluand meets identified needs and other relevant standards. Quality is usually considered to be independent of context and cost. See also *merit* and *value.*

Quasi-experimental designs. Evaluation designs in which groups are not randomly assigned but the evaluation team seeks out a closely similar comparison group with which to compare results. Careful matching of treatment and comparison groups eliminates or greatly reduces the likelihood that rival explanations exist (e.g., the groups were different at the start). See also *causation* and *experimental designs.*

Ranking. Listing evaluands (e.g., products, programs, schools) or evaluees (e.g., candidates for a job, students) in order from highest to lowest quality or value.

Ranking rubric. A guide for classifying evaluands or evaluees into categories that represent their quality or value on some dimension relative to a group of other evaluands or evaluees.

Recipient. Someone who receives a service or an intervention or who participates in a program. See also *impactee.*

Relative merit. The quality or value of something in comparison with one or more other evaluands (e.g., interventions, products, job candidates). See also *ranking.*

Return on investment. The ratio of profits to invested capital. Although this term is (strictly speaking) a numerical ratio, it is also used in the qualitative sense to refer to the magnitude of benefits relative to the resources invested.

Robust. Not vulnerable to weaknesses in one of the sources of evidence. Evaluation findings are usually most robust when they are supported by several independent sources of evidence so that weaknesses in any one of those sources will not invalidate the overall conclusion. See also *triangulation.*

Rolling design. An open-ended, continuous improvement approach to doing evaluation. Instead of rolling out a major evaluation data collection effort all at once, it is done in phases. Starting with something roughly equivalent to a pilot (i.e., small-scale initial data collection effort) and then expanding the scope each time, one evaluates the findings as one progresses through each stage and takes opportunities between phases to continuously improve the data collection instruments and methods to make sure that they capture any important information that arises along the way.

Rubric. A tool that provides an evaluative description of what performance or quality "looks like" at each of two or more defined levels. See also *grading rubic* and *ranking rubic*.

Satisfaction. Happiness or contentment. It is the result of fulfillment of conscious desires (i.e., wants). See also *wants*.

Services. Essentially intangible sets of benefits or activities that are provided (i.e., sold or given) by one party to another (adapted from Zeithaml & Bitner, 2002).

Side effect. An unintended effect of the evaluand.

Side impact. An effect of the evaluand on someone who was not an intended impactee.

Soft hurdle. An overall requirement for entry into a high-rating category. Unlike a bar or hard hurdle, it does not automatically classify an evaluand as "failed" (i.e., it is nonfatal); instead, it places a *limit* on the maximum rating that can be achieved if the evaluand does not clear a particular soft hurdle (e.g., to get an overall "A" for a course, none of the assignments completed during the semester can be lower than a "B–"). See also *bar* and *hard hurdle*.

Stakeholder. Anyone who has a stake in the evaluand. This term includes upstream stakeholders and impactees.

Strategy. The way in which an organization achieves (or moves toward achieving) a high-level purpose or outcome. Strategy may be planned or emergent, but it is usually a combination of the two.

Statistically significant. A result that tells us only that any observed difference (or statistical relationship) is unlikely to be due to chance (e.g., a fluke sample yielding unusual data).

Subcriteria. The elements that make up a broader criterion or dimension of merit. Evaluative criteria (or dimensions) are broken down into subcriteria or subdimensions to more clearly define the criteria and so that they can be more easily assessed using qualitative and/or quantitative methods.

Subdimensions (of merit). See *subcriteria.*

Subjective. Inappropriate application of personal or cultural preferences or biases. It can also mean using informed judgment (an acceptable form of subjectivity in evaluation). It can also refer to someone's inner experience (also an acceptable form of subjectivity in evaluation if inner experiences, such as stress and confidence, are actual or possible effects of the evaluand).

Summative evaluation. An evaluation that is done primarily for reporting or decision-making purposes. See also *formative evaluation.*

Synthesis. "The process of combining a set of ratings or performances on several components or dimensions into an overall rating" (Scriven, 1991, p. 342). It can also be the process of combining a set of ratings or performances on several subdimensions into a rating on one dimension.

System. A set of parts, processes, and/or activities that have some overall purpose or function. Typical examples of systems that one might evaluate include a performance appraisal system, a health care system, and an information and data management system.

Systematic. Methodical, thorough, and not haphazard.

Target market. The intended consumers or recipients of a particular product, service, or program. Target markets are often divided into market segments (i.e., groups of intended consumers with similar needs, interests, or preferences).

Theory-based evaluation. Broadly speaking, any evaluation that uses program theory or program logic as its guiding framework. A good theory-based evaluation goes beyond simply drawing a logic model for the program (or other evaluand) and investigates the links among variables in the logic model to check whether the assumptions underlying it are sound.

Transparent. Clear, well explained, and easily understood by relevant audiences.

Triangulation. Using two or more methods or sources of data to investigate something. It is preferable that the methods and sources have different strengths and weaknesses so that the strengths of one can help counterbalance the weaknesses of the others (the principle of critical multiplism).

Unconscious needs. Needs (met or unmet) that are not known to the person who has them, although they may be known to someone else. See also *conscious needs* and *needs*.

Unmet need. A dimension on which a satisfactory level of functioning has not been achieved. See also *performance need*.

Upstream stakeholders. Individuals who have invested time, effort, money, and/or egos in the design, development, and/or implementation of an evaluand.

Value. Usefulness or benefit to an individual, an organization, or a community in a particular context that often takes cost into account. See also *worth*.

Values (or sources of value). In evaluation, the basis for defining what aspects of the evaluand should be considered to have merit or value in a particular context. Sources of value include impactee needs, ethical and legal standards, and other relevant standards.

Wants. Conscious desires without which dissatisfaction (but not necessarily unsatisfactory functioning) occurs. See also *needs*.

Worth. Value to someone or something. Worth combines merit, context, and (usually) cost. See also *merit*.

REFERENCES

Australian Institute of Aboriginal and Torres Strait Islander Studies. (2000, May). *Guidelines for ethical research in indigenous studies.* Available online: www.aiatsis .gov.au/corp/docs/ethicsguidea4.pdf

Brinkerhoff, R. O. (2003). *The success case method: Find out quickly what's working and what's not.* San Francisco: Berrett-Koehler.

Davidson, E. J. (2001). The meta-learning organization: A model and methodology for evaluating organizational learning capacity. *Dissertation Abstracts International, 62*(5), 1882A. (UMI No. 3015945)

Davidson, E. J. (2003). Linking organizational learning to the bottom line: Methodological issues, challenges, and suggestions. The *Psychologist-Manager Journal, 6*(1), 54–67.

Drucker, P. F. (1954). *The practice of management.* New York: Harper.

Eagly, A., Makhijani, M., & Klonsky, B. (1992). Gender and the evaluation of leaders: A meta-analysis. *Psychological Bulletin, 111,* 3–22.

Guba, E. G., & Lincoln, Y. S. (1989). *Fourth generation evaluation.* Newbury Park, CA: Sage.

House, E. R., & Howe, K. R. (1999). *Values in evaluation and social research.* Thousand Oaks, CA: Sage.

Joint Committee on Standards for Educational Evaluation. (1988). *The personnel evaluation standards.* Thousand Oaks, CA: Corwin.

Joint Committee on Standards for Educational Evaluation. (1994). *The program evaluation standards* (2nd ed.). Thousand Oaks, CA: Corwin.

Joint Committee on Standards for Educational Evaluation. (2003). *The student evaluation standards.* Thousand Oaks, CA: Corwin.

Kamehameha Schools. (2003). *Native Hawaiian guidelines for culturally responsible evaluation and research* (Policy Analysis and System Evaluation). Available online: www.ksbe.edu/services/pase/pdf/evaluationhui/03_04_17.pdf

Lawler, E. E., III, Seashore, S. E., & Mirvis, P. H. (1983). Measuring change: Progress, problems, and prospects. In S. E. Seashore, E. E. Lawler, III, P. H. Mirvis, & C. Cammann (Eds.), *Assessing organizational change: A guide to methods, measures, and practices* (pp. 531–546). New York: John Wiley.

Lipsey, M. W. (1989). *Design sensitivity: Statistical power for experimental research.* Newbury Park, CA: Sage.

Mersman, J. L. (1999, March). *Evaluation of a school-based health program.* Unpublished technical report, Claremont Graduate University.

Mersman, J. L., & Davidson, E. J. (1999, November). *Synthesizing qualitative and quantitative data: Simplicity and validity.* Paper presented at the meeting of the American Evaluation Association, Orlando, FL.

Miron, G., & Nelson, C. D. (1992). *What's public about charter schools?* Thousand Oaks, CA: Corwin Press.

Patton, M. Q. (1990). *Qualitative evaluation and research methods* (2nd ed.). Newbury Park, CA: Sage.

Patton, M. Q. (1997). *Utilization-focused evaluation* (3rd ed.). Thousand Oaks, CA: Sage.

Scriven, M. (1981). *The logic and methodology of evaluation.* Inverness, CA: Edgepress.

Scriven, M. (1991). *Evaluation thesaurus* (4th ed.). Newbury Park, CA: Sage.

Scriven, M. (1993). *Hard-won lessons in program evaluation* (New Directions for Program Evaluation, No. 58). San Francisco: Jossey-Bass.

Scriven, M. (2003). *The Key Evaluation Checklist.* Available online: http://evaluation. wmich.edu/checklists/

Shadish, W. R. (1994). Critical multiplism: A research strategy and its attendant tactics. In L. Sechrest (Ed.), *Program evaluation: A pluralistic enterprise* (New Directions in Program Evaluation, No. 60, pp. 13–57). San Francisco: Jossey-Bass.

Shadish, W. R., Cook, T. D., & Campbell, D. T. (2002). *Experimental and quasi-experimental designs for generalized causal inference.* Boston: Houghton Mifflin.

U.S. Interagency Arctic Research Policy Committee. (n.d.). *Principles for the conduct of research in the Arctic.* Available online: www.ankn.uaf.edu/conduct.html

Villiers, C. (1989, March). Boiled frog syndrome. *Management Today,* pp. 121–127.

Zeithaml, V. A., & Bitner, M. J. (2002). *Services marketing* (3rd ed.). New York: McGraw-Hill.

INDEX

———•◦•———

Absolute merit, 14, 237
  and participatory evaluation, 138
  sample grading rubrics, 138-142
  using rubrics for determining, 137-142
Absolute quality, 137
  versus relative quality, 18-20
  See also Absolute merit
Absolute value, 137
American Evaluation Association:
  Guiding Principles for Evaluators, 210
Analytical evaluation, 102, 104, 237.
  See also Component evaluation;
  Dimensional evaluation; Holistic
  evaluation
"Ask observers" strategy for inferring
  causation, 71-74
Assessment, 2, 237
Australian Institute of Aboriginal and
  Torres Strait Islander Studies, 210

Background and Context (KEC
  checkpoint 1), 5, 6, 8, 9, 11,
  192, 193, 195
Bar, **108**, 110, 156-157, 166, 178-179,
  198, **237**. *See also* Hurdle; Hard
  hurdle; Soft hurdle
Baseline data, 30, 237-238
Benchmarking, 15, 145, 238
"Best practices," 17
Biases, personal and cultural, 89-90
"Big picture" evaluation questions, 2, 4,
  13, 14, 23, 131, 190, 191, 208-209

Bitner, M. J., 247
Brinkerhoff, R. O., 73

Campbell, D. T., 125
Case study, 191
Causation/Causality, 67, 238
  basic principles for inferring, 70-71
  certainty about, 68-70
  See also Causation, strategies for
  inferring; Causation issue
Causation, strategies for inferring,
  67, 71-81
  ask observers (Strategy 1), 71-74
  check whether content of
    evaluand matches outcome
    (Strategy 2), 74
  check whether "dose" is related
    logically to "response"
    (Strategy 5), 78
  control statistically for extraneous
    variables (Strategy 7), 79-80
  identify and check underlying
    causal mechanisms
    (Strategy 8), 80-81
  look for other telltale patterns
    suggesting one cause or another
    (Strategy 3), 75-76
  make comparisons with "control"
    or "comparison" groups
    (Strategy 6), 79
  whether timing of outcomes makes
    sense (Strategy 4), 76-77

Author's Note: **Boldface** entries appear in "Glossary."

Dimensions of merit, 18, 23, 53, 153, 239
  determining importance of, 101
  multiple, 102
  See also Criteria of merit;
    Dimensional evaluation;
    Evaluative criteria, identifying
Direct recipient, 30, 240. *See also*
    Immediate recipient
Distal outcomes, 75
Dose-response idea, 78, 79
Downstream consumers, 30, 240
Downstream impactees, 30-31, 32, 42, 59, 67, 196
  upstream stakeholders versus, 31
Drucker, P., 172, 242

Effect, 4, 240
Evaluand, 5, 240. *See also* Impact;
    Outcome
  different types, 1-2
  finding, 10-11
  goals and, 25
  identifying, 8-9, 11, 13, 23
Evaluand components, determining
    importance of, 101-103, 114-118
Evaluation, 1, 240
  as political, 54-55
  audience, 6, 13, 14
  definition, xi, 131
  ingredients of good, 5-8
  overview, 6
  reasons, 2
  related basic definitions, 1-2
  See also specific types of evaluation
Evaluation approach, evaluation
    purpose and, 3
Evaluation Center, The, xiii
Evaluation plan, 189
**Evaluation-specific logic and
    methodology**, 8, 240
Evaluation project, first:
  advice for choosing, 9-11
Evaluation purpose:
  accountability, 3
  broad, 14

defining main, 4, 6, 13-21
  See also "Big picture" evaluation
    questions; Key Evaluation
    Checklist
Evaluation report, 7, 109
  preliminary checkpoints, 190-192
  See also specific KEC checkpoints
Evaluation-specific logic and
    methodology, xii, xiv, 2, 8
Evaluation steps, 4
Evaluative attitude, 35
Evaluative conclusions, 5, 240.
    See also Explicitly evaluative
    conclusions
Evaluative criteria, determining
    importance of, 100-104, 112-114.
    See also Evaluative criteria,
    strategies for determining
    importance of
Evaluative criteria, identifying, 23-24, 47-49
  basic concepts/tools, 27-29
  See also Consumers; Criterion list;
    Criteria of merit; Dimensions of
    merit; Impactees; Needs
    assessment; Needs assessment
    methods
Evaluative criteria, organizing, 53-54.
    See also Evidence, multiple
    sources of; Key Evaluation
    Checklist
Evaluative criteria, strategies for
    determining importance of:
  literature evidence (Strategy 3), 105, 109-111, 123, 126
  needs/values assessments evidence
    (Strategy 5), 105, 112-117, 118, 123, 126
  program theory and causal linkages
    evidence (Strategy 6), 105, 118, 121-125, 126, 167
  selected stakeholders knowledge
    (Strategy 2), 105, 107-109, 111, 112, 122, 123, 126
  specialist judgment (Strategy 4), 105, 111, 112, 123, 126

ABOUT THE AUTHOR

Jane Davidson is former Associate Director of The Evaluation Center at Western Michigan University, where she launched and directed the world's first fully interdisciplinary Ph.D. in evaluation. She is currently Director of Davidson Consulting Limited (New Zealand). Her Ph.D. is from Claremont Graduate University in organizational behavior, with substantial emphasis on evaluation under the tutelage of Michael Scriven. She has worked in various evaluation, consulting, and quality assurance-related roles in government, business, and education, and she has conducted trainings on coaching skills for managers and supervisors, training needs analysis, and customer service skills. She has published in, or had work accepted for, the *Human Resources Program Evaluation Handbook* (Sage), the *International Handbook of Educational Evaluation* (Kluwer), the *Handbook of Organizational Culture and Climate* (Sage), the *Handbook of Organizational Consulting Psychology* (Sage), and *Foundations and Evaluation: Contexts and Practices for Effective Philanthropy* (Jossey–Bass). She has also published in the journals *New Directions for Evaluation* and the *Psychologist-Manager Journal*.